University of Hertfordshire

Learning and Information Services

College Lane, Hatfield, Hertfordshire, AL10 9AB

For renewal of Standard and One Week Loans,
please visit the website: http://www.voyager.herts.ac.uk

This item must be returned or the loan renewed by the due date.
The University reserves the right to recall items from loan at any time.
A fine will be charged for the late return of items.

4827/KM/DS

ECONOMETRIC FORECASTING AND HIGH-FREQUENCY DATA ANALYSIS

LECTURE NOTES SERIES
Institute for Mathematical Sciences, National University of Singapore

Series Editors: Louis H. Y. Chen and Ka Hin Leung
Institute for Mathematical Sciences
National University of Singapore

ISSN: 1793-0758

Published

Vol. 1   Coding Theory and Cryptology
edited by Harald Niederreiter

Vol. 2   Representations of Real and p-Adic Groups
edited by Eng-Chye Tan & Chen-Bo Zhu

Vol. 3   Selected Topics in Post-Genome Knowledge Discovery
edited by Limsoon Wong & Louxin Zhang

Vol. 4   An Introduction to Stein's Method
edited by A. D. Barbour & Louis H. Y. Chen

Vol. 5   Stein's Method and Applications
edited by A. D. Barbour & Louis H. Y. Chen

Vol. 6   Computational Methods in Large Scale Simulation
edited by K.-Y. Lam & H.-P. Lee

Vol. 7   Markov Chain Monte Carlo: Innovations and Applications
edited by W. S. Kendall, F. Liang & J.-S. Wang

Vol. 8   Transition and Turbulence Control
edited by Mohamed Gad-el-Hak & Her Mann Tsai

Vol. 9   Dynamics in Models of Coarsening, Coagulation, Condensation and Quantization
edited by Weizhu Bao & Jian-Guo Liu

Vol. 10 Gabor and Wavelet Frames
edited by Say Song Goh, Amos Ron & Zuowei Shen

Vol. 11 Mathematics and Computation in Imaging Science and Information Processing
edited by Say Song Goh, Amos Ron & Zuowei Shen

Vol. 12 Harmonic Analysis, Group Representations, Automorphic Forms and Invariant Theory — In Honor of Roger E. Howe
edited by Jian-Shu Li, Eng-Chye Tan, Nolan Wallach & Chen-Bo Zhu

Vol. 13 Econometric Forecasting and High-Frequency Data Analysis
edited by Roberto S. Mariano & Yiu-Kuen Tse

Lecture Notes Series, Institute for Mathematical Sciences,
National University of Singapore

Vol.
13

ECONOMETRIC FORECASTING AND HIGH-FREQUENCY DATA ANALYSIS

Editors

Roberto S. Mariano

Singapore Management University, Singapore & University of Pennsylvania, USA

Yiu-Kuen Tse

Singapore Management University, Singapore

World Scientific

NEW JERSEY · LONDON · SINGAPORE · BEIJING · SHANGHAI · HONG KONG · TAIPEI · CHENNAI

Published by

World Scientific Publishing Co. Pte. Ltd.

5 Toh Tuck Link, Singapore 596224

USA office: 27 Warren Street, Suite 401-402, Hackensack, NJ 07601

UK office: 57 Shelton Street, Covent Garden, London WC2H 9HE

British Library Cataloguing-in-Publication Data
A catalogue record for this book is available from the British Library.

Lecture Notes Series, Institute for Mathematical Sciences,
National University of Singapore — Vol. 13
ECONOMETRIC FORECASTING AND HIGH-FREQUENCY DATA ANALYSIS

Copyright © 2008 by World Scientific Publishing Co. Pte. Ltd.

ISBN-13   978-981-277-895-6
ISBN-10   981-277-895-0

Printed in Singapore by Mainland Press Pte Ltd

CONTENTS

FOREWORD

The Institute for Mathematical Sciences at the National University of Singapore was established on 1 July 2000. Its mission is to foster mathematical research, both fundamental and multidisciplinary, particularly research that links mathematics to other disciplines, to nurture the growth of mathematical expertise among research scientists, to train talent for research in the mathematical sciences, and to serve as a platform for research interaction between the scientific community in Singapore and the wider international community.

The Institute organizes thematic programs which last from one month to six months. The theme or themes of a program will generally be of a multidisciplinary nature, chosen from areas at the forefront of current research in the mathematical sciences and their applications.

Generally, for each program there will be tutorial lectures followed by workshops at research level. Notes on these lectures are usually made available to the participants for their immediate benefit during the program. The main objective of the Institute's Lecture Notes Series is to bring these lectures to a wider audience. Occasionally, the Series may also include the proceedings of workshops and expository lectures organized by the Institute.

The World Scientific Publishing Company has kindly agreed to publish the Lecture Notes Series. This Volume, "Econometric Forecasting and High-Frequency Data Analysis", is the thirteenth of this Series. We hope that through the regular publication of these lecture notes the Institute will achieve, in part, its objective of promoting research in the mathematical sciences and their applications.

October 2007

Louis H.Y. Chen
Ka Hin Leung
Series Editors

PREFACE

This volume contains papers and tutorial notes presented in the Econometric Forecasting and High-Frequency Data Analysis Program jointly organized by the Institute for Mathematical Sciences, National University of Singapore, and the School of Economics, Singapore Management University, in April–May 2004, for which, together with Tilak Abeysinghe, we were Program Co-Chairs. The chapters collected in this volume summarize some recent findings and new results in two key areas in econometrics: econometric forecasting and the analysis of high-frequency financial data.

The paper by Klein and Ozmucur proposes new methods for forecasting macroeconomic variables by combining data with different frequencies. Wallis emphasizes the importance of communicating information about forecast uncertainty, and considers various statistical techniques for assessing the reliability of forecasts. Franses focuses on techniques for forecasting seasonal time series data, including some advanced techniques on modeling seasonal and periodic unit roots. Viewing daily data as aggregates of compound sums of tick-by-tick data, Gourieroux discusses the class of compound autoregressive (Car) processes. Deistler considers the important problem of modeling multivariate time series, including the issues of estimation and model selection.

We are indebted to our Program Committee members for their valuable inputs into the Program, to Louis Chen, Director of IMS, for his unfailing support, and to Lai Fun Kwong of World Scientific, for her endless patience. This volume brings us some fond memory of the Program, the highlight of which was a one-and-a-half day symposium. The symposium culminated in a public forum on "Econometrics Today", which was chaired by Roberto S. Mariano and attended by over 120 participants. The panel, which consists of Lawrence Klein, Robert Engle and Kenneth Wallis, freely shared its candid views about the current state of econometric methodology and its impact on economic research.

October 2007

Roberto S. Mariano
Singapore Management University, Singapore
& University of Pennsylvania, USA

Yiu-Kuen Tse
Singapore Management University, Singapore

FORECAST UNCERTAINTY, ITS REPRESENTATION AND EVALUATION[*]

Kenneth F. Wallis

Department of Economics
University of Warwick
Coventry CV4 7AL, United Kingdom
E-mail: k.f.wallis@warwick.ac.uk

Contents

---

[*]These lectures formed part of the program on Econometric Forecasting and High-Frequency Data Analysis at the Institute for Mathematical Sciences, National University of Singapore, jointly organised by the School of Economics and Social Sciences, Singapore Management University, May 2004; the kind hospitality of both institutions is gratefully acknowledged. The lectures were written up for publication in August 2004. Subsequently some of the material formed the basis of lectures given, under the same general title, as the Sir Richard Stone lectures in London in October 2005. Taking advantage of the passage of time, some of the added material has been updated and incorporated into the present text.

1. Introduction

Forecasts of future economic outcomes are subject to uncertainty. It is increasingly accepted that forecasters who publish forecasts for the use of the general public should accompany their point forecasts with an indication of the associated uncertainty. These lectures first describe the various available methods of communicating information about forecast uncertainty. It is equally important that forecasters' statements about the underlying uncertainty should be reliable. The lectures go on to consider the various available statistical techniques for assessing the reliability of statements about forecast uncertainty.

The lectures draw on and extend material covered in previous survey articles such as Wallis (1995) and, most notably, Tay and Wallis (2000) on density forecasting. While Tay and Wallis discussed applications in macroeconomics and finance, the present lectures are oriented towards macroeconomics, while other lecturers in this program deal with financial econometrics. Relevant research articles are referenced in full, but background material in statistics, econometrics, and associated mathematical methods is not; readers needing to refer to the general literature are asked to consult their favourite textbooks.

This introduction first motivates the lectures by considering the "why" question – why say anything about forecast uncertainty? – and then presents an overview of the issues to be addressed in the two main sections, based on an introductory theoretical illustration.

1.1 *Motivation*

Why not just give a forecast as a single number, for example, inflation next year will be 2.8%? But what if someone else's inflation forecast is 3.1%, is this an important difference, or is it negligible in comparison to the underlying uncertainty? At the simplest level, to acknowledge the uncertainty that is always present in economic forecasting, and that "we all know" that inflation next year is unlikely to be exactly 2.8%, contributes to better-informed discussion about economic policy and prospects. The central banks of many countries now operate an inflation-targeting monetary policy regime, in which forecasts of inflation play an important part, since monetary policy has a delayed effect on inflation. Uncertainty has a crucial role in policy decisions, and considerations of transparency and its impact on the credibility of policy have led many banks to discuss the "risks to the forecast" in their forecast publications. Some have gone further, as described in detail below, and publish a density forecast of inflation, that is, an estimate of the probability distribution of the possible future values of inflation. This represents a complete description of the uncertainty associated with a forecast.

The decision theory framework provides a more formal justification for the publication of density forecasts as well as point forecasts. The decision theory formulation begins with a loss function $L(d,y)$ that describes the consequences of taking decision d today if the future state variable has the value y. If the future were known, then the optimal decision would be the one that makes L as small as possible. But if the future outcome is uncertain, then the loss is a random variable, and a common criterion is to choose the decision that minimises the expected loss. To calculate the expected value of $L(d,y)$ for a range of values of d, in order to find the minimum, the complete probability distribution of y is needed in general. The special case that justifies restricting attention to a point forecast is the case in which L is a quadratic function of y. In this case the certainty equivalence theorem states that the value of d that minimises expected loss $E(L(d,y))$ is the same as the value that minimises $L(d,E(y))$, whatever the distribution of y might be. So in this case only a point forecast, specifically the conditional expectation of the unknown future state variable, is required. In practice, however, macroeconomic forecasters have little knowledge of the identity of the users of forecasts, not to mention their loss functions, and the assumption that these are all quadratic is unrealistic. In many situations the possibility of an unlimited loss is also unrealistic, and bounded loss functions are more reasonable. These are informally referred to as "a miss is as good as a mile" or, quoting Bray and Goodhart (2002), " you might as well be hung for a sheep as a lamb". In more general frameworks such as these, decision-makers require the complete distribution of y.

1.2 *Overview*

A theoretical illustration

We consider the simple univariate model with which statistical prediction theory usually begins, namely the Wold moving average representation of a stationary, non-deterministic series:

$$y_t = \varepsilon_t + \theta_1 \varepsilon_{t-1} + \theta_2 \varepsilon_{t-2} + \cdots, \quad \sum_{j=0}^{\infty} \theta_j^2 < \infty \quad (\theta_0 = 1)$$

$$E(\varepsilon_t) = 0, \quad \operatorname{var}(\varepsilon_t) = \sigma_\varepsilon^2, \quad E(\varepsilon_t \varepsilon_s) = 0, \quad \text{all } t, s \neq t.$$

To construct a forecast h steps ahead, consider this representation at time $t+h$:

$$y_{t+h} = \varepsilon_{t+h} + \theta_1 \varepsilon_{t+h-1} + \cdots + \theta_{h-1} \varepsilon_{t+1} + \theta_h \varepsilon_t + \theta_{h+1} \varepsilon_{t-1} + \cdots .$$

The optimal **point forecast** with respect to a squared error loss function, the "minimum mean squared error" (mmse) forecast, is the conditional expectation $E(y_{t+h} | \Omega_t)$, where Ω_t denotes the relevant information set. In the present case this simply comprises available data on the y-process at the forecast origin, t, hence the mmse h-step-ahead forecast is

$$\hat{y}_{t+h} = \theta_h \varepsilon_t + \theta_{h+1} \varepsilon_{t-1} + \cdots,$$

with forecast error $e_{t+h} = y_{t+h} - \hat{y}_{t+h}$ given as

$$e_{t+h} = \varepsilon_{t+h} + \theta_1 \varepsilon_{t+h-1} + \cdots + \theta_{h-1} \varepsilon_{t+1} .$$

The forecast error has mean zero and variance σ_h^2, where

$$\sigma_h^2 = E\left(e_{t+h}^2\right) = \sigma_\varepsilon^2 \sum_{j=0}^{h-1} \theta_j^2 .$$

The forecast root mean squared error is defined as $RMSE_h = \sigma_h$. The forecast error is a moving average process and so in general exhibits autocorrelation at all lags up to $h-1$: only the one-step-ahead forecast has a non-autocorrelated error. Finally note that the optimal forecast and its error are uncorrelated:

$$E(e_{t+h} \hat{y}_{t+h}) = 0 .$$

An **interval forecast** is commonly constructed as the point forecast plus or minus one or two standard errors, $\hat{y}_{t+h} \pm \sigma_h$, for example. To attach a probability to this statement we need a distributional assumption, and a normal distribution for the random shocks is commonly assumed:

$$\varepsilon_t \sim N\left(0, \sigma_\varepsilon^2\right).$$

Then the future outcome also has a normal distribution, and the above interval has probability 0.68 of containing it. The **density forecast** of the future outcome is this same distribution, namely

$$y_{t+h} \sim N\left(\hat{y}_{t+h}, \sigma_h^2\right).$$

Example

A familiar example in econometrics texts is the stationary first-order autoregression, abbreviated to AR(1):

$$y_t = \phi y_{t-1} + \varepsilon_t, \quad |\phi| < 1.$$

Then in the moving average representation we have $\theta_j = \phi^j$ and the h-step-ahead point forecast is

$$\hat{y}_{t+h} = \phi^h y_t.$$

The forecast error variance is

$$\sigma_h^2 = \sigma_\varepsilon^2 \frac{1 - \phi^{2h}}{1 - \phi^2}.$$

As h increases this approaches the unconditional variance of y, namely $\sigma_\varepsilon^2 / \left(1 - \phi^2\right)$. Interval and density forecasts are obtained by using these quantities in the preceding expressions.

Generalisations

This illustration uses the simplest univariate linear model and treats its parameters as if their values are known. To have practical relevance these constraints need to be relaxed. Thus in Section 2, where methods of measuring and reporting forecast uncertainty are discussed, multivariate models and non-linear models appear, along with conditioning variables and non-normal distributions, and the effects of parameter estimation error and uncertainty about the model are considered.

Forecast evaluation

Given a time series of forecasts and the corresponding outcomes or realisations y_t, $t = 1,...,n$, we have a range of techniques available for the statistical assessment of the quality of the forecasts. For point forecasts these have a long history; for a review, see Wallis (1995, §3). The first question is whether there is any systematic bias in the forecasts, and this is usually answered by testing the null hypothesis that the forecast errors have zero mean, for which a t-test is appropriate. Whether the forecasts have minimum mean squared error cannot be tested, because we do not know what the minimum achievable mse is, but other properties of optimal forecasts can be tested. The absence of correlation between errors and forecasts, for example, is often tested in the context of a realisation-forecast regression, and the non-autocorrelation of forecast errors at lags greater than or equal to h is also testable. Information can often be gained by comparing different forecasts of the same variable, perhaps in the context of an extended realisation-forecast regression, which is related to the question of the construction of combined forecasts.

Tests of interval and density forecasts, a more recent development, are discussed in Section 3. The first question is one of correct coverage: is the proportion of outcomes falling in the forecast intervals equal to the announced probability; are the quantiles of the forecast densities occupied in the correct proportions? There is also a question of independence, analogous to the non-autocorrelation of the errors of point forecasts. The discussion includes applications to two series of density forecasts of inflation, namely those of the US Survey of Professional Forecasters (managed by the Federal Reserve Bank of Philadelphia, see http://www.phil.frb.org/econ/spf/index.html) and the Bank of England Monetary Policy Committee (as published in the Bank's quarterly *Inflation Report*). Finally some recent extensions to comparisons and combinations of density forecasts are considered, which again echo the point forecasting literature.

Section 4 contains concluding comments.

2. Measuring and Reporting Forecast Uncertainty

We first consider methods of calculating measures of expected forecast dispersion, both model-based and empirical, and then turn to methods of reporting and communicating forecast uncertainty. The final section considers some related issues that arise in survey-based forecasts. For a fully-developed taxonomy of the sources of forecast uncertainty see Clements and Hendry (1998).

2.1 *Model-based measures of forecast uncertainty*

For some models formulae for the forecast error variance are available, and two examples are considered. In other models simulation methods are employed.

The linear regression model

The first setting in which parameter estimation error enters that one finds in econometrics textbooks is the classical linear regression model. The model is

$$y = X\beta + u, \quad u \sim N\left(0, \sigma_u^2 I_n\right).$$

The least squares estimate of the coefficient vector, and its covariance matrix, are

$$b = \left(X'X\right)^{-1} X'y, \quad \mathrm{var}(b) = \sigma_u^2 \left(X'X\right)^{-1}.$$

A point forecast conditional on regressor values $c' = [1\ x_{2f}\ x_{3f}\ ...\ x_{kf}]$ is $\hat{y}_f = c'b$, and the forecast error has two components

$$e_f = y_f - \hat{y}_f = u_f - c'(b - \beta).$$

Similarly the forecast error variance has two components

$$\mathrm{var}(e_f) = \sigma_u^2 \left(1 + c'\left(X'X\right)^{-1} c\right).$$

The second component is the contribution of parameter estimation error, which goes to zero as the sample size, n, increases (under standard regression assumptions that ensure the convergence of the second moment matrix $X'X/n$). To make this expression operational the unknown error variance σ_u^2 is replaced by an estimate s^2 based on the sum of squared residuals, which results in a shift from the normal to Student's t-distribution, and interval and density forecasts are based on the distributional result that

$$\frac{y_f - \hat{y}_f}{s\sqrt{1 + c'(X'X)^{-1}c}} \sim t_{n-k} .$$

It should be emphasised that this result refers to a forecast that is conditional on given values of the explanatory variables. In practical forecasting situations the future values of deterministic variables such as trends and seasonal dummy variables are known, and perhaps some economic variables such as tax rates can be treated as fixed in short-term forecasting, but in general the future values of the economic variables on the right-hand side of the regression equation need forecasting too. The relevant setting is then one of a multiple-equation model rather than the above single-equation model. For a range of linear multiple-equation models generalisations of the above expressions can be found in the literature. However the essential ingredients of forecast error – future random shocks and parameter estimation error – remain the same.

Estimation error in multi-step forecasts

To consider the contribution of parameter estimation error in multi-step forecasting with a dynamic model we return to the AR(1) example discussed in Section 1.2. Now, however, the point forecast is based on an estimated parameter:

$$\hat{y}_{t+h} = \hat{\phi}^h y_t .$$

The forecast error again has two components

$$y_{t+h} - \hat{y}_{t+h} = e_{t+h} + \left(\phi^h - \hat{\phi}^h \right) y_t ,$$

where the first term is the cumulated random error defined above, namely

$$e_{t+h} = \varepsilon_{t+h} + \phi\varepsilon_{t+h-1} + \cdots + \phi^{h-1}\varepsilon_{t+1}.$$

To calculate the variance of the second component we first neglect any correlation between the forecast initial condition y_t and the estimation sample on which $\hat{\phi}$ is based, so that the variance of the product is the product of the variances of the factors. Using the result that the variance of the least squares estimate of ϕ is $(1-\phi^2)/n$, and taking a first-order approximation to the non-linear function, we then obtain

$$\mathrm{var}\left(\hat{\phi}^h - \phi^h\right) \approx \frac{\left(h\phi^{h-1}\right)^2\left(1-\phi^2\right)}{n}.$$

The variance of y_t is $\sigma_\varepsilon^2/(1-\phi^2)$, hence the forecast error variance is

$$E\left(y_{t+h} - \hat{y}_{t+h}\right)^2 \approx \sigma_\varepsilon^2\left(\frac{1-\phi^{2h}}{1-\phi^2} + \frac{\left(h\phi^{h-1}\right)^2}{n}\right).$$

The second contribution causes possible non-monotonicity of the forecast error variance as h increases, but goes to zero as h becomes large. As above, this expression is made operational by replacing unknown parameters by their estimates, and the t-distribution provides a better approximation for inference than the normal distribution. And again, generalisations can be found in the literature for more complicated dynamic linear models.

Stochastic simulation in non-linear models

Practical econometric models are typically non-linear in variables. They combine log-linear regression equations with linear accounting identities. They include quantities measured in both real and nominal terms together with the corresponding price variables, hence products and ratios of variables appear. More complicated functions such as the constant elasticity of substitution (CES) production function can also be found. In these circumstances an analytic expression for a forecast does not exist, and numerical methods are used to solve the model.

A convenient formal representation of a general non-linear system of equations, in its structural form, is

$$f\left(y_t, z_t, \alpha\right) = u_t,$$

where f is a vector of functions having as many elements as the vector of endogenous variables y_t, and z_t, α and u_t are vectors of predetermined variables, parameters and random disturbances respectively. This is more general than is necessary, because models are mostly linear in parameters, but no convenient simplification is available. It is assumed that a unique solution for the endogenous variables exists. Whereas multiple solutions might exist from a mathematical point of view, typically only one of them makes sense in the economic context. The solution has no explicit analytic form, but it can be written implicitly as

$$y_t = g\left(u_t, z_t, \alpha\right),$$

which is analogous to the reduced form in the linear case.

Taking period t to be the forecast period of interest, the "deterministic" forecast $\hat{y}_t$ is obtained, for given values of predetermined variables and parameters, as the numerical solution to the structural form, with the disturbance terms on the right-hand side set equal to their expected values of zero. The forecast can be written implicitly as

$$\hat{y}_t = g\left(0, z_t, \alpha\right),$$

and is approximated numerically to a specified degree of accuracy.

Forecast uncertainty likewise cannot be described analytically. Instead, stochastic simulation methods are used to estimate the forecast densities. First R vectors of pseudo-random numbers u_{tr}, $r = 1, ..., R$, are generated with the same properties as those assumed or estimated for the model disturbances: typically a normal distribution with covariance matrix estimated from the model residuals. Then for each replication the model is solved for the corresponding values of the endogenous variables y_{tr}, say, where

$$f\left(y_{tr}, z_t, \alpha\right) = u_{tr}, \ r = 1, ..., R$$

to the desired degree of accuracy, or again implicitly

$$y_{tr} = g\left(u_{tr}, z_t, \alpha\right).$$

In large models attention is usually focused on a small number of key macroeconomic indicators. For the relevant elements of the y-vector the empirical distributions of the y_{tr} values then represent their density forecasts. These are presented as histograms, possibly smoothed using techniques discussed by Silverman (1986), for example.

The early applications of stochastic simulation methods focused on the mean of the empirical distribution in order to assess the possible bias in the deterministic forecast. The non-linearity of g is the source of the lack of equality in the following statement,

$$E\left(y_t | z_t, \alpha\right) = E\left(g\left(u_t, z_t, \alpha\right)\right) \neq g\left(E\left(u_t\right), z_t, \alpha\right) = \hat{y}_t,$$

and the bias is estimated as the difference between the deterministic forecast and the simulation sample mean

$$\bar{y}_t = \frac{1}{R}\sum_{r=1}^{R} y_{tr}.$$

Subsequently attention moved on to second moments and event probability estimates. With an economic event, such as a recession, defined in terms of a model outcome, such as two consecutive quarters of declining real GDP, then the relative frequency of this outcome in R replications of a multi-step forecast is an estimate of the probability of the event. Developments also include study of the effect of parameter estimation error, by pseudo-random sampling from the distribution of $\hat{\alpha}$ as well as that of u_t. For a fuller discussion, and references, see Wallis (1995, §4).

Loss functions

It is convenient to note the impact of different loss functions at this juncture, in the light of the foregoing discussion of competing point forecasts. The conditional expectation is the optimal forecast with respect to a squared error loss function, as noted above, but in routine forecasting exercises with econometric models one very rarely finds the mean stochastic simulation estimate being used. Its computational burden becomes less of a concern with each new generation of computer, but an alternative loss function justifies the continued use of the deterministic forecast.

In the symmetric linear or absolute error loss function, the optimal forecast is the median of the conditional distribution. (Note that this applies only to forecasts of a single variable, strictly speaking, since there is no standard definition of the median of a multivariate distribution. Commonly, however, this is interpreted as the set of medians of the marginal univariate distributions.) Random disturbances are usually assumed to have a symmetric distribution, so that the mean and median are both zero, hence the deterministic forecast $\hat{y}_t$ is equal to the median of the conditional distribution of y_t provided that the transformation $g(\cdot)$ preserves the median. That is, provided that

$$\mathrm{med}\big(g(u_t, z_t, \alpha)\big) = g\big(\mathrm{med}(u_t), z_t, \alpha\big).$$

This condition is satisfied if the transformation is bijective, which is the case for the most common example in practical models, namely the exponential function, whose use arises from the specification of log-linear equations with additive disturbance terms. Under these conditions the deterministic forecast is the minimum absolute error forecast. There is simulation evidence that the median of the distribution of stochastic simulations in practical models either coincides with the deterministic forecast or is very close to it (Hall, 1986).

The third measure of location familiar in statistics is the mode, and in the context of a density forecast the mode represents the most likely outcome. Some forecasters focus on the mode as their preferred point forecast believing that the concept of the most likely outcome is most easily understood by forecast users. It is the optimal forecast under a step or "all-or-nothing" loss function, hence in a decision context in which the loss is bounded or "a miss is as good as a mile", the mode is the best choice of point forecast. Again this applies in a univariate, not multivariate setting: in practice the mode is difficult to compute in the multivariate case (Calzolari and Panattoni, 1990), and it is not preserved under transformation. For random variables X and Y with asymmetric distributions, it is not in general true that the mode of $X + Y$ is equal to the mode of X plus the mode of Y, for example.

Model uncertainty

Model-based estimates of forecast uncertainty are clearly conditional on the chosen model. However the choice of an appropriate model is itself subject to uncertainty. Sometimes the model specification is chosen with reference to an *a priori* view of the way the world works, sometimes it is the result of a statistical model selection procedure. In both cases the possibility that an inappropriate model has been selected is yet another contribution to forecast uncertainty, but in neither case is a measure of this contribution available, since the true data generating process is unknown.

A final contribution to forecast uncertainty comes from the subjective adjustments to model-based forecasts that many forecasters make in practice, to take account of off-model information of various kinds: their effects are again not known with certainty, and measures of this contribution are again not available. In these circumstances some forecasters provide subjective assessments of uncertainty, whereas others turn to *ex post* assessments.

2.2 *Empirical measures of forecast uncertainty*

The historical track record of forecast errors incorporates all sources of error, including model error and the contribution of erroneous subjective adjustments. Past forecast performance thus provides a suitable foundation for measures of forecast uncertainty.

Let y_t, $t = 1,...,n$ be an observed time series and $\hat{y}_t$, $t = 1,...,n$ be a series of forecasts of y_t made at times $t - h$, where h is the forecast horizon. The forecast errors are then $e_t = y_t - \hat{y}_t$, $t = 1,...,n$. The two conventional summary measures of forecast performance are the sample root mean squared error,

$$RMSE = \sqrt{\frac{1}{n}\sum_{t=1}^{n} e_t^2} \ ,$$

and the sample mean absolute error,

$$MAE = \frac{1}{n}\sum_{t=1}^{n} |e_t| \ .$$

The choice between them should in principle be related to the relevant loss function – squared error loss or absolute error loss – although many forecasters report both.

In basing a measure of the uncertainty of future forecasts on past forecast performance we are, of course, facing an additional forecasting problem. Now it is addressed to measures of the dispersion of forecasts, but it is subject to the same difficulties of forecast failure due to structural breaks as point forecasts. Projecting forward from past performance assumes a stable underlying environment, and difficulties arise when this structure changes.

If changes can be anticipated, subjective adjustments might be made, just as is the case with point forecasts, but just as difficult. For example, the UK government publishes alongside its budget forecasts of key macroeconomic indicators the mean absolute error of the past ten years' forecasts. The discussion of the margin of error of past forecasts in the statement that accompanied the June 1979 budget, immediately following the election of Mrs Thatcher's first government, noted the "possibility that large changes in policy will affect the economy in ways which are not foreseen".

A more recent example is the introduction in several countries of a monetary policy regime of direct inflation targeting. It is claimed that this will reduce uncertainty, hence the "old regime" forecast track record may be an unreliable guide to the future uncertainty of inflation. Eventually a track record on the new regime will accumulate, but measures of uncertainty are needed in the meantime. One way to calibrate the variance of inflation in the new regime is to undertake a stochastic simulation study of the performance of a macroeconometric model augmented with a policy rule for the interest rate that targets inflation. Blake (1996) provides a good example, using the model of the UK economy maintained by the National Institute of Economic and Social Research. He finds that inflation uncertainty is indeed reduced in the new regime, although his estimates are of course conditional on the specification of the model and the policy rule. In particular the latter implies the vigorous use of interest rates to achieve the inflation target in the face of shocks, and the price to pay for a stable inflation rate may be higher interest rate variability.

2.3 *Reporting forecast uncertainty*

Interval forecasts and density forecasts are discussed in turn, including some technical considerations. The Bank of England's fan chart is a leading graphical representation, and other examples are discussed.

Forecast intervals

An interval forecast is commonly presented as a range centred on a point forecast, as noted in the Introduction, with associated probabilities calculated with reference to tables of the normal distribution. Then some typical interval forecasts and their coverage probabilities are

$$\hat{y}_t \pm MAE \qquad 57\%$$

$$\hat{y}_t \pm RMSE \qquad 68\%$$

$$\hat{y}_t \pm 2RMSE \qquad 95\%$$

$$\hat{y}_t \pm 0.675RMSE \qquad 50\% \quad \text{(the interquartile range).}$$

In more complicated models other distributions are needed, as noted above. If parameter estimation errors are taken into account then Student's t-distribution is relevant, whereas in complex non-linear models the forecast distribution may have been estimated non-parametrically by stochastic simulation. In the latter case the distribution may not be symmetric, and a symmetric interval centred on a point forecast may not be the best choice. In any event it can be argued that to focus on uncertainty the point forecast should be suppressed, and only the interval reported.

The requirement that an interval (a, b) be constructed so that it has a given probability π of containing the outcome y, that is,

$$\Pr(a \leq y \leq b) = F(b) - F(a) = \pi$$

where $F(\cdot)$ is the cumulative distribution function, does not by itself pin down the location of the interval. Additional specification is required, and the question is what is the best choice. The forecasting literature assumes unimodal densities and considers two possible specifications, namely the shortest interval, with $b - a$ as small as possible, and the central interval, which contains the stated probability in the centre of the distribution, defined such that there is equal probability in each of the tails:

$$\Pr(y < a) = \Pr(y > b) = (1 - \pi)/2 .$$

(This usage of "central" is in accordance with the literature on confidence intervals, see Stuart, Ord and Arnold, 1999, p. 121.) If the distribution of outcomes is symmetric then the two intervals are the same; if the distribution is asymmetric then the shortest and central intervals do not coincide. Each can be justified as the optimal interval forecast with respect to a particular loss function or cost function, as we now show.

It is assumed that there is a cost proportional to the length of the interval, $c_0(b - a)$, which is incurred irrespective of the outcome. The distinction between the two cases arises from the assumption about the additional cost associated with the interval not containing the outcome.

All-or-nothing loss function If the costs associated with the possible outcomes have an all-or-nothing form, being zero if the interval contains the outcome and a constant $c_1 > 0$ otherwise, then the loss function is

$$L(y) = \begin{cases} c_0(b-a)+c_1 & y < a \\ c_0(b-a) & a \le y \le b \\ c_0(b-a)+c_1 & y > b \end{cases}$$

The expected loss is

$$E\big(L(y)\big) = c_0(b-a) + \int_{-\infty}^{a} c_1 f(y)dy + \int_{b}^{\infty} c_1 f(y)dy$$
$$= c_0(b-a) + c_1 F(a) + c_1\big(1 - F(b)\big).$$

To minimise expected loss subject to the correct interval probability consider the Lagrangean

$$\mathcal{L} = c_0(b-a) + c_1 F(a) + c_1\big(1 - F(b)\big) + \lambda\big(F(b) - F(a) - \pi\big).$$

The first-order conditions with respect to a and b give

$$f(a) = f(b) = c_0 / (c_1 - \lambda),$$

thus for given coverage the limits of the optimal interval correspond to ordinates of the probability density function (pdf) of equal height on either side of the mode. As the coverage is reduced, the interval closes in on the mode of the distribution.

The equal height property is also a property of the interval with shortest length $b-a$ for given coverage π. To see this consider the Lagrangean

$$\mathcal{L} = b - a + \lambda\big(F(b) - F(a) - \pi\big).$$

This is a special case of the expression considered above, and the first-order conditions for a minimum again give $f(a) = f(b)$ as required. The shortest interval has unequal tail probabilities in the asymmetric case, and these should be reported, in case a user might erroneously think that they are equal.

Linear loss function Here it is assumed that the additional cost is proportional to the amount by which the outcome lies outside the interval. Thus the loss function is

$$L(y) = \begin{cases} c_0(b-a) + c_2(a-y) & y < a \\ c_0(b-a) & a \le y \le b \\ c_0(b-a) + c_2(y-b) & y > b \end{cases}$$

The expected loss is

$$E(L(y)) = c_0(b-a) + \int_{-\infty}^{a} c_2(a-y)f(y)dy + \int_{b}^{\infty} c_2(y-b)f(y)dy$$

and the first-order conditions for minimum expected loss give

$$c_0 = c_2 \int_{-\infty}^{a} f(y)dy = c_2 \int_{b}^{\infty} f(y)dy .$$

Hence the best forecast interval under a linear loss function is the central interval with equal tail probabilities $\Pr(y < a) = \Pr(y > b)$, the limits being the corresponding quantiles

$$a = F^{-1}\left(\frac{1-\pi}{2}\right), \quad b = F^{-1}\left(\frac{1+\pi}{2}\right).$$

As the coverage, π, is reduced, the central interval converges on the median.

In some applications a pre-specified interval may be a focus of attention. In a monetary policy regime of inflation targeting, for example, the objective of policy is sometimes expressed as a target range for inflation, whereupon it is of interest to report the forecast probability that the future outcome will fall in the target range. This is equivalent to an event probability forecasting problem, the forecast being stated as the probability of the future event "inflation on target" occurring.

Density forecasts

The preceding discussion includes cases where the density forecast has a known functional form and cases where it is estimated by non-parametric methods. In the former case features of the forecast may not be immediately apparent from an algebraic expression for the density, and in both cases numerical presentations are used, either as histograms, with intervals of equal length, or based on quantiles of the distribution. In the present context the conventional discretisation of a distribution based on quantiles amounts to representing the density forecast as a set of central forecast intervals with different coverage probabilities. Graphical presentations are widespread, but before discussing them we present a further density function that is used to represent forecast uncertainty, particularly when the balance of risks to the forecast is asymmetric.

The density forecasts of inflation published by the Bank of England and the Sveriges Riksbank assume the functional form of the two-piece normal distribution (Blix and Sellin, 1998; Britton, Fisher and Whitley, 1998). A random variable X has a two-piece normal distribution with parameters μ, σ_1 and σ_2 if it has probability density function (pdf)

$$f(x) = \begin{cases} A\exp\left(-(x-\mu)^2\big/2\sigma_1^2\right) & x \le \mu \\ A\exp\left(-(x-\mu)^2\big/2\sigma_2^2\right) & x \ge \mu \end{cases}$$

where $A = \left(\sqrt{2\pi}\,(\sigma_1+\sigma_2)\big/2\right)^{-1}$ (John, 1982; Johnson, Kotz and Balakrishnan, 1994; Wallis, 1999). The distribution is formed by taking the left half of a normal distribution with parameters (μ, σ_1) and the right half of a normal distribution with parameters (μ, σ_2), and scaling them to give the common value $f(\mu) = A$ at the mode, as above. An illustration is presented in Figure 1. The scaling factor applied to the left half of the $N(\mu,\sigma_1)$ pdf is $2\sigma_1\big/(\sigma_1+\sigma_2)$ while that applied to the right half of the $N(\mu,\sigma_2)$ pdf is $2\sigma_2\big/(\sigma_1+\sigma_2)$. If $\sigma_2 > \sigma_1$ this reduces the probability mass to the left of the mode to below one-half and correspondingly increases the probability mass above the mode, hence in this case the two-piece normal distribution is positively skewed with mean>median>mode. Likewise, when $\sigma_1 > \sigma_2$ the distribution is negatively skewed. The mean and variance of the distribution are

$$E(X) = \mu + \sqrt{\frac{2}{\pi}}(\sigma_2 - \sigma_1)$$

$$\mathrm{var}(X) = \left(1 - \frac{2}{\pi}\right)(\sigma_2 - \sigma_1)^2 + \sigma_1\sigma_2 \ .$$

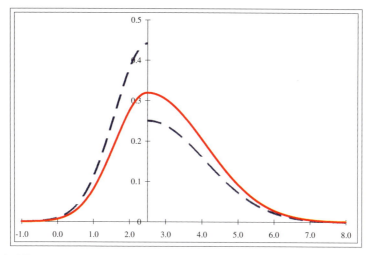

dashed line :   two halves of normal distributions with $\mu = 2.5$,
                     $\sigma_1 = 0.902$ (left) and $\sigma_2 = 1.592$ (right)
solid line :   the two-piece normal distribution

Figure 1. The probability density function of the two-piece normal distribution

The two-piece normal distribution is a convenient representation of departures from the symmetry of the normal distribution, since probabilities can be readily calculated by referring to standard normal tables and scaling by the above factors; however, the asymmetric distribution has no convenient multivariate generalisation.

In the case of the Bank of England, the density forecast describes the subjective assessment of inflationary pressures by its Monetary Policy Committee, and the three parameters are calibrated to represent this judgement, expressed in terms of the location, scale and skewness of the distribution. A point forecast – mean and/or mode – fixes the location of the distribution. The level of uncertainty or scale of the distribution is initially assessed with reference to forecast errors over the preceding ten years, and is then adjusted with respect to known or anticipated future developments. The degree of skewness, expressed in terms of the difference between the mean and the mode, is determined by the Committee's collective assessment of the balance of risks on the upside and downside of the forecast.

Graphical presentations

In real-time forecasting, a sequence of forecasts for a number of future periods from a fixed initial condition (the "present") is often presented as a time-series plot. The point forecast may be shown as a continuation of the plot of actual data recently observed, and limits may be attached, either as standard error bands or quantiles, becoming wider as the forecast horizon increases. Thompson and Miller (1986) note that "typically forecasts and limits are graphed as dark lines on a white background, which tends to make the point forecast the focal point of the display." They argue for and illustrate the use of selective shading of quantiles, as "a deliberate attempt to draw attention away from point forecasts and toward the *uncertainty* in forecasting" (1986, p. 431, emphasis in original).

In presenting its density forecasts of inflation the Bank of England takes this argument a stage further, by suppressing the point forecast. The density forecast is presented graphically as a set of forecast intervals covering 10, 20, 30,..., 90% of the probability distribution, of lighter shades for the outer bands. This is done for quarterly forecasts up to two years ahead, and since the dispersion increases and the intervals "fan out" as the forecast horizon increases, the result has become known as the "fan chart". Rather more informally, and noting its red colour, it also became known as the "rivers of blood". (In their recent textbook, Stock and Watson (2003) refer to the fan chart using only the "river of blood" title; since their reproduction is coloured green, readers are invited to use their imagination.)

An example of the Bank of England's presentation of the density forecasts is shown in Figure 2. This uses the shortest intervals for the assigned probabilities, which converge on the mode. (The calibrated parameter values for the final quarter's forecast are also used in the illustration of the two-piece normal distribution in Figure 1.) As the distribution is asymmetric the probabilities in the upper and lower same-shade segments are not equal. The Bank does not report the consequences of this, which are potentially misleading. For the final quarter Wallis (1999, Table 1) calculates the probability of inflation lying below the darkest 10% interval as 32½%, and correspondingly a

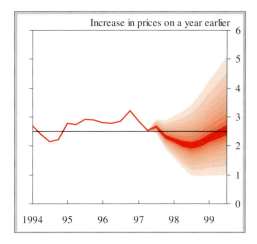

Figure 2. The August 1997 *Inflation Report* fan chart

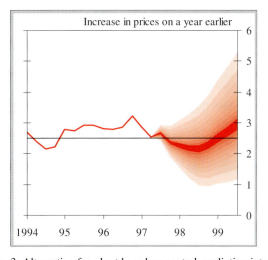

Figure 3. Alternative fan chart based on central prediction intervals

probability of 57½% that inflation will lie above the middle 10% interval. Visual inspection of the fan chart does not by itself reveal the extent of this asymmetry. Similarly the lower and upper tail probabilities in the final quarter are 3.6% and 6.4% respectively.

An alternative presentation of the same density forecasts by Wallis (1999) is shown in Figure 3: this uses central intervals defined by percentiles, with equal tail probabilities, as discussed above. There is no ambiguity about the probability content of the upper and lower bands of a given shade: they are all 5%, as are the tail probabilities. It is argued that a preference for this alternative fan chart is implicit in the practice of the overwhelming majority of statisticians of summarising densities by presenting selected percentiles.

Additional examples

We conclude this section by describing three further examples of the reporting of forecast uncertainty by the use of density forecasts. First is the National Institute of Economic and Social Research in London, England, which began to publish density forecasts of inflation and GDP growth in its quarterly *National Institute Economic Review* in February 1996, the same month in which the Bank of England's fan chart first appeared. The forecast density is assumed to be a normal distribution centred on the point forecast, since the hypothesis of unbiased forecasts with normally distributed errors could not be rejected in testing the track record of earlier forecasts. The standard deviation of the normal distribution is set equal to the standard deviation of realised forecast errors at the same horizon over a previous period. The distribution is presented as a histogram, in the form of a table reporting the probabilities of outcomes falling in various intervals. For inflation, those used in 2004, for example, were: less than 1.5%, 1.5 to 2.0%, 2.0 to 2.5%, and so on.

A second example is the budget projections prepared by the Congressional Budget Office (CBO) of the US Congress. Since January 2003 the uncertainty of the CBO's projections of the budget deficit or surplus under current policies has been represented as a fan chart. The method of construction of the density forecast is described in CBO (2003); in outline it follows the preceding paragraph, with a normal distribution calibrated to the historical record. On the CBO website (www.cbo.gov) the fan chart appears in various shades of blue.

Our final example is the work of Garratt, Lee, Pesaran and Shin (2003). They have previously constructed an eight-equation conditional vector error-correction model of the UK economy. In the present article they develop density and event probability forecasts for inflation and growth, singly and jointly, based on this model. These are computed by stochastic simulation allowing for parameter uncertainty. The density forecasts are presented by plotting the estimated cumulative distribution function at three forecast horizons.

2.4 *Forecast scenarios*

Variant forecasts that highlight the sensitivity of the central forecast to key assumptions are commonly published by forecasting agencies. The US Congressional Budget Office (2004), for example, presents in addition to its baseline budget projections variants that assume lower real growth, higher interest rates or higher inflation. The Bank of England has on occasion shown the sensitivity of its central projection for inflation to various alternative assumptions preferred by individual members of the Monetary Policy Committee: with respect to the behaviour of the exchange rate, the scale of the slowdown in the global economy, and the degree of spare capacity in the domestic economy, for example. The most highly developed and documented use of forecast scenarios is that of the CPB Netherlands Bureau for Economic Policy Analysis, which is a good example for fuller discussion.

Don (2001), who was CPB Director 1994-2006, describes the CPB's practice of publishing a small number of scenarios rather than a single forecast, arguing that this communicates forecast uncertainty more properly than statistical criteria for forecast quality, since "*ex post* forecast errors can at best provide a rough guide to *ex ante* forecast errors". Periodically the CPB publishes a medium-term macroeconomic outlook for the Dutch economy over the next Cabinet period, looking four or five years ahead. The outlook is the basis for the CPB's analysis of the platforms of the competing parties at each national election, and for the programme of the new Cabinet. It comprises two scenarios, which in the early outlooks were termed "favourable" and "unfavourable" in relation to the exogenous assumptions supplied to the model of the domestic economy. "The idea is that these scenarios show between which margins economic growth in the Netherlands for the projection period is likely to lie, barring extreme conditions. There is no numerical probability statement; rather the flavour is informal and subjective, but coming from independent experts" (Don, 2001, p.172). The first sentence of this quotation almost describes an interval forecast, but the word "likely" is not translated into a probability statement, as noted in the second sentence.

The practical difficulty facing the user of these scenarios is not knowing where they lie in the complete distribution of possible outcomes. What meaning should be attached to the words "favourable" and "unfavourable"? And how likely is "likely"? Indeed, in 2001, following a review, the terminology was changed to "optimistic" and "cautious". The change was intended to indicate that the range of the scenarios had been reduced, so that "optimistic" is less optimistic than "favourable" and "cautious" is less pessimistic than "unfavourable". It was acknowledged that this made the probability of the actual outcome falling outside the bands much larger, but no quantification was given. (A probability range for potential GDP growth, a key element of the scenarios, can be found in Huizinga (2001), but no comparable estimate of actual outcomes.) All the above terminology lacks precision and is open to subjective interpretation, and ambiguity persists in the absence of a probability statement. Its absence also implies that *ex post* evaluation of the forecasts can only be undertaken descriptively, and that no systematic statistical evaluation is possible.

The objections in the preceding two sentences apply to all examples of the use of scenarios in an attempt to convey uncertainty about future outcomes. How to assess the reliability of statements about forecast uncertainty, assuming that these are quantitative, not qualitative, is the subject of Section 3 below.

2.5 *Uncertainty and disagreement in survey forecasts*

In the absence of direct measures of future uncertainty, early researchers turned to the surveys of forecasters that collected their point forecasts, and suggested that the disagreement among forecasters invariably observed in such surveys might serve as a useful proxy measure of uncertainty. In 1968 the survey now known as the Survey of Professional Forecasters (SPF) was inaugurated, and since this collects density forecasts as well as point forecasts in due course it allowed study of the relationship between direct measures of uncertainty and such proxies, in a line of research initiated by Zarnowitz and Lambros (1987) that remains active to the present time.

The SPF represents the longest-running series of density forecasts in macroeconomics, thanks to the agreement of the Business and Economic Statistics Section of the American Statistical Association and the National Bureau of Economic Research jointly to establish a quarterly survey of macroeconomic forecasters in the United States, originally known as the ASA-NBER survey. Zarnowitz (1969) describes its objectives, and discusses the first results. In 1990 the Federal Reserve Bank of Philadelphia assumed responsibility for the survey, and changed its name to the Survey of Professional Forecasters. Survey respondents are asked not only to report their point forecasts of several variables, but also to attach a probability to each of a number of preassigned intervals, or bins, into which future GNP growth and inflation might fall. In this way, respondents provide their density forecasts of these two variables, in the form of histograms. The probabilities are then averaged over respondents to obtain the mean or aggregate density forecasts, again in the form of histograms, and these are published on the Bank's website. A recent example is shown in Table 1.

Zarnowitz and Lambros (1987) define "consensus" as the degree of agreement among point forecasts of the same variable by different forecasters, and "uncertainty" as the dispersion of the corresponding probability distributions. Their emphasis on the distinction between them was motivated by several previous studies in which high dispersion of point forecasts had been interpreted as indicating high uncertainty, as noted above. Access to a direct measure of uncertainty now provided the opportunity for Zarnowitz and Lambros to check this presumption, among other things. Their definitions are made operational by calculating time series of: (a) the mean of the standard deviations calculated from the individual density forecasts, and (b) the standard deviations of the corresponding sets of point forecasts, for two variables and four forecast

Table 1. SPF mean probability of possible percent changes in GDP and prices, quarter 4, 2006

	2005–2006	2006–2007
Real GDP		
≥ 6.0	0.11	0.39
5.0 to 5.9	0.30	0.72
4.0 to 4.9	2.41	3.30
3.0 to 3.9	73.02	19.43
2.0 to 2.9	19.49	48.30
1.0 to 1.9	3.30	19.59
0.0 to 0.9	0.92	5.43
−1.0 to −0.1	0.21	1.88
−2.0 to −1.1	0.16	0.62
< −2.0	0.07	0.33
GDP price index		
≥ 8.0	0.17	0.20
7.0 to 7.9	0.28	0.28
6.0 to 6.9	0.37	0.93
5.0 to 5.9	1.17	1.59
4.0 to 4.9	5.65	5.04
3.0 to 3.9	40.48	23.96
2.0 to 2.9	48.20	49.93
1.0 to 1.9	3.13	15.63
0.0 to 0.9	0.52	2.24
< 0	0.02	0.20

Notes. Number of forecasters reporting is 46. Released 13 November 2006.
Source: http://www.phil.frb.org/files/spf/spfq406.pdf (Table 4).

horizons. As the strict sense of "consensus" is unanimous agreement, we prefer to call the second series a measure of disagreement. They find that the uncertainty (a) series are typically larger and more stable than the disagreement (b) series, thus measures of uncertainty based on the forecast distributions "should be more dependable". The two series are positively correlated, however, hence in the absence of direct measures of uncertainty a measure of disagreement among point forecasts may be a useful proxy.

A formal relationship among measures of uncertainty and disagreement can be obtained as follows. Denote n individual density forecasts of a variable y at some future time as $f_i(y)$, $i = 1,...,n$. In the SPF these are expressed numerically, as histograms, but the statistical framework also accommodates density forecasts that are expressed analytically, for example, via the normal or two-piece normal distributions. For economy of notation time subscripts and references to the information sets on which the forecasts are conditioned are suppressed. The published mean or aggregate density forecast is then

$$f_A(y) = \frac{1}{n}\sum_{i=1}^{n} f_i(y),$$

which is an example of a finite mixture distribution. The finite mixture distribution is well known in the statistical literature, though not hitherto in the forecasting literature; it provides an appropriate statistical model for a combined density forecast. (Note that in this section n denotes the size of a cross-section sample, whereas elsewhere it denotes the size of a time-series sample. We do not explicitly consider panel data at any point, so the potential ambiguity should not be a problem.)

The moments about the origin of $f_A(y)$ are given as the same equally-weighted sum of the moments about the origin of the individual densities. We assume that the individual point forecasts are the means of the individual forecast densities and so denote these means as $\hat{y}_i$; the individual variances are σ_i^2. Then the mean of the aggregate density is

$$\mu_1' = \frac{1}{n}\sum_{i=1}^{n} \hat{y}_i = \hat{y}_A,$$

namely the average point forecast, and the second moment about the origin is

$$\mu_2' = \frac{1}{n}\sum_{i=1}^{n}\left(\hat{y}_i^2 + \sigma_i^2\right).$$

Hence the variance of f_A is

$$\sigma_A^2 = \mu_2' - \mu_1'^2 = \frac{1}{n}\sum_{i=1}^{n}\sigma_i^2 + \frac{1}{n}\sum_{i=1}^{n}\left(\hat{y}_i - \hat{y}_A\right)^2.$$

This expression decomposes the variance of the aggregate density, σ_A^2, a possible measure of collective uncertainty, into the average individual uncertainty or variance, plus a measure of the dispersion of, or disagreement between, the individual point forecasts. The two components are analogous to the measures of uncertainty and disagreement calculated by Zarnowitz and Lambros, although their use of standard deviations rather than variances breaks the above equation; in any event Zarnowitz and Lambros seem unaware of their role in decomposing the variance of the aggregate distribution. The decomposition lies behind more recent analyses of the SPF data, by Giordani and Soderlind (2003), for example, although their statistical framework seems less appropriate. The choice of measure of collective uncertainty – the variance of the aggregate density forecast or the average individual variance – is still under discussion in the recent literature.

(*Note.* This use of the finite mixture distribution was first presented in the May 2004 lectures, then extended in an article in a special issue of the *Oxford Bulletin of Economics and Statistics*; see Wallis, 2005.)

3. Evaluating Interval and Density Forecasts

Decision theory considerations suggest that forecasts of all kinds should be evaluated in a specific decision context, in terms of the gains and losses that resulted from using the forecasts to solve a sequence of decision problems. As noted above, however, macroeconomic forecasts are typically published for general use, with little knowledge of users' specific decision contexts, and their evaluation is in practice based on their statistical performance. How this is done is the subject of this section, which considers interval and density forecasts in turn, and includes two applications.

3.1 *Likelihood ratio tests of interval forecasts*

Given a time series of interval forecasts with announced probability π that the outcome will fall within the stated interval, *ex ante*, and the corresponding series of observed outcomes, the first question is whether this coverage probability is correct *ex post*. Or, on the other hand, is the relative frequency with which outcomes were observed to fall inside the interval significantly different from π? If in n observations there are n_1 outcomes falling in their respective forecast intervals and n_0 outcomes falling outside, then the *ex post* coverage is $p = n_1/n$. From the binomial distribution the likelihood under the null hypothesis is

$$L(\pi) \propto \left(1-\pi\right)^{n_0} \pi^{n_1},$$

and the likelihood under the alternative hypothesis, evaluated at the maximum likelihood estimate p, is

$$L(p) \propto \left(1-p\right)^{n_0} p^{n_1}.$$

The likelihood ratio test statistic $-2 \log\left(L(\pi)/L(p)\right)$ is denoted LR_{uc} by Christoffersen (1998), and is then

$$\mathrm{LR}_{uc} = 2\left(n_0 \log(1-p)/(1-\pi) + n_1 \log(p/\pi)\right).$$

It is asymptotically distributed as chi-squared with one degree of freedom, denoted χ_1^2, under the null hypothesis.

The LR_{uc} notation follows Christoffersen's argument that this is a test of *unconditional* coverage, and that this is inadequate in a time-series context. He defines an efficient sequence of interval forecasts as one which has correct *conditional* coverage and develops a likelihood ratio test of this hypothesis, which combines the test of unconditional coverage with a test of independence. This supplementary hypothesis is directly analogous to the requirement of lack of autocorrelation of orders greater than or equal to the forecast lead time in the errors of a sequence of efficient point forecasts. It is implemented in a two-state (the outcome lies in the interval or not) Markov chain, as a likelihood ratio test of the null hypothesis that successive observations are statistically independent, against the alternative hypothesis that the observations are from a first-order Markov chain.

A test of independence against a first-order Markov chain alternative is based on the matrix of transition counts $[n_{ij}]$, where n_{ij} is the number of observations in state i at time $t-1$ and j at time t. The maximum likelihood estimates of the transition probabilities are the cell frequencies divided by the corresponding row totals. For an interval forecast there are two states – the outcome lies inside or outside the interval – and these are denoted 1 and 0 respectively. The estimated transition probability matrix is

$$P = \begin{bmatrix} 1-p_{01} & p_{01} \\ 1-p_{11} & p_{11} \end{bmatrix} = \begin{bmatrix} n_{00}/n_{0\cdot} & n_{01}/n_{0\cdot} \\ n_{10}/n_{1\cdot} & n_{11}/n_{1\cdot} \end{bmatrix},$$

where replacing a subscript with a dot denotes that summation has been taken over that index. The likelihood evaluated at P is

$$L(P) \propto \left(1-p_{01}\right)^{n_{00}} p_{01}^{n_{01}} \left(1-p_{11}\right)^{n_{10}} p_{11}^{n_{11}} .$$

The null hypothesis of independence is that the state at t is independent of the state at $t-1$, that is, $\pi_{01} = \pi_{11}$, and the maximum likelihood estimate of the common probability is $p = n_{\cdot 1}/n$. The likelihood under the null, evaluated at p, is

$$L(p) \propto \left(1-p\right)^{n_{\cdot 0}} p^{n_{\cdot 1}} .$$

This is identical to $L(p)$ defined above if the first observation is ignored. The likelihood ratio test statistic is then

$$\mathrm{LR}_{\mathrm{ind}} = -2 \log\left(L(p)/L(P)\right)$$

which is asymptotically distributed as χ_1^2 under the independence hypothesis.

Christoffersen proposes a likelihood ratio test of conditional coverage as a joint test of unconditional coverage and independence. It is a test of the original null hypothesis against the alternative hypothesis of the immediately preceding paragraph, and the test statistic is

$$\mathrm{LR}_{\mathrm{cc}} = -2 \log\left(L(\pi)/L(P)\right) .$$

Again ignoring the first observation the test statistics obey the relation

$$\mathrm{LR}_{\mathrm{cc}} = \mathrm{LR}_{\mathrm{uc}} + \mathrm{LR}_{\mathrm{ind}} .$$

Asymptotically $\mathrm{LR}_{\mathrm{cc}}$ has a χ_2^2 distribution under the null hypothesis. The alternative hypothesis for $\mathrm{LR}_{\mathrm{ind}}$ and $\mathrm{LR}_{\mathrm{cc}}$ is the same, and these tests form an ordered nested sequence.

3.2 *Chi-squared tests of interval forecasts*

It is well known that the likelihood ratio tests for such problems are asymptotically equivalent to Pearson's chi-squared goodness-of-fit tests. For general discussion and proofs, and references to earlier literature, see Stuart, Ord and Arnold (1999, ch 25). In discussing this equivalence for the Markov chain tests they develop, Anderson and Goodman (1957) note that the chi-squared tests, which are of the form used in contingency tables, have the advantage that "for many users of these methods, their motivation and their application seem to be simpler". This point of view leads Wallis (2003) to explore the equivalent chi-squared tests for interval forecasts, and their extension to density forecasts.

To test the unconditional coverage of interval forecasts, the chi-squared statistic that is asymptotically equivalent to LR_{uc} is the square of the standard normal test statistic of a sample proportion, namely

$$X^2 = n(p-\pi)^2 / \pi(1-\pi).$$

The asymptotic result rests on the asymptotic normality of the binomial distribution of the observed frequencies, and in finite samples an exact test can be based on the binomial distribution.

For testing independence, the chi-squared test of independence in a 2×2 contingency table is asymptotically equivalent to LR_{ind}. Denoting the matrix $[n_{ij}]$ of observed frequencies alternatively as

$$\begin{bmatrix} a & b \\ c & d \end{bmatrix},$$

the statistic has the familiar expression

$$X^2 = \frac{n(ad-bc)^2}{(a+b)(c+d)(a+c)(b+d)}.$$

Equivalently, it is the square of the standard normal test statistic for the equality of two binomial proportions. In finite samples computer packages such as StatXact are available to compute exact *P*-values, by enumerating all possible tables that give rise to a value of the test statistic greater than or equal to that observed, and cumulating their null probabilities.

Finally for the conditional coverage joint test, the asymptotically equivalent chi-squared test compares the observed contingency table with the expected frequencies under the joint null hypothesis of row independence and correct coverage probability π. In the simple formula for Pearson's statistic memorised by multitudes of students, $\Sigma (O - E)^2 / E$, the observed (O) and expected (E) frequencies are, respectively,

$$\begin{bmatrix} a & b \\ c & d \end{bmatrix} \text{ and } \begin{bmatrix} (1-\pi)(a+b) & \pi(a+b) \\ (1-\pi)(c+d) & \pi(c+d) \end{bmatrix}.$$

The test has two degrees of freedom since the column proportions are specified by the hypothesis under test and not estimated. The statistic is equal to the sum of the squares of two standard normal test statistics of sample proportions, one for each row of the table. Although the chi-squared statistics for the separate and joint hypotheses are asymptotically equivalent to the corresponding likelihood ratio statistics, in finite samples they obey the additive relation satisfied by the LR statistics only approximately, and not exactly.

To illustrate the two approaches to testing we consider the data on the SPF mean density forecasts of inflation, 1969-1996, analysed by Diebold, Tay and Wallis (1999) and used by Wallis (2003) to illustrate the chi-squared tests. The series of forecasts and outcomes are shown in Figure 4. The density forecasts are represented by box-and-whisker plots, the box giving the interquartile range and the whiskers the 10th and 90th percentiles; these are obtained by linear interpolation of the published histograms. For the present purpose we treat the interquartile range as the relevant interval forecast. Taking the first observation as the initial condition for the transition counts leaves 27 further observations, of which 19 lie inside the box and 8 outside. Christoffersen's LR_{uc} statistic is equal to 4.61, and Pearson's chi-squared statistic is equal to 4.48. The asymptotic critical value at the 5% level is 3.84, hence the null hypothesis of correct coverage, unconditionally, with $\pi = 0.5$, is rejected.

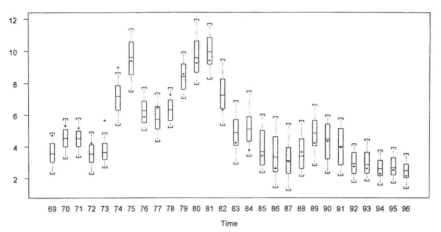

Note: outcomes are denoted by diamonds; forecast inter-quartile ranges by boxes.
Source: Diebold, Tay and Wallis (1999).

Figure 4. US inflation: SPF mean density forecasts and outcomes, 1969-1996

The matrix of transition counts is

$$\begin{bmatrix} 5 & 4 \\ 3 & 15 \end{bmatrix}$$

which yields values of the LR_{ind} and X^2 statistics of 4.23 and 4.35 respectively. Thus the null hypothesis of independence is rejected. Finally, summing the two likelihood ratio statistics gives the value 8.84 for LR_{cc}, whereas the direct chi-squared statistic of the preceding paragraph is 8.11, which illustrates the lack of additivity among the chi-squared statistics. Its exact P-value in the two binomial proportions model is 0.018, indicating rejection of the conditional coverage joint hypothesis. Overall the two asymptotically equivalent approaches give different values of the test statistics in finite samples, but in this example they are not sufficiently different to result in different conclusions.

3.3 *Extension to density forecasts*

For interval forecasts the calibration of each tail may be of interest, to check the estimation of the balance of risks to the forecast. If the forecast is presented as a central interval, with equal tail probabilities, then the expected frequencies under the null hypothesis of correct coverage are $n(1-\pi)/2$, $n\pi$, $n(1-\pi)/2$ respectively, and the chi-squared statistic comparing these with the observed frequencies has two degrees of freedom.

This is a step towards goodness-of-fit tests for complete density forecasts, where the choice of the number of classes, k, into which to divide the observed outcomes is typically related to the size of the sample. The conventional answer to the question of how class boundaries should be determined is to use equiprobable classes, so that the expected class frequencies under the null hypothesis are equal, at n/k. With observed class frequencies n_i, $i = 1,..., k$, $\Sigma n_i = n$, the chi-squared statistic for testing goodness-of-fit is

$$X^2 = \sum_{i=1}^{k} \frac{(n_i - n/k)^2}{(n/k)} \ .$$

It has a limiting χ^2_{k-1} distribution under the null hypothesis.

The asymptotic distribution of the test statistic rests on the asymptotic k-variate normality of the multinomial distribution of the observed frequencies. Placing these in the $k \times 1$ vector x, under the null hypothesis this has mean vector $\mu = (n/k,...,n/k)$ and covariance matrix

$$V = (n/k)\left[I - ee'/k\right],$$

where e is a $k \times 1$ vector of ones. The covariance matrix is singular, with rank $k-1$. Defining its generalised inverse V^-, the limiting distribution of the quadratic form $(x-\mu)'V^-(x-\mu)$ is then χ^2_{k-1} (Pringle and Rayner, 1971, p.78). Since the above matrix in square brackets is symmetric and idempotent it coincides with its generalised inverse, and the chi-squared statistic given in the preceding paragraph is equivalently written as

$$X^2 = (x-\mu)'\left[I - ee'/k\right](x-\mu)\big/(n/k)$$

(note that $e'(x-\mu) = 0$). There exists a $(k-1) \times k$ transformation matrix A such that (Rao and Rao, 1998, p.252)

$$AA' = I, \quad A'A = [I - ee'/k].$$

Hence defining $y = A(x - \mu)$ the statistic can be written as an alternative sum of squares

$$X^2 = y'y/(n/k)$$

where the $k-1$ components $y_i^2/(n/k)$ are independently distributed as χ_1^2 under the null hypothesis.

Anderson (1994) introduces this decomposition in order to focus on particular characteristics of the distribution of interest. For example, with $k = 4$ and

$$A = \frac{1}{2} \begin{bmatrix} 1 & 1 & -1 & -1 \\ 1 & -1 & -1 & 1 \\ 1 & -1 & 1 & -1 \end{bmatrix}$$

the three components focus in turn on departures from the null distribution with respect to location, scale and skewness. Such decompositions are potentially more informative about the nature of departures from the null distribution than the single "portmanteau" goodness-of-fit statistic. Anderson (1994) claims that the decomposition also applies in the case of non-equiprobable classes, but Boero, Smith and Wallis (2004) show that this is not correct. They also show how to construct the matrix A from Hadamard matrices.

The test of independence of interval forecasts in the Markov chain framework generalises immediately to density forecasts grouped into k classes. However the matrix of transition counts is now $k \times k$, and with sample sizes that are typical in macroeconomic forecasting this matrix is likely to be sparse once k gets much beyond 2 or 3, the values relevant to interval forecasts. The investigation of possible higher-order dependence becomes even less practical in the Markov chain approach, since the dimension of the transition matrix increases with the square of the order of the chain. In these circumstances other approaches based on transformation rather than grouping of the data are more useful, as discussed next.

3.4 *The probability integral transformation*

The chi-squared goodness-of-fit tests suffer from the loss of information caused by grouping of the data. The leading alternative tests of fit all make use, directly or indirectly, of the probability integral transform. In the present context, if a forecast density $f(y)$ with corresponding distribution function $F(y)$ is correct, then the transformed variable

$$u = \int_{-\infty}^{y} f(x)dx = F(y)$$

is uniformly distributed on $(0,1)$. For a sequence of one-step-ahead forecasts $f_{t-1}(y)$ and corresponding outcomes y_t, a test of fit can then be based on testing the departure of the sequence $u_t = F_{t-1}(y_t)$ from uniformity. Intuitively, the u-values tell us in which percentiles of the forecast densities the outcomes fell, and we should expect to see all the percentiles occupied equally in a long run of correct probability forecasts. The advantage of the transformation is that, in order to test goodness-of-fit, the "true" density does not have to be specified.

Diebold, Gunther and Tay (1998), extending the perspective of Christoffersen (1998) from interval forecasts to density forecasts, show that if a sequence of density forecasts is correctly conditionally calibrated, then the corresponding u-sequence is iid $U(0,1)$. They present histograms of u for visual assessment of unconditional uniformity, and various autocorrelation tests.

A test of goodness-of-fit that does not suffer the disadvantage of grouping can be based on the sample cumulative distribution function of the u-values. The distribution function of the $U(0,1)$ distribution is a 45-degree line, and the Kolmogorov-Smirnov test is based on the maximum absolute difference between this null distribution function and the sample distribution function. Miller (1956) provides tables of critical values for this test. It is used by Diebold, Tay and Wallis (1999) in their evaluation of the SPF mean density forecasts of inflation. As in most classical statistics, the test is based on an assumption of random sampling, and although this corresponds to the joint null hypothesis of independence and uniformity in the density forecast context, little is known about the properties of the test in respect of departures from independence. Hence to obtain direct information about possible directions of departure from the joint null hypothesis, separate tests have been employed, as noted above. However standard tests for autocorrelation face difficulties when the variable is bounded, and a further transformation has been proposed to overcome these.

3.5 *The inverse normal transformation*

Given probability integral transforms u_t, we consider the inverse normal transformation

$$z_t = \Phi^{-1}(u_t)$$

where $\Phi(\cdot)$ is the standard normal distribution function. Then if u_t is iid $U(0,1)$, it follows that z_t is iid $N(0,1)$. The advantages of this second transformation are that there are more tests available for normality, it is easier to test autocorrelation under normality than uniformity, and the normal likelihood can be used to construct likelihood ratio tests.

We note that in cases where the density forecast is explicitly based on the normal distribution, centred on a point forecast $\hat{y}_t$ with standard deviation σ_t, as in some examples discussed above, then the double transformation returns the standardised value of the outcome $(y_t - \hat{y}_t)/\sigma_t$, which could be calculated directly.

Berkowitz (2001) proposes likelihood ratio tests for testing hypotheses about the transformed series z_t. In the AR(1) model

$$z_t - \mu = \phi(z_{t-1} - \mu) + \varepsilon_t, \quad \varepsilon_t \sim N\left(0, \sigma_\varepsilon^2\right)$$

the hypotheses of interest are $\mu = 0$, $\sigma_\varepsilon^2 = 1$ and $\phi = 0$. The exact likelihood function of the normal AR(1) model is well known; denote it $L(\mu, \sigma_\varepsilon^2, \phi)$. Then a test of independence can be based on the statistic

$$\mathrm{LR}_{\mathrm{ind}} = -2\left(\log L(\hat{\mu}, \hat{\sigma}_\varepsilon^2, 0) - \log L(\hat{\mu}, \hat{\sigma}_\varepsilon^2, \hat{\phi})\right)$$

and a joint test of the above three hypotheses on

$$\mathrm{LR} = -2\left(\log L(0,1,0) - \log L(\hat{\mu}, \hat{\sigma}_\varepsilon^2, \hat{\phi})\right)$$

where the hats denote estimated values. However this approach does not provide tests for more general departures from iid $N(0,1)$, in particular non-normality.

Moment-based tests of normality are an obvious extension, with a long history. Defining the central moments

$$\mu_j = E(z - \mu)^j$$

the conventional moment-based measures of skewness and kurtosis are

$$\beta_1 = \frac{\mu_3^2}{\mu_2^3} \text{ and } \beta_2 = \frac{\mu_4}{\mu_2^2}$$

respectively. Sometimes $\sqrt{\beta_1}$ and $(\beta_2 - 3)$ are more convenient measures; both are equal to zero if z is normally distributed. Given the equivalent sample statistics,

$$\hat{\mu}_j = \frac{1}{n} \sum_{t=1}^{n} (z_t - \bar{z})^j, \quad \sqrt{b_1} = \frac{\hat{\mu}_3}{\hat{\mu}_2^{3/2}}, \quad b_2 = \frac{\hat{\mu}_4}{\hat{\mu}_2^2},$$

Bowman and Shenton (1975) showed that the test statistic

$$B = n \left(\frac{\left(\sqrt{b_1} \right)^2}{6} + \frac{(b_2 - 3)^2}{24} \right)$$

is asymptotically distributed as χ_2^2 under the null hypothesis of normality. This test is often attributed to Jarque and Bera (1980) rather than Bowman and Shenton. Jarque and Bera's contributions were to show that B is a score or Lagrange multiplier test statistic and hence asymptotically efficient, and to derive a correction for the case of hypotheses about regression disturbances, when the statistic is based on regression residuals. However the correction drops out if the residual sample mean is zero, as is the case in many popular regression models, such as least squares regression with a constant term.

A second possible extension, due to Bao, Lee and Saltoglu (2007), is to specify a flexible alternative distribution for ε_t that nests the normal distribution, for example a semi-nonparametric density function, and include the additional restrictions that reduce it to normality among the hypotheses under test.

Bao, Lee and Saltoglu also show that the likelihood ratio tests are equivalent to tests based on the Kullback-Leibler information criterion (KLIC) or distance measure between the forecast and "true" densities. For a density forecast $f_1(y)$ and a "true" density $f_0(y)$ the KLIC distance is defined as

$$I(f_0, f_1) = E_0 \big(\log f_0(y) - \log f_1(y) \big).$$

With E replaced by a sample average, and using transformed data z, a KLIC-based test is equivalent to a test based on

$$\log g_1(z) - \log \phi(z),$$

the likelihood ratio, where g_1 is the forecast density of z and ϕ is the standard normal density. Equivalently, the likelihood ratio statistic measures the distance of the forecast density from the "true" density. Again the transformation from $\{y\}$ to $\{z\}$ obviates the need to specify the "true" density of y, but some assumption about the density of z is still needed for this kind of test, such as their example in the previous paragraph. Berkowitz specifies g_1 as autoregressive $N\big(\mu, \sigma^2\big)$, as discussed above.

3.6 *The Bank of England's inflation forecasts*

To illustrate some of these procedures we present an evaluation of the Bank of England's density forecasts of inflation, drawn from Wallis (2004). The density forecast first published in the Bank of England's quarterly *Inflation Report* in February 1996 became the responsibility of the Monetary Policy Committee (MPC) on its establishment in 1997, when the Bank was given operational independence. Our evaluation follows the practice of the analyses of the MPC's forecasting record published in the August issue of the *Inflation Report* each year since 1999, by starting from the MPC's first inflation projection published in August 1997, and by focusing on the one-year-ahead forecasts. Strictly speaking, the forecasts are conditional projections, based on the assumption that interest rates remain at the level just agreed by the MPC. They begin with a current-quarter forecast, and extend up to eight quarters ahead. Nevertheless it is argued that the one-year-ahead projections can be evaluated as unconditional forecasts, using standard forecast evaluation procedures, since inflation does not react quickly to changes in the interest rate. On the other hand the inflation outcome two years ahead is likely to be influenced by intervening policy shifts, whose impact is difficult to estimate when comparing the outcome to a forecast with a strong judgemental component, as here. The two-year projection has played an important part in establishing policy credibility, with the central projection seldom deviating far from the inflation target.

The forecast parameters, inflation outcomes and associated u-values for 22 one-year-ahead forecasts are shown in Table 2. Forecasts are dated by the publication date of the *Inflation Report* in which they appear, and the inflation outcome refers to the corresponding quarter one year later. The inflation measure is the annual percentage change in the quarterly Retail Prices Index excluding mortgage interest payments (RPIX, Office for National Statistics code CHMK). Over the sample period 1997q3-2003q4 its mean is 2.40 and its standard deviation is 0.34.

With respect to the asymmetry of the forecast densities, it is seen that 13 of them exhibit positive skewness, with the mean exceeding the mode, whereas five are symmetric and four are negatively skewed. The balance of risks was thought to be on the upside of the forecast more often than not, although the average of the Bank's preferred skew measure (mean minus mode), at 0.075, is small.

Evaluations of point forecasts typically focus on the conditional expectation, the mean of the forecast density, and the *Inflation Report* forecast analyses follow suit, despite the focus on the mode, the most likely outcome, in the MPC's forecast commentary and press releases. The mean forecasts in Table 2 have an average error of zero (0.01, to be precise), thus these forecasts are unbiased. The tendency to overestimate inflation in the early part of the sample is offset by the more recent underestimation. Important contributions to this experience were the unanticipated persistence of the strength of sterling in the early years, followed more recently by surprisingly high house price inflation, which contributes to the housing depreciation component of RPIX inflation.

Table 2. Bank of England Monetary Policy Committee inflation forecasts: One-year-ahead forecasts and outcomes ($n = 22$)

Inflation Report	(1) Mode	(2) Mean	(3) Std. Dev.	(4) Outcome	(5) *u*
Aug 97	1.99	2.20	0.79	2.55	0.68
Nov 97	2.19	2.72	0.75	2.53	0.45
Feb 98	2.44	2.53	0.50	2.53	0.51
May 98	2.37	2.15	0.66	2.30	0.56
Aug 98	2.86	3.00	0.62	2.17	0.08
Nov 98	2.59	2.72	0.64	2.16	0.19
Feb 99	2.52	2.58	0.62	2.09	0.22
May 99	2.23	2.34	0.60	2.07	0.34
Aug 99	1.88	2.03	0.59	2.13	0.58
Nov 99	1.84	1.79	0.55	2.11	0.72
Feb 00	2.32	2.42	0.57	1.87	0.17
May 00	2.47	2.52	0.55	2.26	0.32
Aug 00	2.48	2.48	0.54	2.38	0.43
Nov 00	2.19	2.24	0.56	1.95	0.31
Feb 01	2.09	2.04	0.55	2.37	0.72
May 01	1.94	1.89	0.55	1.86	0.47
Aug 01	1.96	1.96	0.55	2.00	0.52
Nov 01	2.06	2.26	0.60	2.61	0.73
Feb 02	2.13	2.33	0.59	2.89	0.83
May 02	2.05	2.05	0.52	2.90	0.95
Aug 02	2.31	2.31	0.51	2.87	0.87
Nov 02	2.41	2.41	0.48	2.58	0.64

Notes on sources: (1), (2): Bank of England spreadsheets, see
http://www.bankofengland.co.uk/inflationreport/irprobab.htm;
(3), (5): calculated using code written in the Gauss Programming Language by Michael
Clements. The standard deviation is the square root of the variance given on p. 20; u is
the probability integral transform of the inflation outcome in the forecast distribution;
(4): annual percentage growth in quarterly RPIX, ONS code CHMK

The standard deviation of the forecast errors is 0.42, indicating that
the standard deviation of the fan chart distributions is an overestimate. A
90% confidence interval is (0.34, 0.56), and the recent entries in column
(3) of Table 2 cluster around its upper limit. The dispersion of the fan
charts has tended to decrease over the period, perhaps in recognition of a
decline in the volatility of inflation, although the realised uncertainty is
less than that assumed by the MPC at any time. This finding can be
expected to dominate assessments of the goodness-of-fit of the complete

distributions. A simple approach is to assess the coverage of the interquartile range, as in the SPF illustration in Section 3.2. We find that, rather than containing the nominal 50% of the outcomes, they actually contain some two-thirds of the outcomes, with 15 of the 22 u-values falling between 0.25 and 0.75. The forecast interquartile ranges were too wide. More generally the class frequencies in the four classes defined by the quartiles, which are equiprobable under the hypothesis of correct distributions, are 4, 6, 9, 3. The chi-squared goodness-of-fit statistic is 3.82, compared to the asymptotic critical value at the 5% level of 7.81. The data show little evidence of asymmetry, although it is only the first three outcomes in 2003 that have delivered this finding by falling in the uppermost quarter of the fan charts.

A more complete picture of the correspondence or otherwise of the fan chart forecasts to the correct distribution is given in Figure 5. This compares the sample distribution function of the observed u-values with the uniform distribution function, the 45° line representing the hypothesis that the densities are correct. It is again seen that there are fewer

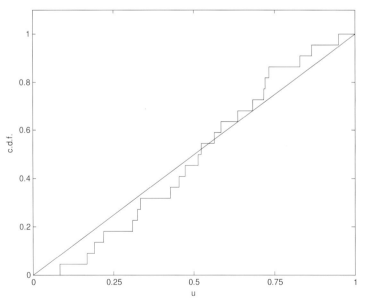

Figure 5. Bank of England Monetary Policy Committee inflation forecasts: cumulative distribution functions of sample u-values ($n=22$) and uniform distribution

observations than there "should" be in the outer ranges of the forecasts, with the sample distribution function being correspondingly steeper than the 45° line in the central region. The fan charts fanned out too much. Whether exaggerated views of uncertainty led to undue caution in the setting of interest rates is an open research question.

3.7 *Comparing density forecasts*

A recent development in density forecasting is the comparative evaluation of forecasts, given the existence in some circumstances of competing density forecasts of the same outcome. This is a reflection, to date a small one, of the extensive literature on the comparison of point forecasts. In both cases such forecasts are sometimes genuinely competitive, having been constructed by different groups using different models or methods, and sometimes artificially competitive, a competing "benchmark" or "naïve" forecast having been constructed by forecasters wishing to undertake a comparative evaluation of their own forecasts. Either way, two activities are usually distinguished, namely hypothesis testing – is there a significant difference in forecast performance? – and model selection – which forecast is best? And in each activity, how sensitive are the results to the choice of measure of performance? We consider three groups of possible measures of performance, namely scoring rules, test statistics and distance measures, and an equivalence between them.

Scoring rules have been principally developed in probability forecasting, which has a long history in meteorology and medicine. The two leading measures are the quadratic probability or "Brier" score and the logarithmic score, which can be readily adapted to density forecasts. Given a series of density forecasts presented as k-bin histograms with bin probabilities p_{jt}, $j = 1,...,k$, and defining an indicator variable $I_{jt} = 1$ if the outcome y_t, $t = 1,...,n$, falls in bin j, otherwise $I_{jt} = 0$, the quadratic probability score is

$$QPS = \frac{1}{n}\sum_{t=1}^{n}\sum_{j=1}^{k}\left(p_{jt} - I_{jt}\right)^2, \quad 0 \le QPS \le 2.$$

The logarithmic score, abbreviated to *Slog*, is

$$Slog = \frac{1}{n}\sum_{t=1}^{n}\sum_{j=1}^{k} I_{jt} \log\left(p_{jt}\right) \quad \text{or} \quad \frac{1}{n}\sum_{t=1}^{n} \log\left(f_{t-1}\left(y_t\right)\right)$$

if $f_{t-1}(y)$ is a continuous (one-step-ahead) forecast density. It is entirely possible that different rankings of competing forecasts are given by the different scoring rules.

For two density forecasts $f_1(y)$ and $f_2(y)$, Bao, Lee and Saltoglu (2007) consider the KLIC difference

$$I\left(f_0, f_1\right) - I\left(f_0, f_2\right).$$

Again replacing E by a sample average, but without transforming the data, a likelihood ratio test of equal forecast performance can be based on the sample average of

$$\log f_2\left(y_t\right) - \log f_1\left(y_t\right).$$

Amisano and Giacomini (2007) develop the same test by starting from the logarithmic score as a comparative measure of forecast performance. Using outcomes $\{y\}$ rather than transformed data $\{z\}$ (or $\{u\}$) is preferred, because the need to specify and/or estimate the density of z (or u) is avoided. This is not an issue in comparing goodness-of-fit statistics of competing forecasts based on transforms, such as statistics assessing departures from uniformity of $\{u\}$. While these can be readily applied to model selection problems, few hypothesis testing procedures are as yet available.

Comparisons of the goodness-of-fit of competing forecasts may also be undertaken as a preliminary to determining the weights that might be employed in the construction of a combined forecast. Mitchell and Hall (2005) consider combinations of two competing density forecasts of UK inflation, using weights based on their relative Berkowitz LR test statistics, which they interpret as "KLIC weights". They find that the combined forecast performs worse than the better of the two individual forecasts. That combining with an inferior forecast could improve matters seems counter intuitive, but for point forecasts this is what the original result of Bates and Granger (1969) shows, if the "optimal" weights are used. Their result is that a linear combination of two competing point forecasts using the optimal (variance minimising) weight in general has a smaller forecast mse than either of the two competing forecasts. The only case in which no improvement is possible is that in which one forecast is already the minimum mse forecast; its optimal weight is then 1, and there is no gain in combining with an inferior forecast. Bates and Granger work analytically in the widely accepted least squares framework, but there is as yet no comparable setting in which to consider density forecast combination (Wallis, 2005).

4. Conclusion

It is now widely recognised that a point forecast is seldom sufficient for well-informed decision-making in the face of an uncertain future, and that it needs to be supplemented with some indication of the degree of uncertainty. The first main section of these lecture notes surveys the different ways in which economic forecasters measure and report uncertainty, and discusses some of the technical issues that arise. It is seen that much progress has been made in recent years in measuring and reporting forecast uncertainty. However there is still reluctance in some quarters to adopt the international language of uncertainty, namely probability.

The second main section surveys recent research on statistical methods for the evaluation of interval and density forecasts. The discussion aims to convey the principles and key ideas that underlie these methods, and some technical issues of interest to specialists are left on one side. These include the distinction between in-sample and out-of-sample analysis, the effects of parameter estimation error, finite-sample issues and the use of the bootstrap to estimate exact p-values, and the possibility of direct estimation of the "true" $f_0(y)$. Their importance and possible resolution is often related to the size of the available sample of data, and there is a major contrast in this respect between macroeconomic forecasting, which is our main concern, and financial analysis based on high-frequency data, discussed elsewhere in this program. In both fields many outstanding research problems remain, and this is an active and fruitful area in which to work.

References

Amisano, G. and Giacomini, R. (2007). Comparing density forecasts via weighted likelihood ratio tests. *Journal of Business and Economic Statistics*, 25, 177-190.

Anderson, G.J. (1994). Simple tests of distributional form. *Journal of Econometrics*, 62, 265-276.

Anderson, T.W. and Goodman, L.A. (1957). Statistical inference about Markov chains. *Annals of Mathematical Statistics*, 28, 89-110.

Bao, Y., Lee, T-H. and Saltoglu, B. (2007). Comparing density forecast models. *Journal of Forecasting*, 26, 203-255.

Bates, J.M. and Granger, C.W.J. (1969). The combination of forecasts. *Operational Research Quarterly*, 20, 451-468.

Berkowitz, J. (2001). Testing density forecasts, with applications to risk management. *Journal of Business and Economic Statistics*, 19, 465-474.

Blake, A.P. (1996). Forecast error bounds by stochastic simulation. *National Institute Economic Review*, No.156, 72-79.

Blix, M. and Sellin, P. (1998). Uncertainty bands for inflation forecasts. Working Paper No.65, Sveriges Riksbank, Stockholm.

Boero, G., Smith, J. and Wallis, K.F. (2004). Decompositions of Pearson's chi-squared test. *Journal of Econometrics*, 123, 189-193.

Bowman, K.O. and Shenton, L.R. (1975). Omnibus test contours for departures from normality based on $\sqrt{b_1}$ and b_2. *Biometrika*, 62, 243-250.

Bray, M. and Goodhart, C.A.E. (2002). "You might as well be hung for a sheep as a lamb": the loss function of an agent. Discussion Paper 418, Financial Markets Group, London School of Economics.

Britton, E., Fisher, P.G. and Whitley, J.D. (1998). The *Inflation Report* projections: understanding the fan chart. *Bank of England Quarterly Bulletin*, 38, 30-37.

Calzolari, G. and Panattoni, L. (1990). Mode predictors in nonlinear systems with identities. *International Journal of Forecasting*, 6, 317-326.

Christoffersen, P.F. (1998). Evaluating interval forecasts. *International Economic Review*, 39, 841-862.

Clements, M.P. and Hendry, D.F. (1998). *Forecasting Economic Time Series*. Cambridge: Cambridge University Press.

Congressional Budget Office (2003). The uncertainty of budget projections: a discussion of data and methods. Congressional Budget Office Report, US Congress, Washington DC.

Congressional Budget Office (2004). *The Budget and Economic Outlook: Fiscal Years 2005 to 2014; Appendix A: The Uncertainty of Budget Projections; Appendix B: How Changes in Economic Assumptions Can Affect Budget Projections*. Congressional Budget Office, US Congress, Washington DC.

Diebold, F.X., Gunther, T.A. and Tay, A.S. (1998). Evaluating density forecasts with applications to financial risk management. *International Economic Review*, 39, 863-883.

Diebold, F.X., Tay, A.S. and Wallis, K.F. (1999). Evaluating density forecasts of inflation: the Survey of Professional Forecasters. In *Cointegration, Causality, and Forecasting: A Festschrift in Honour of Clive W.J. Granger* (R.F. Engle and H. White, eds), pp.76-90. Oxford: Oxford University Press.

Don, F.J.H. (2001). Forecasting in macroeconomics: a practitioner's view. *De Economist*, 149, 155-175.

Garratt, A., Lee, K., Pesaran, M.H. and Shin, Y. (2003). Forecast uncertainties in macroeconometric modeling: an application to the UK economy. *Journal of the American Statistical Association*, 98, 829-838.

Giordani, P. and Soderlind, P. (2003). Inflation forecast uncertainty. *European Economic Review*, 47, 1037-1059.

Hall, S.G. (1986). The importance of non-linearities in large forecasting models with stochastic error processes. *Journal of Forecasting*, 5, 205-215.

Huizinga, F. (2001). Economic outlook 2003-2006. *CPB Report*, 2001/4, 16-22.

Jarque, C.M. and Bera, A.K. (1980). Efficient tests for normality, homoscedasticity and serial independence of regression residuals. *Economics Letters*, 6, 255-259.

John, S. (1982). The three-parameter two-piece normal family of distributions and its fitting. *Communications in Statistics – Theory and Methods*, 11, 879-885.

Johnson, N.L., Kotz, S. and Balakrishnan, N. (1994). *Continuous Univariate Distributions*, 2nd ed., vol. 1. New York: Wiley.

Miller, L.H. (1956). Table of percentage points of Kolmogorov statistics. *Journal of the American Statistical Association*, 51, 111-121.

Mitchell, J. and Hall, S.G. (2005). Evaluating, comparing and combining density forecasts using the KLIC with an application to the Bank of England and NIESR "fan" charts of inflation. *Oxford Bulletin of Economics and Statistics*, 67, 995-1033.

Pringle, R.M. and Rayner, A.A. (1971). *Generalized Inverse Matrices with Applications to Statistics*. London: Charles Griffin.

Rao, C.R. and Rao, M.B. (1998). *Matrix Algebra and its Applications to Statistics and Econometrics*. Singapore: World Scientific Publishing Co.

Silverman, B.W. (1986). *Density Estimation for Statistics and Data Analysis*. London: Chapman and Hall.

Stock, J.H. and Watson, M.W. (2003). *Introduction to Econometrics*. Boston, MA: Pearson Education.

Stuart, A., Ord, J.K. and Arnold, S. (1999). *Kendall's Advanced Theory of Statistics*, 6th ed., vol. 2A. London: Edward Arnold.

Tay, A.S. and Wallis, K.F. (2000). Density forecasting: a survey. *Journal of Forecasting*, 19, 235-254. Reprinted in *A Companion to Economic Forecasting* (M.P. Clements and D.F. Hendry, eds), pp.45-68. Oxford: Blackwell, 2002.

Thompson, P.A. and Miller, R.B. (1986). Sampling the future: a Bayesian approach to forecasting from univariate time series models. *Journal of Business and Economic Statistics*, 4, 427-436.

Wallis, K.F. (1995). Large-scale macroeconometric modeling. In *Handbook of Applied Econometrics* (M.H. Pesaran and M.R. Wickens, eds), pp.312-355. Oxford: Blackwell.

Wallis, K.F. (1999). Asymmetric density forecasts of inflation and the Bank of England's fan chart. *National Institute Economic Review*, No.167, 106-112.

Wallis, K.F. (2003). Chi-squared tests of interval and density forecasts, and the Bank of England's fan charts. *International Journal of Forecasting*, 19, 165-175.

Wallis, K.F. (2004). An assessment of Bank of England and National Institute inflation forecast uncertainties. *National Institute Economic Review*, No.189, 64-71.

Wallis, K.F. (2005). Combining density and interval forecasts: a modest proposal. *Oxford Bulletin of Economics and Statistics*, 67, 983-994.

Zarnowitz, V. (1969). The new ASA-NBER survey of forecasts by economic statisticians. *American Statistician*, 23(1), 12-16.

Zarnowitz, V. and Lambros, L.A. (1987). Consensus and uncertainty in economic prediction. *Journal of Political Economy*, 95, 591-621.

THE UNIVERSITY OF PENNSYLVANIA MODELS FOR HIGH-FREQUENCY MACROECONOMIC MODELING

Lawrence R. Klein

University of Pennsylvania, Department of Economics
3718 Locust Walk, Philadelphia, PA 19104, USA
E-mail: lrk@ssc.upenn.edu

Suleyman Ozmucur

University of Pennsylvania, Department of Economics
3718 Locust Walk, Philadelphia, PA 19104, USA
E-mail: ozmucur@ssc.upenn.edu

1. Introduction

Forecasting of economic activity requires the use of all available information. However, data are collected at different frequencies. For example, stock prices are available instantaneously (real time), but industrial production data are available monthly, at best. This necessitates building models which utilize data at different frequencies. This was the starting point for high-frequency macro-econometric models initiated by Klein & Sojo (1989). The approach of combining data at different frequencies is not restricted to macro-econometric models (Abeysinghe, 1998, 2000; Shen, 1996). Recently, Mariano & Murasawa (2002) construct an index of coincident indicators utilizing quarterly GDP figures and monthly indicators such as personal income, industrial production, employment, and manufacturing & trade sales.

Since GDP, the most comprehensive economic indicator, is available quarterly in many countries, initially it may only be feasible to provide forecasts for quarterly GDP and the GDP deflator. It may also be feasible to provide forecasts for components of GDP whenever high-frequency data are made available for likely indicators related to individual components.

Our long-standing conviction stands intact that detailed structural model building is the best kind of system for understanding the macro economy through its causal dynamic relationships, specified by received economic analysis. There are, however, some related approaches, based on indicator analysis that are complementary for use in high frequency analysis. For most economies, the necessary data base for structural model building, guided by consistent social accounting systems (national income and product accounts, input-output accounts, national balance sheets) are, at best, available only at annual frequencies. Many advanced industrial countries can provide the accounts at quarterly frequencies, but few, if any, can provide them at monthly frequencies.

A more complete understanding of cyclical and other turbulent dynamic movements might need even higher frequency observation, i.e. weekly, daily, or real time. It would not be impossible to construct a structural model from monthly data, but a great deal of interpolation and use of short cut procedures would have to be used; so we have turned to a specific kind of indicator method to construct econometric models at this high frequency. No doubt, systems of monthly accounts of national income and product will become available, in due course, for construction of complete structural models, and indicator analysis will probably then be used for even higher frequency, say, for a weekly model.

In a festschrift volume, honoring the business cycle indicator research of Geoffrey H. Moore, there is already a chapter that shows how leading indicators, that he found to be useful, already appear in some form or other in quarterly structural models.[1] This represents an ex-post treatment, in the sense that many forward-looking variables were quite naturally and understandably used in quarterly model construction and some turned out to be among the leading indicators that Geoffrey Moore developed, quite independently. A current quarter model may be used to estimate initial conditions (Klein & Sojo, 1989).

---

[1] See Klein (1990).

In step with new technological developments in the information sector of modern economies, attention has been paid to the use of newly available computer power, data resources, telecommunication facilities and other technical changes that made higher frequency analysis of economic statistics possible.

In a few countries, new methods of high frequency analysis (monthly or higher) have already been applied and are entirely plausible for countries such as Singapore and India, where data collection and thriving "new economy" activities have been firmly established. [2] There are excellent structural models available for India, and these have been applied on an annual basis for economic analysis (forecasting, policy implementation and quantitative historical analysis). [3] There have also been studies that use indicators. It remains to examine how these two approaches may be used in a complementary way.

The paper is in four sections. The second section deals with the methodology of the current quarter model (CQM) and performance of alternative models. The methodology used in "survey corner" is presented in the third section. Results are also compared with the help of various model selection criteria. Major conclusions are stated in the final section.

2. The Methodology of the Current Quarter Model (CQM)

There are at least three well-known accounting approaches to GDP measurement, and it is equally well-known (for several decades) that they rarely provide the same results.

Method 1. GDP is the sum of <u>final</u> purchases. This is known as demand-side estimation and happens to be the officially favored method for the USA, but not for all nations. It finds textbook expression in the accounting definition.

GDP = C(consumption) + I(investment) + G (government purchases)
   + X (exports) – M(imports).

---

[2] See, Klein (2000)
[3] See Mammen (1999), and Palanivel & Klein (2002).

In input-output accounting, it is usually displayed in the form of column sums of a rectangular matrix at the right-hand-side of the square inter-industry delivery matrix.

Method 2. GDP is the sum of income payments to the <u>original</u> factors of production.

It also is expressed in textbooks as

GDP = W(wages) + IN(interest) + P(profits) + R(rent/royalty)
+ IT(indirect tax) – S(subsidies).

In input-output accounting it is usually displayed as row sums of a rectangular matrix across the bottom of the square inter-industry matrix.

Method 3. GDP is the sum of value-added across all sectors of production. Value-added is written as

GDP = GP(gross production) – IP(intermediate production) = VA(value added).

If all statistical reports were accurate and if all economic agents were cooperative respondents or reporters, these three methods should give identical estimates. A very recent discrepancy between Method 1 and Method 2 for the USA, 2001, fourth quarter is estimated at $186 billion (seasonally adjusted annual rate). While this is a small percentage of the (unknown) total GDP of the USA, it is a very, very significant amount. It is as large as many important national policy initiatives that are meant to stabilize the economy. Revisions since 2001 change discrepancy from a large negative to a small plus, but cyclical swings are still strong. It does not go away, and it is not a random series. It has a well-established serial pattern and is closely correlated with important economic variables (Klein & Makino, 2000). The nonrandom serial correlation found in data of the discrepancy between different measures of GDP for the USA has been found in other national data, but not always between Methods 1 and 2, but sometimes between 1 and 3. Some countries do not have full statistics for Method 2.

It should be noted that there are similarities between Methods 2 and 3; they both aim for estimates of <u>value-added</u>, but Method 2 does this on an individual sector or industry basis, and Method 2 uses direct estimates of factor payments, while Method 3 derives factor payments (total or by sector) as a residual. It gets to value-added indirectly.

The methodology used in CQM is essentially based on Klein & Sojo (1989), and Klein & Park (1993, 1995). Real GDP and the GDP deflator are estimated using the expenditure side model (Method 1), and the income side model (Method 2).

In the expenditure side and the income side models, bridge equations are used to relate quarterly components to monthly indicators[4]. Bridge equations are statistical relationships between quarterly figures and averages of monthly indicators. For example, private fixed investment in information processing and related equipment (INV) in National Income and Products Accounts (NIPA)-which is available quarterly, is related to the quarterly average of manufacturers' shipments (SHIPMENT) of information technology-which is available monthly. These monthly indicators are the ones used by the US Department of Commerce, Bureau of Economic Analysis which is responsible for publishing the National Income and Products Accounts for the US (US Department of Commerce, 2002a, 2002b, 2002c). There are about 200 bridge equations in the US model. The detail is partly dictated by the composition of basic tables of the Commerce Department (US Department of Commerce, 2002a, 2002b, 2002c).

$$\text{DLOG(INV)} = 0.019 + 0.919 \text{ DLOG(SHIPMENT)} + 0.315 \text{ AR(1)} + 0.294 \text{ AR(2)} - 0.244 \text{ AR(3)}$$
$$(7.43) \quad (9.38) \qquad\qquad (3.77) \qquad (3.51) \qquad (-2.95)$$

$$R^2 = 0.531, \text{SEE} = .019, \text{F} = 38.14, \text{D.W.} = 2.01, n = 140 \ (1969 \text{ Q1} - 2003 \text{ Q4}).$$

---

[4] Augmented Dickey-Fuller (1979), Phillips-Perron (1991), and Kwiatkowski, Phillips, Schmidt, and Shin (KPSS) (1992) unit root tests were implemented to study time series properties of the series used in the model. Almost all variables are non-stationary, integrated of order one, i.e. I(1). The monthly changes or percentage changes of these variables are integrated of order zero, I (0). Eviews by Quantitative Micro Software is used in all the calculations. Critical values used in testing are based on MacKinnon (1991). For modeling non-stationary processes see, Clements & Hendry (1998, 2002), and Engle & Granger (1987, 1991).

Forecasts of monthly indicators are obtained by standard Box-Jenkins (1976) ARIMA equations. For example, month-to-month change in non-farm payroll employment is expressed as auto-regressive process of orders 1, 2, and a moving average of order 2, i.e. (ARIMA (2, 1, 2)). These monthly forecasts are averaged for the quarter and then related to quarterly variables in the model. There are over a hundred monthly indicators in the most recent version of the Current Quarter Model (CQM). It is possible to include some structural variables in this equation, such as real interest rate and real credits. However, that will increase the data requirement significantly. One has to get forecasts of those variables for the coming six months. It is not difficult to imagine the added difficulty, if one has to repeat this for about 100 such equations. This is the trade-off that one has to face and make a decision.

$$D(EMPLOYMENT) = 0.137 + 0.241\ AR(1) + 0.678^*\ AR(2) - 0.346^*\ MA(2)$$
$$(2.33)\quad (3.75)\quad\quad (9.36)\quad\quad\quad (-3.27)$$

$R^2 = 0.589$, SEE = .109, F = 114.2, D.W. = 2.08, $n = 243$ (January 1984 – March 2004).

Since figures based on the production method (Method 3) are released with a lag, it is not used in the US model. Instead the principal components methodology is used. The following monthly indicators are used to form the principal components which are to be used in the estimation of real GDP (Klein & Park, 1993, 1995): Real manufacturing shipments, real manufacturing orders, real manufacturing unfilled orders, real retail sales, real money supply, index of industrial production, non-farm payroll employment, average number of hours worked, housing starts, real effective exchange rate, federal funds rate, interest rate spread (prime rate – treasury bill rate), interest rate spread (10 year bond yield – 1 year bond yield). The following monthly indicators are used to form the principal components which are to be used in the estimation of the GDP deflator: consumer price index, producer price index (finished goods), producer price index (intermediate goods), import price index, farm price index, average number of hours worked, average hourly wages. Three principal components were significant in explaining growth in real GDP.

DLOG(GDPR)*100 = 0.719 + 0.981 Z1 – 0.144* Z2 + 0.045* Z5

(14.46) (8.81)   (–2.92)   (2.41)

$R^2 = 0.612$, SEE = .351, F = 29.48, D.W. = 1.81, $n = 60$ (1984 Q1– 2003 Q4).

The arithmetic average of the expenditure side model, the income side model and the principal components model is given as the final forecast presented in weekly reports. The weights of alternative methods may be adjusted based on forecast errors (Diebold, 2004; Granger & Newbold, 1973, 1986; Klein &Young, 1980).

The University of Pennsylvania Current Quarter Model has generated a great deal of interest in high-frequency models. Models for various countries have been built: Japan by Inada; Mexico by Coutino (2002); Hong Kong by Chan (2000); and France by Courbis. Recently models were built for members of the European Union (Grassman and Keereman, 2001; Baffigi, Golinelli and Parigi, 2002), for USA (Payne, 2000), and Russia (Klein, Eskin and Roudoi, 2003). In Asian countries, production or value added method (Method 3) is the most common method used in calculation of the GDP[5]. The expenditure method (Method 1) is the next most common method used. The income method (Method 2) is not as common as in the United States.

Releases may contain some information on basic data and evaluation of weekly events and official releases. Reports by Chan (2003), Coutino (2003), Inada (2003), and Klein & Ozmucur (2004a) are examples of such releases. The principal point is, to be ready as soon as any partial data are made available during a week, to re-calculate projections.

Performances of alternative models are based on ex-ante forecasting accuracy of these models[6]. At the time of forecasting, no quarterly

---

[5] What indicators may be useful in explaining real economic activity? These indicators may depend on availability of data and the structural characteristics of the economy. As an example, Klein & Ozmucur (2003) use twenty monthly indicators in calculating principal components to get estimates of China's GDP, although the focus of that paper was different than the present one. It interpreted history rather than estimated the future.

[6] See Klein (1991), Wallis (1995), Wallis & Whitley (1991). Diebold & Mariano (1995) propose a formal test for model comparisons. A survey on model comparison criteria is done by Mariano (2002). See, also Theil (1961) for criteria for measuring model performance.

information was available for the quarter of interest. For example, the 2003Q4 forecast of GDP growth is based only on monthly indicators which are forecasted econometrically. Although, forecasts are provided every week, only forecasts following the release dates are compared in this paper. For example, advance estimate of real GDP growth for 2003Q4 was given on our weekly report of February 2, 2004. Preliminary estimate was used in the March 1, 2004 report, while the final estimate was used in the weekly report of March 29, 2004. These are denoted by ADVANCE, PRELIMINARY, and FINAL. Estimates are obtained from the expenditure side model (EXPENDITURE), the income side model (INCOME), the principal components model (PRINCOM), and the average of three methods (AVERAGE). Periods prior to advance estimate are shown after the underscore. For example, AVERAGE_1 refers to forecasts of December 29, 2003 (the date of the report where the final estimate of 2003Q3 was available). Similarly, AVERAGE_2 refers to the forecast obtained two-months ahead of the advance estimate for Q4. This was dated December 1, 2003 (preliminary estimate of 2003Q3 was made available). On the other hand, AVERAGE_3 refers to the forecast obtained three-months ahead of the advance estimate for Q4. The date of that forecast was November 3, 2003 (advance estimate of 2003Q3 was made available). Since forecasts for the current quarter and the following quarter are estimated in the model, it is possible to make comparisons for up to six-month-ahead forecasts. Forecasts given in reports of September 29, 2003 (AVERAGE_4), September 1, 2003 (AVERAGE_5), and August 4, 2003 (AVERAGE_6) may be used to make comparisons with the 2003Q4 actual figure. It should be noted that in comparisons with the preliminary and the final estimate of the real GDP growth, involve additional one and two periods, respectively. For example, AVERAGE_1 is a one-month ahead forecast if compared with the advance estimate. It is a two-month ahead forecast if compared with the preliminary and a three-month ahead forecast if compared with the final estimate of real GDP growth.

There are 28 forecasts (1997:Q1-2003Q4) where actual figures are also available (Figure 1)[7]. A mechanical (naïve) model which has last quarter's growth rate is used as the benchmark model. Average absolute error for real GDP growth is 1.36 for the expenditure side model, 1.59 for the income side model, 1.30 for the principal components model, and 1.01 for the average of the three (Table 1). The average absolute error for the mechanical model (no-change model) is 1.88. Similar results are obtained in the ordering for the two-period and three-period-ahead forecasts. All in all, the average forecast gives the lowest mean absolute error, while the naïve model gives the highest mean absolute error. These results are supported by the correlation coefficients between forecasts and actual values (Table 2), and prediction-realization diagrams (Figures 2, and 3). It is clear from these results that there is an advantage of combining forecasts. Forecast errors also decrease with added information, as one gets close to the release date. It is also important to see that the expenditure side model performs relatively better when real GDP growth rate is increasing, and the principal components model performs relatively better when the growth rate is decreasing (Table 3).

When compared with the mechanical (naïve or no-change) model, Diebold & Mariano statistics are significant at the five percent level for all models except the expenditure side model. This may be due to large errors in the expenditure side model during the early years of our analysis. Diebold & Mariano (DM) statistics are 0.87 for the expenditure side model, 2.95 for the income side model, 1.92 for the principal components model, and 2.48 for the average. In summary, models perform significantly better than the mechanical model.

3. The Methodology of the Survey Corner[8]

Many indicators are helpful in improving statistical performance for forecasting and policy analysis. We do believe, however, that no single

---

[7] Model performance results for the 1990Q2-1994Q2 period are provided in Klein & Park (1995). Periods before 1997, as well as variables such as the deflator for personal consumption expenditures, may be included in the future.

[8] See, Klein & Ozmucur (2002b).

indicator (or type of indicator) can do the necessary work by itself. The principal components, which are estimated linear functions of the whole set of indicators that we choose to represent the movement of the economy as a whole, the methodology is used as a short-cut and quick method to a full scale structural econometric model.

Table 1. Absolute values of forecasts of alternative models.

Absolute Errors (1997:1–2003:4)					
	EXPEND._1	INCOME_1	PRINCOM_1	AVERAGE_1	NAIVE_1
Mean	1.36	1.59	1.30	1.01	1.88
Median	1.34	1.49	0.93	0.77	1.37
Maximum	3.94	5.69	3.82	3.07	5.62
Minimum	0.00	0.16	0.07	0.01	0.06
Std. Dev.	1.19	1.28	1.11	0.92	1.44
Skewness	0.82	1.51	0.95	1.09	1.05
Kurtosis	2.77	5.76	2.79	3.07	3.40
	EXPEND._2	INCOME_2	PRINCOM_2	AVERAGE_2	NAIVE_2
Mean	1.71	1.58	1.54	1.39	2.13
Median	1.49	1.43	1.32	1.01	1.87
Maximum	4.52	7.29	4.85	3.92	6.19
Minimum	0.00	0.02	0.03	0.03	0.31
Std. Dev.	1.44	1.47	1.21	1.02	1.57
Skewness	0.63	2.27	1.21	0.80	0.88
Kurtosis	2.18	9.42	4.08	2.70	3.17
	EXPEND._3	INCOME_3	PRINCOM_3	AVERAGE_3	NAIVE_3
Mean	1.86	1.97	1.80	1.67	2.15
Median	1.56	1.78	1.63	1.33	1.74
Maximum	4.78	6.36	5.29	4.39	6.40
Minimum	0.19	0.14	0.03	0.20	0.07
Std. Dev.	1.33	1.67	1.43	1.25	1.55
Skewness	0.67	1.12	0.65	0.63	1.08
Kurtosis	2.30	3.95	2.58	2.36	3.60

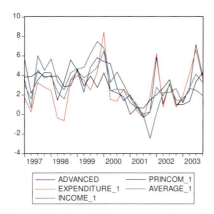

Figure 1. Real GDP Growth Forecasts by Alternative Models.

Table 2. Correlation Coefficients Between real GDP growth rates and Model Estimates (numbers following the model name refer to number of months before the advanced estimate).

	Correlation Coefficients		
	ADVANCE	PRELIMINARY	FINAL
EXPENDITURE_1	0.67	0.62	0.63
INCOME_1	0.54	0.48	0.47
PRINCOM_1	0.58	0.58	0.57
AVERAGE_1	0.76	0.71	0.70
EXPENDITURE_2	0.48	0.45	0.47
INCOME_2	0.44	0.38	0.37
PRINCOM_2	0.43	0.40	0.40
AVERAGE_2	0.65	0.59	0.60
EXPENDITURE_3	0.40	0.30	0.29
INCOME_3	0.27	0.21	0.19
PRINCOM_3	0.26	0.18	0.15
AVERAGE_3	0.41	0.31	0.28
ADVANCED	1.00	0.96	0.96
PRELIMINARY	0.96	1.00	0.99
FINAL	0.96	0.99	1.00

Note: Comparisons with the preliminary and the final estimate of the real GDP growth, involve additional one and two periods, respectively. For example, AVERAGE_1 is a one-month ahead forecast if compared with the advance estimate. It is a two-month ahead forecast if compared with the preliminary and a three-month ahead forecast if compared with the final estimate of real GDP growth.

Lawrence R. Klein and Suleyman Ozmucur

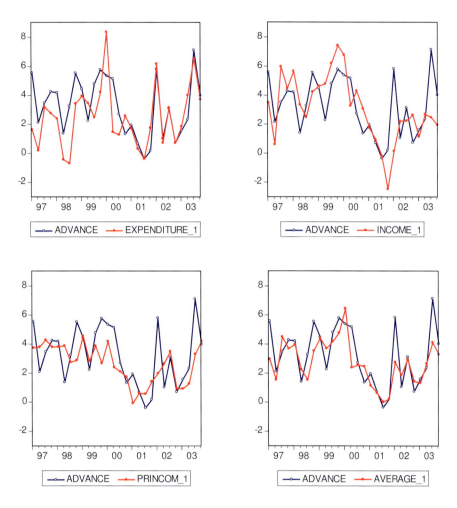

Figure 2a. Real GDP Growth Forecasts by Alternative Models.

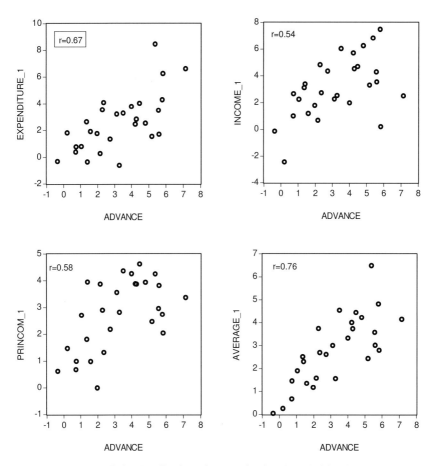

Figure 2b. Prediction-Realization Diagrams for One-Month-Ahead Forecasts.

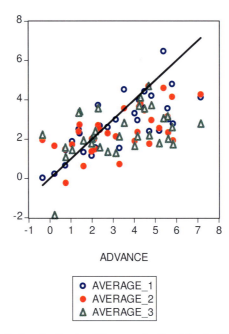

Figure 2c. Prediction-Realization Diagrams for One-Month-Ahead Forecasts.

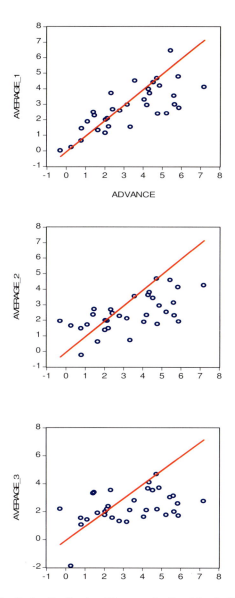

Figure 2d. Prediction-Realization Diagrams for One-Month-Ahead Forecasts.

Lawrence R. Klein and Suleyman Ozmucur

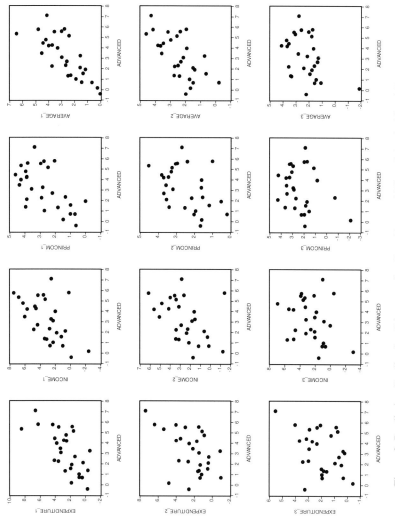

Figure 3. Prediction-Realization Diagrams for One, Two and Three-Month-Ahead Forecasts.

Table 3. Absolute values of errors of alternative models.

Sample: 1997:1 2003:4 IF ADVANCE<ADVANCE(−1)				
	EXPEND._1	INCOME_1	PRINCOM_1	AVERAGE_1
Mean	1.256	1.402	0.947	0.787
Median	1.225	1.555	0.585	0.705
Maximum	3.680	2.500	2.740	2.780
Minimum	0.000	0.160	0.070	0.070
Std. Dev.	1.123	0.738	0.881	0.707
Skewness	0.761	−0.673	0.912	1.586
Kurtosis	2.709	2.371	2.555	5.545
Observations	14	14	14	14

Sample: 1997:1 2003:4 IF ADVANCE>ADVANCE(−1)				
	EXPEND._1	INCOME_1	PRINCOM_1	AVERAGE_1
Mean	1.456	1.780	1.655	1.234
Median	1.520	1.360	1.150	0.915
Maximum	3.940	5.690	3.820	3.070
Minimum	0.050	0.190	0.410	0.010
Std. Dev.	1.293	1.666	1.228	1.072
Skewness	0.803	1.218	0.702	0.638
Kurtosis	2.623	3.520	2.058	1.973
Observations	14	14	14	14

Timeliness, flexibility, and foresight are important properties of indicators, and we are especially interested in information that reflects subjective feelings of participants in the economy. Results of surveys covering consumers, producers or managers are useful in forecasting major macroeconomic variables, like personal consumption expenditures, personal income flows, industrial production, employment, and financial market averages. Our results indicate that models including survey results perform better than those that do not include survey results.

In the USA, there was extreme uncertainty following the terrorist attack of September 11, 2001. Many conflicting judgments were expressed in the financial media concerning consumption, the largest single expenditure component in GDP. Our use of the model presented here enabled sensible, objective forecasts to be made in advance of each month since then.

The surveys of investors provide fresh insight on the functioning of the US economy. Surveys are very informative, not only for the present critical situation but for analysis of the economy in a more normal environment.

The economic information system is vast and developing in many dimensions. The information is more and more frequent – decennial, annual, quarterly, monthly, weekly, daily, hourly, ... real time. The scope is both macro and microeconomic. The history dates from colonial times and grows intensively, mainly as a result of advances in the use of information technology. Our ability to process this enormous information flow is made possible by the advances in computer science, both in terms of hardware and software supply.

Vast as this information flow has become, it is focused on objective, quantitative information such as prices, transaction volumes, production, sales, costs, exports, imports, interest rates, exchange rates, and so on. These pieces of information are all readily available in quantitative form, but they often lack a qualitative dimension. They are objective but economic decision making has a large subjective component. It is this subjective and qualitative property that finds expression in responses to surveys of human populations. There are some well-known surveys of households, firms, and bureaucrats but few, if any, of investors[9]. This is the dimension in economic behavior that has been missing, but is now filled by the results of the surveys of investor optimism.

The population that is being sampled every month has well-considered thoughts about the economy, their personal economic circumstances and other relevant issues. The qualitative responses in coded quantitative index form provide both microeconomic and macroeconomic information that enables one to determine their influence on performance of markets, consumption patterns, and production patterns.

Subjective feelings are always important for the economy, but the present situation highlights their extreme significance because personal attitudes have quickly and radically been changed as a result of

---

[9] See Adams (1964), Adams & Green (1965), Bram & Ludvigson (1998), Carroll, Fuhrer,& Wilcox (1994), Cashell (2003), Eppright, Arguea, & Huth (1998), Garner(2002), Howrey(2001), Klein & Ozmucur (2001), Lee, Elango & Schnaars (1997), Lovell & Tien (2000), Matsusaka & Sbordone (1995), Pain & Weale (2001) for predictive power of surveys.

calculated terrorism within US boundaries. Consumers and producers are no longer being guided mainly by objective market signals, and surveys of the investor population can quickly fill the void in our analyses of the economy.

The emphasis on leading, coincident, and lagging indicators for spotting or interpreting cyclical phases is very interesting, but this methodology seems to extract less from the data than is plausible, certainly less than can be sought with the new technologies. It is not purely a matter of the contributions of each individual series, examined one at a time, in trying to unfold the cyclical story, but more a matter of trying to interpret the collective message (or signal) of the group as a whole. Much of macro-econometric model building focuses attention on the final adding-up to obtain total GDP or some related aggregates from the system as a whole, at the same time that the parts are examined.

The phases of the cycle that are generated by a combination of specific shocks, together with aggregate signals, may be due to shifting forces, sometimes on the demand side, sometimes on the supply side, sometimes from pressures in market-clearing, sometimes from natural causes; sometimes from geopolitical causes, sometimes from cumulative effects of small random errors, and so on. It seems to be too narrow to base ultimate decision making on 10-15 sensitive leaders, particularly for their timing.

Short of building the ultimate high-frequency model with many potential inlets of disturbance to the economy, our approach is to measure the collective impact of several high frequency indicators at many closely spaced time intervals – weekly or even daily in this high, interconnected global environment, and let their aggregate measured impact show where the economy is going[10]. Both timing and magnitude will matter, and the specific indicators that account for observed change need not always be the same. We are looking for a generalization of the traditional indicator approach. To be specific, we collect and combine the

---

[10] See Liu & Hwa (1974) for a monthly econometric model for the US. Liu & Hall (2001) estimate monthly GDP for the US using Kalman filter methodology. See, Hamilton (1994a, 1994b), Harvey (1987, 1989), Kalman (1960, 1961), Kalman & Bucy (1961), Kim &Nelson (1999), Stock &Watson (1991, 2002) for the application of Kalman filters.

joint effects of 20 to 30 (or even more) high frequency indicators. Each is separately measured, but the signal evolves from an aggregative measure.

We propose to form <u>principal components</u> of the monthly indicators whose periodic values appear at either different or similar time points of each month. An indicator will be denoted as

$$I_{it} = \text{the } i\text{-th indicator value at month } t.$$
$$i = 1,2,\ldots, 30$$

The actual number of indicators will depend on the status of the data files of the economy being studied, and 30 need not be the limit of what can be used.

Another kind of variable will be an anticipatory or expectational variable, giving some subjective impression in advance, based on sampling human populations. Surveys of ordinary households, <u>investing</u> households, business executives, or possibly public officials may be used. These will be written as

S_{it} = sample survey response of the i-th economic agent at month t. The agents are asked to respond to future intentions or judgments, to contemporary or recent feelings or intentions.

The outcome of the economic decision will be X_{it} = i-th economic measurement or outcome such as consumer spending by households, business production or capital formation by firms, or financial market price averages by investors.

Having formed principal components of relevant indicators, we plan to regress important substantive variables jointly on sample survey indexes, allowing lagged (carry-over) effects from earlier sample results, generally of the most recent past months, as well as the current month, and also upon those principal components that show significant relationships to the chosen substantive variables (consumer spending, industrial production, capital formation, or financial market averages).

It is noteworthy that these substantive variables constitute some of the important <u>coincident</u> indicators of the US economy, while consumer surveys are one of the <u>leading</u> indicators of the US economy, as are the financial market (i.e. stock market) averages.

The method of principal component analysis is a well-known technique often used in social and psychological measurement (Anderson,

$1984)^{11}$. In econometrics, it has been used for reduction of large data collections into more manageable form, especially to deal with problems of multicollinearity and shortage of degrees of freedom.

If we write for the i-th principal component

$$PC_{it} = \sum_{i=1}^{24} \gamma_i I_{it}$$

our procedure can be stated as one that estimates regression relationships between the specific economic variables that we want to project and the principal components, which, in turn, are based on the primary indicators.

$$X_{it} = \sum_{j=1}^{n_i} \alpha_{ij} PC_{jt} + \beta_{iq} S_{t-q} + e_{it}$$

$n_i < 24$, is the subset of principal components that are found to be significantly related to X_{it}, a magnitude that we are trying to project.

S_{t-q} = coefficient of a relevant Survey index referring to the q-th period (lag). In many cases we distribute the lag in S_t over a few recent months.

$$e_{it} = \text{random error.}$$

Simultaneously, in estimating the coefficients in the above relationship we also represent e_{it} as an ARIMA process

$$e_{it} = \sum_{j=1}^{3} \rho_{ij} e_{it-j} + \sum_{j=1}^{3} \mu_{ij} u_{it-j}$$

where both e_{it} and u_{it} are independent random variables. The "noise" in this process comes from e_{it}.

There is much data processing and analysis in these various steps, but the structure of the system pays much attention to the underlying structure of the social accounts. It is not a purely empirical approach. In particular, it depends very much on the structure of a social accounting system, involving national income and product accounts (NIPA), the

---

[11] See Nagar & Basu (1999), and Nagar & Rahman (2002).

input-output accounts (IO), and the flow-of-funds accounts (F/F). It should be noticed that appropriate accounting balance among these three accounts seems to track the GDP, which is close to, but not directly identified as the end result of aggregate economic activity, but is a very important summary statistic, which is the objective of much economic analysis. It is well known that GDP can be expressed as the sum of all <u>final</u> expenditures, as shown in the NIPA system. This represents the demand side of the economy. But, as we indicated above, GDP can also be expressed as the sum of all payments to the <u>primary</u> factors of production that are responsible for aggregate output. The primary factors are labor, capital, land, and public services. This represents the supply side of the economy. The sum of all primary factor payments can also be evaluated for each sector of the economy as the sum, sector-by-sector, of <u>gross</u> sector output less <u>intermediate</u> sector output, to obtain sectoral value-added. These totals can be computed from a full IO table. By double entry accounting principles, the independent computation of these three estimates of GDP should be identical, but errors and emissions of observation infiltrate each method in practice, so the three sums do not necessarily agree. They may differ from each other by <u>at least</u> as much as one or two percent, and this can be important, especially since it does not turn out to be a random variable; therefore in choosing indicator variables, there must be strong representation from the demand side of the accounts, from the supply side, and from sectoral production flows. Also there should be consistency with the F/F accounts, dealing with saving and investment balances, from which specific indicators can be extracted.

The accounting balances arise from double-entry bookkeeping and even from quadruple-entry bookkeeping in the F/F accounts, which are important for financial market clearing. Hence, the indicator list should contain interest rates, inflation rates, exchange rates, and prices of factor inputs. In the applications, described below, the diversification of indicators follows those principles very carefully.

Also, since the objectives are forecasting, there should be indicators for the future, in the form of forward and futures market variables in addition to the anticipatory components of sample surveys. In this sense, a great deal of economic analysis goes into the selection of indicators.

We form principal components of indicators by extracting the characteristic root of correlation matrices among indicator values. The normalized variables in correlation analysis avoid sensitivity to units of measurement. Since the terrorist attacks of September 11, 2001 in the US, it has been widely noted that these variables have all had key roles in supporting the US economy in an entirely new environmental situation, and we have been following their patterns, month-by-month, in regularly updated studies of their movement on the basis of equations that affect the general economy, people's attitudes, and stochastic dynamic (ARIMA) error terms.

An important early economic use of principal components, though not expressly for indicator analysis, was introduced by Richard Stone, more than 50 years ago. He regressed objective measured variables on components, for his purposes of analysis.[12] Each of the four variables (consumer spending, industrial production, employment, and financial market averages) noted in the previous section have been estimated using principal components of economy-wide indicators, and a corresponding sample survey. Following the regression of the designated series to be explained, we present diagnostic test statistics for serial correlation and normality of distribution of residuals. These are followed by extrapolation of the dependent variable from equations that are re-estimated every month, up to the last month prior to extrapolation. Each re-estimated equation is extrapolated one-month ahead. The regression that is presented is only the last case in the sequence of re-estimates. The specification remains unchanged in this sequence.

Twenty-four indicators are used to calculate principal components to be used in the prediction of monthly employment. These indicators are: new orders (%chg) , housing starts (%chg), number of building permits (%chg), average hourly earnings (%chg), average hours worked (%chg), consumer price index (%chg), producer price index (%chg), real retail sales (%chg), trade-weighted real exchange rate (%chg), real money supply (%chg), real consumer credit (%chg), inventory/sales ratio (chg), ratio of budget revenues to budget expenditures (chg), federal funds rate

---

[12] See Richard Stone, "On the Interdependence of Blocks of Transactions", *Supplement to the Journal of the Royal Statistical Society* IX(1, 1947), 1-45.

(chg), prime rate (chg), corporate bond rate (chg), 3-month treasury bill rate (chg), 1-year bond yield (chg), 10-year bond yield (chg), S & P 500 index (%chg), Dow-Jones index (%chg), real personal income (%chg), manufacturing & trade sales (%chg), new claims for unemployment insurance (chg).

The final equation estimated using 243 observations (January 1984 – March 2004) includes two principal components, the employment index of the Institute for Supply Management (ISM)[13], and autoregressive and moving average processes of residuals. The determination coefficient (R^2) for the equation is 0.638, and all parameters associated with principal components and the Index are significant at the five percent level, most of them at the one percent level. There is no serial correlation in residuals based on Durbin-Watson, Breusch-Godfrey Lagrange Multiplier test and Lyung-Box-Pierce Q test, but the Jarque-Bera test indicates that they are not normally distributed, and Engle's test indicates that there is no autoregressive-conditional heteroscedasticity. Ramsey's RESET test indicates that there is no misspecification, and Chow breakpoint test indicates stability in the relationship.

D(EMPLOYMENT) = –615.804 + 11.361*PC2 – 10.293*PC4 + 6.368*ISM_EMP

            (–4.96)   (2.46)   (–2.11)   (7.73)

        + 4.776*ISM_EMP(–1) + 3.184*ISM_EMP(–2) + 1.592*ISM_EMP(–3)

         (7.73)   (7.73)   (7.73)

        + [AR(1) = 0.97, MA(1) = –0.77]

         (63.0)   (–12.7)

R^2 = 0.638, SEE = 102.37, F = 83.50, D.W. = 2.10, Jarque-Bera = 8.1, Lyung-Box Q(2) = 1.54, Q(12) = 11.18, Breusch-Godfrey LM(2) = 1.64, LM(12) = 12.72, Engle ARCH(1) = 1.83, Ramsey RESET(2) = 1.13, Chow breakpoint (1994:01) = 4.49, n = 243, (January 1984–March 2004).

---

[13] See Bretz (1990), Dasgupta & Lahiri (1992), Klein & Moore (1991), Pelaez (2003), Torda (1985) for the use of ISM (formerly NAPM) surveys. Palaez (2003) proposes the use of different weights to improve the predictive power of the composite index. See, Garcia-Ferrer & Bujosa-Brun (2000) for the use of business surveys in OECD countries.

The real consumer expenditures (CONS) is related to selected principal components (selected on the basis of statistical significance), to polynomial distributed lag (Almon lag) of the UBS index of investor optimism and an ARIMA of the error term.

DLOG(CONS)*100 = 0.244 + 0.0187*PC1 + 0.1018*PC2 + 0.0467*PC10 + 0.0945*PC14

       (16.54) (2.58)   (7.35)   (2.72)   (3.18)

    + 0.000386*UBS + 0.000289*UBS(−1) + 0.000193*UBS(−2)

      (6.32)   (6.32)   (6.32)

    + 0.0000965*UBS(−3) + [AR(1) = 0.341, MA(1) = −0.981]

      (6.32)   (3.49)   (−130.18)

R^2 = 0.636, SEE = 0.256, F = 19.21, D.W. = 2.01, n = 85, (February 1997– February 2004).

The Maximum likelihood estimation of the GARCH(1,1) model (Engle, 1982; Bollershov, 1986) for the S&P 500 with price/earnings ratio (PE) and two principal components (PC1, and PC4) yields the following results[14]:

DLOG(S&P500) = 0.0078 + 0.1479*DLOG(PE(−1)) − 0.00497*PC1 − 0.00509*PC4

      (5.40)   (4.64)   (−5.84)   (−4.13)

   s^2 = 0.000083 + 0.1664 $u(t-1)^2$ + 0.7732 $s(t-1)^2$

    (1.826)   (3.82)   (11.54)

R^2 = 0.104, SEE = 0.034, F = 7.05, D.W. = 1.71, n = 372, (February 1973– January 2004).

Principal component analysis is based on our general point of view that a country's (any country's) economic growth is highly multivariate. No single measured economic activity can account for anything as complex as a modern economy. We examine many time series, select

---

[14] See Chauvet & Potter (2000), and Niemera (1991) for leading indicators of the stock market index. Boughton & Branson (1991), Dasgupta & Lahiri (1991), Gibson & Lazaretou (2001), Roth (1991) propose leading indicators for inflation.

those that seemed to have a priori importance. In order to conserve degrees of freedom we narrowed the list of right hand side variables in the regression as much as possible. This has been an important motivation in adopting the principal component methodology. What is more, these components account for a high degree of variation of the total set. Also, by construction, the components are mutually uncorrelated; therefore we can handle the multicollinearity problem from a statistical point of view. Each component depends, in some way or another, on the whole set of indicators, yet their inter-correlation, which is naturally high, does not confound the interpretation of the regression estimates, and we have plausible associations between GDP growth and individual indicator growth.

It should be noted that results of consumer sentiment or business expectation surveys are useful in improving forecasts. In general, such survey results improve forecast accuracy. Klein & Ozmucur (2001, 2002b) show that the index of investor optimism and the index of consumer confidence improve forecasts of real personal consumption expenditures, while the index of purchasing managers improves forecasts of industrial production and employment. Klein, Mariano & Ozmucur (2001) show that results of business expectation surveys in Singapore improves employment forecasts. Results of surveys covering subjective evaluations of managers or households should be used whenever available.

Forecasts are useful not only for studying the short term developments of the economy, but also for adjusting lower frequency macro-econometric models so that they are solved from up-to-date initial conditions (Klein & Sojo, 1989, Klein & Park, 1995). Comparisons are based on ex-ante forecasting accuracy of these models. These forecasts are based on no available information for the month of interest, except survey results. For example, the April 2004 forecast of employment is based on indicator variables which are forecasted econometrically. Since "Survey Corner" forecasts have been available since March 2003, forecasts are compared for the period beginning in March 2003. There are 13 forecasts (March 2003–March 2004) for employment and 12 forecasts for industrial production (March 2003–February 2004) where actual figures are also available. A mechanical (naïve) model which has last month's change or percentage change is used as the benchmark model. Results are presented in Tables 4 and 5. Since general interest is in the month-to-month change in non-farm payroll employment and month-to-month growth in industrial production index, forecasts and error statistics are presented as changes or percent changes. Survey corner performs better than the current quarter model (monthly ARIMA equation) and the naive model. Average absolute error for month-to-month changes in employment are 74 thousand for the "survey corner", 80 thousand for the "current quarter model", and 92 thousand for the

Table 4. Forecasts Based on Alternative Models at the beginning of the month (Changes in Non-farm Payroll Employment).

	actual	forecast	forecast	forecast
	actual	survey corner	CQM	Naive
2003.01	143		−6	−101
2003.02	−308		4	143
2003.03	−108	−41	−4	−308
2003.04	−48	−83	−72	−108
2003.05	−17	−94	−86	−48
2003.06	−30	−51	0	−17
2003.07	−44	−22	−4	−30
2003.08	−93	−8	−19	−44
2003.09	57	−2	−24	−93
2003.10	126	−25	20	57
2003.11	57	20	113	126
2003.12	1	120	112	57
2004.01	112	151	65	1
2004.02	21	144	79	112
2004.03	308	187	72	21
2004.04		201	167	308
average absolute error		74	80	92

Table 5. Forecasts Based on Alternative Models at the beginning of the month (Percentage Changes in Industrial Production).

	actual	forecast	forecast	forecast
	actual	survey corner	CQM	Naive
2003.01	0.73		−0.01	
2003.02	0.09		0.20	
2003.03	−0.54	−0.37	0.15	0.09
2003.04	−0.45	−0.67	−0.06	−0.54
2003.05	0.18	0.09	−0.14	−0.45
2003.06	0.09	0.18	−0.02	0.18
2003.07	0.46	0.16	0.04	0.09
2003.08	0.09	0.09	0.16	0.46
2003.09	0.36	0.09	0.16	0.09
2003.10	0.27	0.45	0.21	0.36
2003.11	0.89	0.45	0.21	0.27
2003.12	0.08	0.44	0.41	0.89
2004.01	0.79	0.44	0.28	0.08
2004.02	0.73	0.44	0.36	0.79
2004.03		0.44	0.56	
2004.04		0.43	0.53	
average absolute error		0.23	0.35	0.40

"naïve model". Correlation coefficients between actual and forecasted month-to-month changes in employment are 0.64 for the survey corner, 0.46 for the current quarter model and 0.47 for the naïve model (Figure 4). Average absolute error for month-to-month percent changes in industrial production index are 0.23% for the "survey corner", 0.35% for the "current quarter model", and 0.40% for the "naïve model". Correlation coefficients between actual and forecasted month-to-month percent changes in industrial production index are 0.82 for the survey corner, 0.42 for the current quarter model, and 0.35 for the naïve model (Figure 5).

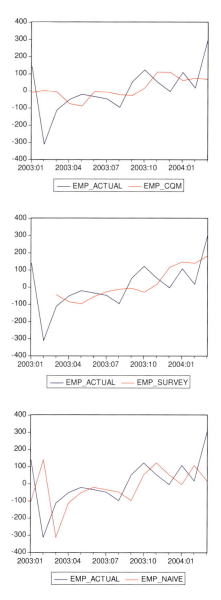

Figure 4. Actual and Extrapolation of Monthly Changes in Non-Farm Payroll Employment.

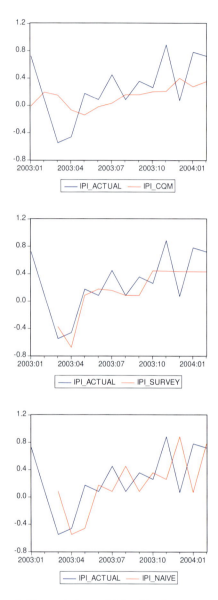

Figure 5. Actual and Extrapolation of Monthly Percentage Changes in Industrial Production.

4. Conclusion

Forecasts are useful not only for studying the short term developments of the economy, but also for adjusting lower frequency macro-econometric models so that they are solved from up-to-date initial conditions. The advantage of combining forecasts is clear from results provided by the Current Quarter Model. It is also clear that forecast errors decrease with added information, as one gets close to the release date. It is also important to see that the expenditure side model performs relatively better when real GDP growth rate is increasing, and the principal components model performs relatively better when the growth rate is decreasing. This indicates a possibility of improving forecasts by using different weights at different stages of the economy.

Results of consumer sentiment or business expectation surveys are useful in improving forecasts. Surveys are very informative, not only for the present critical situation but for analysis of the economy in a more normal environment.

References

Abeysinghe, T. (1998). "Forecasting Singapore's quarterly GDP with monthly external trade". *International Journal of Forecasting*, 14, 505-513.

Abeysinghe, T. (2000). "Modeling variables of different frequencies". *International Journal of Forecasting*, 16, 117-119.

Adams, Gerard F. (1964). "Consumer Attitudes, Buying Plans, and Purchases of Durable Goods: A Principal Components, Time Series Approach". *The Review of Economics and Statistics*. Vol. 46, No. 4 (November, 1964). 347-355.

Adams, Gerard F. & Edward W. Green (1965). "Explaining and Predicting Aggregative Consumer Attitudes". *International Economic Review*. Vol. 6, No. 3 (September, 1965). 275-293.

Anderson, T.W. (1984). *An Introduction to Multivariate Statistical Analysis (2nd ed.)*. John Wiley. New York.

Baffigi, Alberto, Roberto Golinelli and Giuseppe Parigi (2002). *Real-Time GDP Forecasting in the Euro Area*. Project LINK Fall Meeting. University of Bologna, Bologna, Italy, October 7-11, 2002.

Boughton, J.M. and W.H. Branson (1991). "Commodity Prices as a Leading Indicator of Inflation" in K. Lahiri & G.H. Moore (eds.) *Leading Economic Indicators, New Approaches and Forecasting Records*. Cambridge University Press. New York. pp. 305-338.

Bollersev, T. (1986). "Generalized Autoregressive Conditional Heteroskedasticity", *Journal of Econometrics*, 31 (3), 307-327.

Box, G.E.P and G. M. Jenkins (1976). *Time Series Analysis: Forecasting and Control*, rev. ed. Holden-Day. San Francisco.

Bram, Jason & Sydney Ludvigson (1998). "Does Consumer Confidence Forecast Household Expenditure? A Sentiment Index Horse Race". *Federal Reserve Bank of New York Economic Policy Review*. June 1998. 59-78.

Bretz, Robert J. (1990). "Behind the Economic Indicators of the NAPM Report on Business". *Business Economics*. Vol. 25, No. 3. 42-48.

Carroll, Christopher D., Jeffrey C. Fuhrer, David W. Wilcox (1994). "Does Consumer Sentiment Forecast Household Spending? If So Why?". *American Economic Review*. December. 1397-1408.

Cashell, B.W. (2003). "Measures of Consumer Confidence: Are They Useful?" *Congressional Research Service, Library of Congress*, June 2, 2003.

Chan, Chi-Shing (2000). *High Frequency Macroeconomic Forecasting Model for Hong Kong*. APEC Study Center. Hong Kong Institute of Economic and Business Strategy, University of Hong Kong. May 2000.

Chauvet, Marcelle & Simon Potter (2000). "Coincident and Leading Indicators of the Stock Market". *Journal of Empirical Finance*. Vol. 7. 87-111.

Clements, M.P. and D.F. Hendry (1998). *Forecasting Economic Time Series*. Cambridge University Press. Cambridge.

Clements, M.P. and D.F. Hendry, eds (2002). *A Companion to Economic Forecasting*. Blackwell. Oxford.

Coutino, Alfredo (2002). *A High-Frequency Forecasting Model for the Mexican Economy.* Submitted unpublished Ph.D. thesis. Autonomous University of Madrid

Coutino, Alfredo (2003). *A High-Frequency Model for Mexico.* Project LINK web-site. <http://www.chass.utoronto.ca/LINK>

Dasgupta, S. and K. Lahiri (1991). "A leading Indicator of Inflation Based on Interest Rates" in K.Lahiri & G.H. Moore (eds.) *Leading Economic Indicators, New Approaches and Forecasting Records.* Cambridge University Press. New York. pp. 339-353.

Dasgupta, S. & Kajal Lahiri (1992). "A Comparative Study of Alternative Methods of Quantifying Qualitative Survey Responses Using NAPM Data". *Journal of Business & Economic Statistics.* Vol. 10, Issue 4 (October, 1992). 391-400.

Dickey-Fuller (1979). "Distribution of the Estimators for Autoregressive Time Series with a Unit Root". *Journal of the American Statistical Association,* Vol. 74, 427-431.

Diebold, F.X., (2004). *Elements of Forecasting (3rded.),* South-Western, Ohio.

Diebold, F.X. and G.D. Rudebusch (1989). "Scoring the Leading Indicators" *Journal of Business,* 62, 369-391.

Diebold, F.X. and R.S. Mariano (1995). "Comparing Predictive Accuracy". *Journal of Business and Economic Statistics,* 13, 253-265.

Engle, R.F. (1982). "Autoregressive Conditional Heteroscedasticity, with estimates of the Variance of United Kingdom Inflations", *Econometrica,* Vol. 50, 987-1007.

Engle, R.F. and C.W.J. Granger (1987). "Cointegration and error-correction: representation, estimation, and testing". *Econometrica,* Vol. 55, 251-276.

Engle, R.F. and C.W.J. Granger, eds. (1991). *Long-Run Economic Relationships.* Oxford University Press, Oxford.

Eppright, David R., Nestor M. Arguea, William L. Huth (1998). "Aggregate Consumer Expectation Indexes as Indicators of Future Consumer Expenditures". *Journal of Economic Psychology.* Vol. 19, 215-235.

Garcia-Ferrer, Antonio and Marcus Bujosa-Brun (2000). "Forecasting OECD Industrial Turning Points Using Unobserved Components Models with Business Survey Data". *International Journal of Forecasting*. Vol. 16, 207-227.

Garner, Alan C. (2002). "Consumer Confidence After September 11". *Federal Reserve Bank of Kansas City Economic Review*. Second Quarter 2002. 1-21.

Gibson, Heather D. & Sophia Lazaretou (2001). "Leading Inflation Indicators for Greece". Economic Modelling. Vol. 18, 325-348.

Granger, C.W.J. (1969). "Investigating Causal Relationships by Econometric Models and Cross-Spectral Methods", *Econometrica*, 37, 424-438.

Granger, C.W.J. and P. Newbold (1973). "Some Comments on the Evaluation of Economic Forecasts", *Applied Economics*, Vol. 5, 35-47.

Granger, C.W.J. and P. Newbold (1986). *Forecasting Economic Time Series (2nd ed.)*. Academic Press. New York.

Granger, C.W.J. and Y. Jeon (2003). "Interactions Between Large Macro Models and Time Series Analysis", *International Journal of Finance and Economics*, Vol. 8, 1-10.

Grassman, Peter and Filip Keereman (2001). *An Indicator-based Short-term Forecast for Quarterly GDP in the Euro Area.* Directorate-general for Economic and Financial Affairs of the European Commission. Economic paper No. 154. June 2001.

Hamilton, James D. (1994a). *Time Series Analysis*. Princeton University Press. Princeton.

Hamilton, James D. (1994b). "State-Space Models", in R.F. Engle and D.L. McFadden (eds.) *Handbook of Econometrics, Vol. 4*. Elsevier, pp. 3014-3077.

Harvey, Andrew C. (1987). "Applications of the Kalman Filter in Econometrics", in T. Bewley (ed.) *Advances in Econometrics*, Fifth World Congress of the Econometric Society, Vol. 1, pp. 285-313.

Harvey, Andrew C. (1989). *Forecasting, Structural Time Series Models and the Kalman Filter*, Cambridge University Press, Cambridge.

Howrey, E.P. (1991). "New Methods for Using Monthly Data to Improve Forecast Accuracy", in L.R. Klein (ed.) *Comparative Performance of U.S. Econometric Models*. Oxford University Press. New York and Oxford. pp. 227-249.

Howrey, E. Philip (2001). "The Predictive Power of the Index of Consumer Sentiment". *Brookings Papers on Economic Activity*, 1:2001. 175-216.

Inada, Yoshihisa (2003). *A High-Frequency Model for Japan*. Project LINK web-site. <http://www.chass.utoronto.ca/LINK>

Ingetino, Robert and Bharat Trehan (1996). "Using Monthly Data to Predict Quarterly Output", *FRBSF Economic Review*, No.3, 3-11.

Kalman, R.E. (1960). "A New Approach to Linear Filtering and Prediction Problems", *Journal of Basic Engineering, Transactions ASME*, Series D, Vol. 82, 35-45.

Kalman, R.E. (1961). "New Methods in Wiener Filtering Theory", in J.L. Bogdanoff and F. Kozin (eds.), *Proceedings of the First Symposium of Engineering Applications of Random Function Theory and Probability*, Wiley, New York, pp. 270-388.

Kalman, R.E. and R.S. Bucy (1961). "New Results in Linear Filtering and Prediction Theory", *Journal of Basic Engineering, Transactions ASME*, Series D, Vol. 83, 95-108.

Kim, Chang-Jin and Charles R. Nelson (1999). *State-Space Models with Regime Switching*, MIT Press, Cambridge, Massachusetts.

Kitchen, John and Ralph Monaco (2003). "Real-Time Forecasting in Practice, The U.S. Treasury Staff's Real-Time GDP Forecast System". *Business Economics*, October 2003, 10-19.

Klein, L.R. (1971). *An Essay on the Theory of Economic Prediction*. Markham Publishing Company. Chicago.

Klein, L.R. with W. Welfe (1983). *Lectures in Econometrics*. North-Holland. Amsterdam.

Klein, L. R. (1990). "Cyclical Indicators in Econometric Models", in Philip E. Klein, ed., *Analyzing Modern Business Cycles*, Armonk: M.E. Sharpe, Inc., pp. 97-106.

Klein, L.R. (ed.) *Comparative Performance of U.S. Econometric Models*. Oxford University Press. New York and Oxford.

Klein, L. R. (2000). "Essay on the Accuracy of Economic Prediction", *International Journal of Applied Economics and Econometrics*, 9 (Spring, 2000), 29-69.

Klein, L.R., Vladimir Eskin and Andrei Roudoi (2003). *Empirical Regularities in the Russian Economy*. Project LINK Spring Meeting. United Nations, New York, April 23-25, 2003.

Klein, L.R. and J Makino (2000). "Economic Interpretations of the Statistical Discrepancy", *Journal of Economic and Social Measurement*, Vol. 26, 11-29.

Klein, L.R., R.S. Mariano, and S. Ozmucur (2001). *Quarterly Manpower Forecasting Model of Singapore*. Report prepared for Singapore Ministry of Manpower. December 2001 (mimeo).

Klein, L.R., and S. Ozmucur (2001)." The Use of Surveys in Macroeconomic Forecasting" in W. Welfe (ed.) *Macromodels'2001*. University of Lodz. Poland.

Klein, L.R., and S. Ozmucur (2002a)." Consumer Behavior under the Influence of Terrorism within the United States". *The Journal of Entrepreneurial Finance & Business Ventures*, Vol. 7, Issue 3 (Fall 2002), 1-15.

Klein, L.R., and S. Ozmucur (2002b). *Some Possibilities for Indicator Analysis in Economic Forecasting*. Project LINK Fall Meeting. University of Bologna. October 2002. Bologna. Italy (mimeo).

Klein, L.R., and S. Ozmucur (2003). "The estimation of China's Economic Growth Rate", *Journal of Economic and Social Measurement*, Volume 28, Number 4 / 2002 / 2003, pp. 187-202.

Klein, L.R., and S. Ozmucur (2004a). *University of Pennsylvania Current Quarter Model of the United States Economy Forecast Summary*. April 5, 2004. (mimeo). Project LINK web-site. <http://www.chass.utoronto.ca/LINK>

Klein, L.R., and S. Ozmucur (2004b). *University of Pennsylvania Monthly Projections of the United States Economy, Survey Corner*. April 2, 2004. (mimeo).

Klein, L.R. and J.Yong Park (1993). "Economic Forecasting at High-Frequency Intervals". *Journal of Forecasting*, Vol. 12. pp. 301-319.

Klein, L.R. and J.Yong Park (1995). "The University of Pennsylvania Model for High-Frequency Economic Forecasting". *Economic & Financial Modelling*, Autumn 1995. pp. 95-146.

Klein, L.R. and E. Sojo (1989). "Combinations of High and Low Frequency Data in Macroeconometric Models", in L.R. Klein and J. Marquez (eds.), *Economics in Theory and Practice: An Eclectic Approach.* Kluwer Academic Publishers, pp. 3-16.

Klein, L.R. and R.M. Young (1980). *An Introduction to Econometric Forecasting and Forecasting Models.* D.C. Heath & Company, Lexington, Massachusetts.

Klein, P.A. and G.H. Moore (1991). "Purchasing Management Survey Data: Their Value as Leading Indicators" in K. Lahiri & G.H. Moore (eds.) *Leading Economic Indicators, New Approaches and Forecasting Records.* Cambridge University Press. New York. pp. 403-428.

Kwiatkowski, Phillips, Schmidt, and Shin (KPSS) (1992). "Testing the null of stationary against the alternative of a unit root". *Journal of Econometrics*, Vol. 54, 159-178.

Lee, Myung-Soo, B. Elango, Steven P. Schnaars (1997). "The Accuracy of the Conference Board's Buying Plans Index: A Comparison of Judgmental vs. Extrapolation Forecasting Methods". *International Journal of Forecasting.* Vol. 13. 127-135.

Liu, H. & S.G. Hall (2001). "Creating High-frequency National Accounts with State-space Modelling: A Monte Carlo Experiment". *Journal of Forecasting*, 20, 441-449.

Liu, T-C and E-C Hwa (1974). "A Monthly Econometric Model of the U.S. Economy", *International Economic Review*, 15, Issue 2 (June 1974), 328-365.

Lovell, Michael C. & Pao-Lin Tien (2000). "Economic Discomfort and Consumer Sentiment". *Eastern Economic Journal.* Vol. 26, No. 1 (Winter 2000). 1-8.

MacKinnon J. G. (1991). "Critical Values for co-integration tests". In R. Engle and C. W. Granger (eds.) *Long-Run Economic Relationships.* Oxford University Press. Oxford.

Mammen, Thampy (1999). *India's Economic Prospects: A Macroeconomic and Econometric Analysis* Singapore: World Scientific Publishers.

Mariano, R.S. (2002). "Testing Forecast Accuracy", in Clements, M.P. and D.F. Hendry, eds. *A Companion to Economic Forecasting.* Blackwell. Oxford.

Mariano, R.S. and Y. Murasawa (2002). "A New Coincident Index of Business Cycles Based on Monthly and Quarterly Series". *Journal of Applied Econometrics*, Vol.

Martens, Martin (2002). "Measuring and Forecasting S & P 500 Index-Futures Volatility Using High-Frequency Data". *The Journal of Futures Markets.* Vol. 22, No. 6. 497-518.

Matsusaka, John G. & Argia M. Sbordone (1995). "Consumer Confidence and Economic Fluctuations". *Economic Inquiry.* Vol. 33 (April). 296-318.

McGuckin, Robert H., Ataman Ozyildirim, Victor Zarnowitz (2001*). The Composite Index of Leading Economic Indicators: How to Market It More Timely.* NBER Working Paper 8430. August 2001.

Nagar, A.L. and Sudip Ranjan Basu (1999). *Weighting Socio-Economic Indicators of Human Development (A Latent Variable Approach)*, National Institute of Public Finance and Policy, New Delhi (mimeo).

Nagar, A.L. and T. Rahman (2002). *Measurement of Quality of Life.* (mimeo).

Niemera, M.P. (1991). "Using Composite Leading Indicators of Consumption to Forecast Sales and to Signal Turning Points in the Stock Market" in K. Lahiri & G.H. Moore (eds.) *Leading Economic Indicators, New Approaches and Forecasting Records.* Cambridge University Press. New York. pp. 355-371.

Pain, Nigel & Martin Weale (2001). "The Information Content of Consumer Surveys". *National Institute Economic Review.* No. 178 (October, 2001). 44-47.

Palanivel, T. and L.R. Klein (2002). "Economic Reforms and Growth Prospects in India", *Macroeconomics and Monetary Policy*, M.S. Alhuwalia et al., eds. Oxford: Oxford University Press.

Parigi, Guiseppe & Guiseppe Schlitzer (1997). "Predicting Consumption of Italian Households by Means of Survey Indicators". *International Journal of Forecasting.* Vol. 13. 197-209.

Payne, David (2000). "Predicting GDP Growth before the BEA's Advance GDP Release*". Business Economics.* April, 2000. pp. 54-63.

Pelaez, R.F. (2003). "A Reassessment of the Purchasing Manager's Index". *Business Economics.* October, 2003, 35-41.

Phillips P.C.B. and P. Perron (1988). "Testing for a unit root in time series regressions". *Biometrica*, Vol. 75, 335-346.

Quantitative Micro Software (2002). *Eviews 4.1 User's Guide*. Irvine, California. <www.eviews.com>

Roth, H. L (1991). "Leading Indicators of Inflation" in K.Lahiri & G.H. Moore (eds.) *Leading Economic Indicators, New Approaches and Forecasting Records*. Cambridge University Press. New York. pp. 275-301.

Stock, J.H. and M.W. Watson (1991). "A Probability Model of the Coincident Economic Indicators" in K.Lahiri & G.H. Moore (eds.) *Leading Economic Indicators, New Approaches and Forecasting Records*. Cambridge University Press. New York. pp. 63-89.

Stock, J.H. and M.W. Watson (2002). "Macroeconomic Forecasting Using Diffusion Indexes". *Journal of Business & Economic Statistics*, 20, No. 2 (April, 2002), 147-162.

Stone, R. (1947). "On the Interdependence of Blocks of Transactions", *Supplement to the Journal of the Royal Statistical Society* IX (1, 1947), 1-45.

Theil, H. (1961). *Economic Forecasts and Policy (2nd ed.)*. North-Holland. Amsterdam.

Torda, T.S. (1985). "Purchasing Management Index Provides Early Clue on Turning Points". *Business America*, U.S. Department of Commerce, June 24.

US Department of Commerce, Bureau of Economic Analysis (2002a). "Annual Revision of the National Income and Product Accounts: Annual Estimates, 1999-2001, and Quarterly Estimates, 1999:I-2002:I". *Survey of Current Busi*ness. August, 2002.

US Department of Commerce, Bureau of Economic Analysis (2002b). "Annual NIPA revision Annual NIPA Revision: Newly Available Tables". *Survey of Current Busi*ness. October, 2002.

US Department of Commerce, Bureau of Economic Analysis (2002c). "Updated Summary NIPA Methodologies". *Survey of Current Busi*ness. October, 2002.

Wallis, K. (1995). "Large-Scale Macroeconometric Modeling" in M.H. Pesaran and M.R. Wickens, eds., Handbook of Applied Econometrics. Blackwell. Oxford.

Wallis, K. and J.D. Whitley (1991). "Sources of Error in Forecasts and Expectations:UK Economic Models, 1984-88". *Journal of Forecasting*, 10, 231-253.

FORECASTING SEASONAL TIME SERIES*

Philip Hans Franses

Econometric Institute, Erasmus University Rotterdam,
P.O. Box 1738, NL-3000 DR Rotterdam, The Netherlands
E-mail: franses@few.eur.nl

This chapter deals with seasonal time series in economics and it reviews models that can be used to forecast out-of-sample data. Some of the key properties of seasonal time series are reviewed, and various empirical examples are given for illustration. The potential limitations to seasonal adjustment are reviewed. The chapter further addresses a few basic models like the deterministic seasonality model and the airline model, and it shows what features of the data these models assume to have. Then, the chapter continues with more advanced models, like those concerning seasonal and periodic unit roots. Finally, there is a discussion of some recent advances, which mainly concern models which allow for links between seasonal variation and heteroskedasticity and non-linearity.

Keywords and phrases: Forecasting, seasonality, unit roots, periodic models, cointegration.

1. Introduction

This chapter deals with seasonal time series in economics and it reviews models that can be used to forecast out-of-sample data. A seasonal time series is assumed to be a series measured at a frequency t where this series shows certain recurrent patterns within a frequency T, with $t = ST$. For example, quarterly data (t) can show different means and variances within a year $(4T)$. Similar phenomena can appear for hourly data within days, daily data within weeks, monthly data within years, and so on. Examples of data with pronounced recurrent patterns are quarterly nondurable consumption,

---

*Work on this chapter started when the author was enjoying the hospitality of the Institute of Mathematical Statistics, National University of Singapore (April 2004). Thanks are due to Dick van Dijk and Marnik Dekimpe for their help with the data. All computations have been made using Eviews (version 4.1). Details of estimation results not reported in this chapter can be obtained from the author. A full list of relevant references is also available.

monthly industrial production, daily retail sales (within a week), hourly referrals after broadcasting a TV commercial (within a day), and stock price changes measured per minute within a day.

A trend is important to extrapolate accurately when forecasting longer horizons ahead. Seasonality is important to properly take care of when forecasting the next S or kS out-of-sample data, with k not very large, hence the medium term. This chapter reviews models that can be usefully implemented for that purpose. The technical detail is kept at a moderate level, and extensive reference will be made to the studies which contain all the details. Important books in this context are Hylleberg (1992), Ghysels and Osborn (2001), and Franses and Paap (2004). The recent survey of Brendstrup et al. (2004) is excellent, also as it contains a useful and rather exhaustive list of references.

The outline of this chapter is a follows. In Section 2, I discuss some of the key properties of seasonal time series. I use a few empirical examples for illustration. Next, I discuss the potential limitations to seasonal adjustment. In Section 3, I review basic models like the deterministic seasonality model and the airline model, and show features of the data these models assume they have. In Section 4, I continue with more advanced models, like those concerning seasonal and periodic unit roots. Section 5 deals with some recent advances, which mainly concern models which allow for links between seasonal variation and heteroskedasticity and non-linearity. Section 6 concludes with a summary of important future research areas.

2. Seasonal Time Series

This section deals with various features of seasonally observed time series that one might want to capture in an econometric time series model. Next, the discussion focuses on what it is that one intends to forecast. Finally, I address the issue why seasonal adjustment often is problematic.

How do seasonal time series look like?

In this chapter I use a few series for illustration. The typical tools to see how seasonal variation in a series might look like, and hence which time series models might be considered to start with, are (i) graphs (over time, or per season), (ii) autocorrelations (usually after somehow removing the trend, where it is not uncommon to use the first differencing filter $\Delta_1 y_t = y_t - y_{t-1}$), (iii) the R^2 of a regression of $\Delta_1 y_t$ on S seasonal dummies

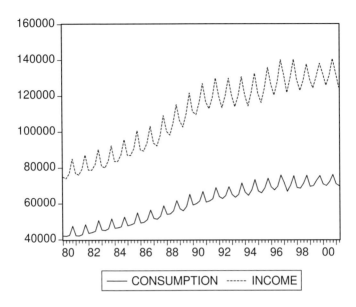

Figure 1: Quarterly consumption and income per quarter in Japan

or on S (or less) sines and cosines, (iv) a regression of squared residuals from a time series model for $\Delta_1 y_t$ on an intercept and $S - 1$ seasonal dummies (to check for seasonal variation in error variance), and finally (v) autocorrelations per season (to see if there is periodicity). With periodicity one typically means that correlations within or across variables can change with the season, see Franses and Paap (2004) for an up to date survey. It should be noted that these are all just first-stage tools, to see in which direction one could proceed. They should not be interpreted as final models or methods, as they usually do not fully capture all relevant aspects of the time series.

The first set of series concerns private consumption and GDP for Japan, quarterly observed, for the period 1980.1-2001.2 (Data source is www.economagic.com). The graphs of these two series appear in Figure 1. The graphs display an upward moving trend for both series, pronounced intra-year variation, and it seems that this variation is common across the two series.

Figure 2 zooms in on the Japanese consumption series (now in natural logarithms, hence the notation LC) by plotting the quarterly observations against the year (Q_1, Q_2, Q_3 and Q_4). This way one can get a better

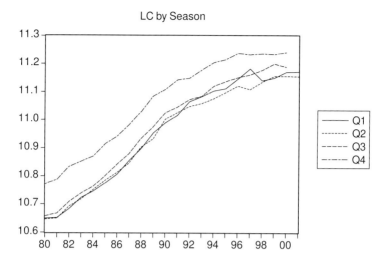

Figure 2: Annual consumption in Japan, observed per quarter

picture of whether seasonal patterns change over time, as then these lines would intersect. These graphs were introduced in Franses (1991, 1994) and now appear in Eviews (version 4.1) as "split seasonals". For the Japanese consumption series one can observe that there is a slight change in seasonality towards the end of the sample, but mostly the seasonal pattern seems rather stable over time.

For these two series, after taking natural logs, the R^2 of the "seasonal dummy regression" for $\Delta_1 y_t$, that is,

$$\Delta_1 y_t = \sum_{s=1}^{4} \delta_s D_{s,t} + \varepsilon_t, \tag{1}$$

is 0.927 for log(consumption) and for log(income) it is 0.943. The $D_{s,t}$ variables obtain a value 1 in seasons s and a 0 elsewhere. Note that it is unlikely that $\hat{\varepsilon}_t$ matches with a white noise time series, but then still, the values of these R^2 measures are high. Franses, Hylleberg and Lee (1995) show that the size of this R^2 can be misinterpreted in case of neglected unit roots, but for the moment this regression is informative.

A suitable first-attempt model for both Japanese log(consumption) and log(income) is

$$\Delta_1 y_t = \sum_{s=1}^{4} \delta_s D_{s,t} + \rho_1 \Delta_1 y_{t-1} + \varepsilon_t + \theta_4 \varepsilon_{t-4} \tag{2}$$

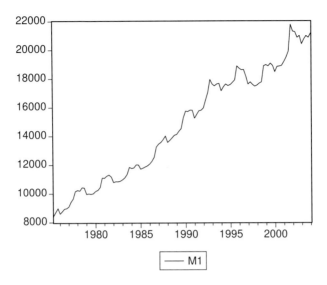

Figure 3: Quarterly M1 in Australia

where ρ_1 is estimated to be -0.559 (0.094) and -0.525 (0.098), respectively (with standard errors in parentheses), and where θ_4 is estimated to be 0.441 (0.100) and 0.593 (0.906), respectively. Relative to (1), the R^2 of these models have increased to 0.963 and 0.975, respectively, suggesting that constant deterministic seasonality seems to account for the majority of trend-free variation in the data.

The next series is quarterly observed M1 for Australia for 1975.2 to and including 2004.1 (Data source: www.economagic.com), see Figure 3. Again, one can observe a marked upward trend, and there are also signs of seasonality, but this time the type of seasonality is a bit unclear. This might be caused by the dominance of the trend, and hence one might want to have a look at the time series without a trend. There are many ways to de-trend a time series, but for the current purpose it is again convenient to take the natural logarithm and then first differences, approximately amounting to quarterly growth rates. The graph of quarterly growth in M1 appears in Figure 4.

Figure 4 clearly shows there is seasonality in M1 growth[1]. A regression of the growth rates (differences in logs) for this variable on four seasonal

---

[1]Interestingly, this seasonality seems to concern intervals of 2 years instead of the usual 1 year, but for the moment this is not pursued any further.

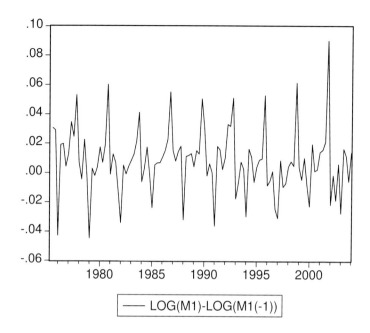

Figure 4: Quarterly growth in M1 in Australia

dummies gives an R^2 of 0.203. Fitting autoregressive models of order 8, 7, 6 and so on, while checking for the absence of residual correlation, reveals that an AR(5) model fits the data for $\Delta_1 y_t$ reasonably well, although the residuals are not entirely "white". The R^2 increases to 0.519, with strong significant parameters for lags 3, 4, and 5, and hence, seasonality for this series cannot fully be captured by deterministic seasonality.

Next, a regression of the squares of the residuals from the AR(5) model on an intercept and 3 seasonal dummies gives an F-value of 5.167, with a p-value of 0.002. Hence, this series seems to display seasonal variation in the variance. One cause for this finding is that a better model for this series could be a periodic time series model, which implies seasonal heteroskedasticity if a non-periodic model is fitted, see Franses and Paap (2004). When I fit an AR(2) model for each of the seasons, that is, I regress $\Delta_1 y_t$ on $\Delta_1 y_{t-1}$ and $\Delta_1 y_{t-2}$ but allow for different parameters for the seasons, then the estimation results for quarters 1 to 4 are (0.929, 0.235), (0.226, 0.769), (0.070, −0.478), and (0.533, −0.203). This suggests that different models for different seasons might be useful, hence a periodic model.

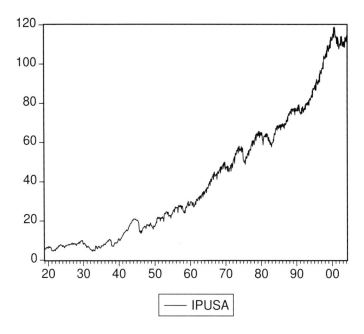

Figure 5: Monthly index of total industrial production in the USA

The next series to consider is the index of monthly total industrial production for the USA, covering 1919.01-2004.02 (Data source: www.economagic.com), and its graph is given in Figure 5. Again a trend is clearly visible, and also at times one can observe dips, which are typically assumed to correspond with recessions. There is ample literature on the supposed non-linearity of this time series, see for example Franses and van Dijk (2004) and the references therein, but this is neglected here for the moment, see Section 5. Additionally, as Figure 6 indicates, there seems to be a change in the variance in this series.

A regression of Δ_1 of log(industrial production) on $S = 12$ seasonal dummies gives an R^2 of 0.374. Adding lags at 1, 12 and 13 to this auxiliary regression model improves the fit to 0.524 (for 1008 data points), with parameters 0.398, 0.280 and −0.290. There is no obvious residual autocorrelation. The sum of these autoregressive parameters is 0.388. This implies that certainly for forecasts beyond the 12 month horizon, constant seasonality dominates. Testing for seasonal heteroskedasticity in the way outlined above for Australian M1 does not suggest any such variation.

Philip Hans Franses

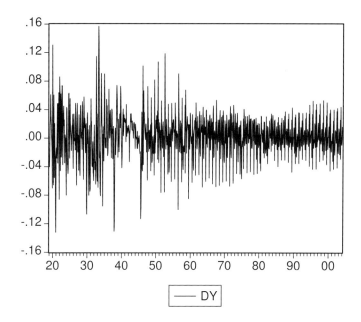

Figure 6: Monthly growth in industrial production in the USA

The next series are the monthly returns of 10 decile portfolios (ranked according to market capitalization), for the New York Stock Exchange, ranging from 1926.08 to 2002.12[2]. These returns might be best described by the simple regression model

$$y_t = \sum_{s=1}^{12} \delta_s D_{s,t} + \varepsilon_t \qquad (3)$$

$$\varepsilon_t = \rho_1 \varepsilon_{t-1} + u_t. \qquad (4)$$

One might expect a "January effect", in particular for the smaller stocks, see Haugen and Lakonishok (1987).

Comparing the estimated parameters for the decile models and their associated standard errors suggests that only a few parameters are significant. Figure 7 depicts the estimates of $\hat{\delta}_s$ for the first two and for the last two deciles, where the first decile usually gets a significant positive parameter. Also the R^2 values are higher for lower deciles. Clearly, the graphs in Figure 7 suggest the presence of a January effect for the smaller stocks.

[2]Data source is http://mba.tuck.dartmouth.edu/pages/faculty/ken.french/

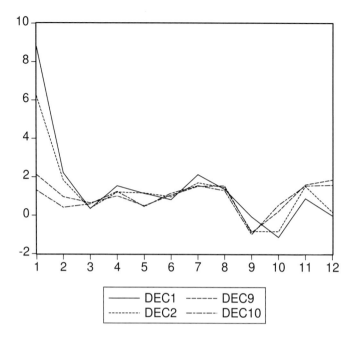

Figure 7: Deciles

The parameters for the seasonal dummies in the regression model in (4) are often not significant. In practice, this is a phenomenon that is quite common for disaggregated data. For example, for weekly sales of instant decaf coffee (observed in the stores of a retail chain in the Netherlands, for 1994 week 29 to 1998 week 28), one might consider

$$y_t = \sum_{s=1}^{52} \delta_s D_{s,t} + \varepsilon_t, \tag{5}$$

but this involves a large amount of parameters, and most likely, many of these will not be statistically relevant. One can then reduce this number by deleting certain $D_{s,t}$ variables, but this might complicate the interpretation. In that case, a more sensible model is

$$y_t = \mu + \sum_{k=1}^{26} [\alpha_k \cos(\frac{2\pi kt}{52}) + \beta_k \sin(\frac{2\pi kt}{52})] + \varepsilon_t, \tag{6}$$

where $t = 1, 2, \dots$. A cycle within 52 weeks (an annual cycle) corresponds with $k = 1$, and a cycle within 4 weeks corresponds with $k = 13$. Other

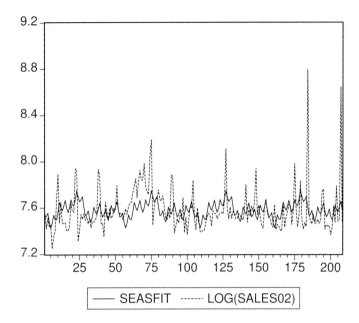

Figure 8: Deterministic seasonal cycles in coffee sales

interpretable cycles would correspond with 2 weeks, 13 weeks and 26 weeks ($k = 26$, 4 and 2, respectively). Note that $\sin(\frac{2\pi kt}{52})$ is equal to 0 for $k = 26$, hence the intercept μ in (6). One may now decide to include only those cycles that make sense from an interpretation point of view.

Figure 8 shows the fit of the model in (6), where ε_t is assumed an AR(1) process, and where only cycles within 2, 4, 13, 26 and 52 weeks are considered. Hence, there are only 9 variables to characterize seasonality. The R^2 measure is 0.139, suggesting that there is moderate deterministic seasonality in this weekly series.

What do we want to forecast?

For seasonal data with seasonal frequency S, one usually considers forecasting 1-step ahead, $\frac{S}{2}$-steps ahead or S-steps ahead. One may also want to forecast the sum of 1 to S steps ahead, that is, say, a year.

There is no general rule that says that forecasting data at the T frequency is better done using data for that particular frequency than by using data at a higher frequency, and then sum the forecasts. For example, when the purpose is to forecast two years ahead, and one has monthly data, one can choose to use a model for the annual data or for the monthly data. There are less annual data than monthly data, so one has less information to specify a model. On the other hand, monthly data show seasonality that one has to capture and such data also might have more outlying observations which may affect model construction.

Also, if the aim is to forecast a full year ahead, one might perhaps, at least in principle, consider modelling seasonally adjusted data. Of course, these adjusted data should not show any seasonality, and the adjustment method should not have introduced data features that were not there to begin with. As I will discuss next, there are however some problematic aspects of seasonally adjusted data.

Why is seasonal adjustment often problematic?

It is common practice to seasonally adjust quarterly or monthly observed macroeconomic time series, like GDP and unemployment. A key motivation is that practitioners seem to want to compare the current observation with that in the previous month or quarter, without considering seasonality. As many series display seasonal fluctuations which are not constant over time, at least not for the typical time span considered in practice, there is a debate in the statistics and econometrics literature about which method is most useful for seasonal adjustment. Roughly speaking, there are two important methods. The first is the Census X-11 method, initiated by Shiskin and Eisenpress (1957), and the second one uses model-based methods, see for example Maravall (1995). Interestingly, it seems that with the new Census X-12 method, the two approaches have come closer together, see Findley et al. (1998). In Franses (2001) I address the question why one would want to seasonally adjust in the first place, and what follows in this subsection draws upon that discussion.

Except for macroeconomics, there is no economic discipline in which the data are seasonally adjusted prior to analysis. It is hard to imagine, for example, that there would be a stock market index, with returns corrected for day-of-the-week effects. Also, seasonality in sales or market shares is of particular interest to a manager, and seasonal adjustment of marketing data would simply result in an uninteresting time series.

Generally, the interest in analyzing macroeconomic data concerns the trend and the business cycle. In case the data have stochastic trends, one usually resorts to well-known techniques for common trends analysis and cointegration, see for example Engle and Granger (1991). To understand business cycle fluctuations, for example in the sense of examining which variables seem to be able to predict recessions, one can use nonlinear models like the (smooth transition) threshold model and the Markov-switching model, see Granger and Teräsvirta (1993) and Franses and van Dijk (2000) for surveys.

Consider a seasonally observed time series y_t, where t runs from 1 to n. In practice one might be interested in the seasonally adjusted observation at time n or $n-1$. The main purpose of seasonal adjustment is to separate the observed data into two components, a nonseasonal component and a seasonal component. These components are not observed, and have to be estimated from the data. It is assumed that

$$y_t = \hat{y}_t^{NS} + \hat{y}_t^{S}, \tag{7}$$

where $\hat{y}_t^{NS}$ is the estimated nonseasonal component, and $\hat{y}_t^{S}$ is the estimated seasonal component. This decomposition assumes an additive relation. When this is not the case, one can transform y_t until it holds for the transformed data. For example, if the seasonal fluctuations seem multiplicative with the trend, one typically considers the natural logarithmic transformation.

As said, there are two commonly used approaches to estimate the components in (7). The first is coined Census X-12. This approach applies a sequence of two-sided moving average filters like

$$w_0 + \sum_{i=1}^{m} w_i (L^i + L^{-i}), \tag{8}$$

where L is the familiar backward shift operator, and where the value of m and the weights w_i for $i = 0, 1, \ldots, m$ are set by the practitioner. It additionally contains a range of outlier removal methods, and corrections for trading-day and holiday effects. An important consequence of two-sided filters is that to adjust observation y_n, one needs the observations at time $n + 1$, $n + 2$ to $n + m$. As these are not yet observed at n, one has to rely on forecasted values, which are then treated as genuine observations. Of course, this automatically implies that seasonally adjusted data should be revised after a while, especially if the newly observed realizations differ from those forecasts. Interesting surveys of this method are given in Bell and Hillmer (1984), Hylleberg (1986), and more recently in Findley et al. (1998).

The second approach involves model-based methods. These assume that the seasonal component can be described by a model like for example

$$(1 + L + L^2 + L^3)y_t^S = \varepsilon_t. \tag{9}$$

With an estimate of the variance of ε_t, and with suitable starting-values, one can estimate the seasonal component using Kalman-filtering techniques, see Harvey (1989). Given $\hat{y}_t^S$, one can simply use (7) to get the estimated adjusted series.

A few remarks can be made. The first amounts to recognizing that seasonally adjusted data are *estimated data*. In practice this might be forgotten, which is mainly due to the fact that those who provide the seasonally adjusted data tend not to provide the associated standard errors. This is misleading. Indeed, a correct statement would read "this month's unemployment rate is 7.8, and after seasonal adjustment it is 7.5 plus or minus 0.3". The Census X-12 method cannot generate standard errors, but for the model-based methods it is not difficult to do so. Koopman and Franses (2003) propose a method which also allows for business cylce-dependent confidence intervals around seasonally adjusted data.

Obviously, when $\hat{y}_t^{NS}$ is saved and $\hat{y}_t^S$ is thrown away, one cannot reconstruct the original series y_t. Moreover, if the original series y_t can be described by an econometric time series model with innovations ε_t, it is unclear to what extent these innovations are assigned to either $\hat{y}_t^{NS}$, $\hat{y}_t^S$ or to both. Hence, when one constructs an econometric time series model for the adjusted series $\hat{y}_t^{NS}$, the estimated innovations in this model are not the "true" innovations. This feature makes impulse-response analysis less interesting.

The key assumption is the relation in (7). For some economic time series this relation does not hold. For example, if the data can best be described by a so-called periodic time series model, where the parameters vary with the seasons, see Section 4 below, one cannot separate out a seasonal component and reliably focus on the estimated nonseasonal component. There are a few theoretical results about what exactly happens if one adjusts a periodic series, and some simulation and empirical results are available, see Franses (1996), Ooms and Franses (1997) and Del Barrio Castro and Osborn (2004). Generally, seasonally adjusted periodic data still display seasonality.

Given the aim of seasonal adjustment, that is, to create time series which are more easy to analyze for trends and business cycles, it is preferable that seasonally adjusted data (1) show no signs of seasonality, (2) do not have trend properties that differ from those of the original data, and (3) that they do not have other non-linear properties than the original data. Unfortunately, it turns out that most publicly available adjusted data do not have all of these properties. Indeed, it frequently occurs that $\hat{y}_t^{NS}$ can be modeled using a seasonal ARMA model, with highly significant parameters at seasonal lags in both the AR and MA parts of the model. The intuition for this empirical finding may be that two-sided filters as in (8) can be shown to assume quite a number of so-called seasonal unit roots, see Section 3 below. Empirical tests for seasonal unit roots in the original series however usually suggest a smaller number of such roots, and by assuming too many such roots, seasonal adjustment introduces seasonality in the MA part of the model. Furthermore, and as mentioned before, if the data correspond with a periodic time series process, one can still fit a periodic time series model to the adjusted data. The intuition here is that linear moving average filters treat all observations as equal.

Would seasonal adjustment leave the trend property of the original data intact? Unfortunately not, as many studies indicate. The general finding is that the persistence of shocks is higher, which in formal test settings usually corresponds with more evidence in favor of a unit root. In a multivariate framework this amounts to finding less evidence in favor of cointegration, that is, of the presence of stable long-run relationships, and thus more evidence of random walk type trends. The possible intuition of this result is that two-sided filters make the effects of innovations to appear in $2m + 1$ adjusted observations, thereby spuriously creating a higher degree of persistence of shocks. Hence, seasonal adjustment incurs less evidence of long-run stability.

Non-linear data do not become linear after seasonal adjustment, but there is some evidence that otherwise linear data can display non-linearity after seasonal adjustment, see Ghysels, Granger and Siklos (1996). Additionally, non-linear models for the original data seem to differ from similar models for the adjusted data. The structure of the non-linear model does not necessarily change, it merely concerns the parameters in these models. Hence, one tends to find other dates for recessions for adjusted data than for unadjusted data. A general finding is that the recessions for adjusted data last longer. The intuition for this result is that expansion data are used to adjust recession data and the other way round. Hence, regime switches get smoothed away or become less pronounced.

In sum, seasonally adjusted data may still display some seasonality, can have different trend properties than the original data have, and also can have different non-linear properties. It is my opinion that this suggests that these data may not be useful for their very purpose.

3. Basic Models

This section deals with a few basic models that are often used in practice. They also often serve as a benchmark, in case one decides to construct more complicated models. These models are the constant deterministic seasonality model, the seasonal random walk, the so-called airline model and the basic structural time series model.

The deterministic seasonality model

This first model is useful in case the seasonal pattern is constant over time. This constancy can be associated with various aspects. First, for some of the data we tend to analyze in practice, the weather conditions do not change, that is, there is an intra-year climatological cycle involving precipitation and hours of sunshine that is rather constant over the years. For example, the harvesting season is reasonably fixed, it is known when lakes and harbors are ice-free, and our mental status also seems to experience some fixed seasonality. In fact, consumer survey data (concerning consumer confidence) show seasonality, where such confidence is higher in January and lower in October, as compared with other months. Some would say that such seasonality in mood has an impact on stock market fluctuations, and indeed, major stock market crashes tend to occur more often in the month of October. Other regular phenomena concern calender-based festivals and holidays. Finally, institutional factors as tax years, end-of-years bonuses, and school holidays, can make some economic phenomena to obey a regular seasonal cycle.

A general model for constant seasonality in case there are S seasons is

$$y_t = \mu + \sum_{k=1}^{\frac{S}{2}} [\alpha_k \cos(\frac{2\pi k t}{S}) + \beta_k \sin(\frac{2\pi k t}{S})] + u_t, \qquad (10)$$

where $t = 1, 2, ...$ and u_t is some ARMA type process. This expression makes explicit that constant deterministic seasonality can also be viewed as a sum of cycles, defined by sines and cosines. For example, for $S = 4$, one has

$$y_t = \mu + \alpha_1 \cos(\frac{1}{2}\pi t) + \beta_1 \sin(\frac{1}{2}\pi t) + \alpha_2 \cos(\pi t) + u_t, \tag{11}$$

where $\cos(\frac{1}{2}\pi t)$ equals $(0, -1, 0, 1, 0, -1,...)$ and $\sin(\frac{1}{2}\pi t)$ is $(1, 0, -1, 0, 1, 0,...)$ and $\cos(\pi t)$ is $(-1, 1, -1, 1,...)$. The μ is included as $\sin(\pi t)$ is zero everywhere.

The expression in terms of sines and cosines is also relevant as it matches more naturally with the discussion below on filters. For example, if one considers $y_t + y_{t-2}$ for quarterly data, which can be written as $(1 + L^2)y_t$, then $(1 + L^2)\cos(\frac{1}{2}\pi t) = 0$ and $(1 + L^2)\sin(\frac{1}{2}\pi t) = 0$. This means that this filter effectively cancels part of the deterministic seasonal variation. Additionally, it holds that $(1 + L)\cos(\pi t) = 0$, and of course, $(1 - L)\mu = 0$. This shows that deterministic seasonality can be removed by applying the transformation $(1 - L)(1 + L)(1 + L^2) = 1 - L^4$. In words it means that comparing the current quarter with the same quarter last year effectively removes the influence of deterministic seasonality, if there would be any, or that of a trends, again if there would be any. I will return to this transformation later on.

Naturally, there is a one-to-one link between the model in (10) and the model which has the familiar S seasonal dummy variables. For $S = 4$, one has

$$y_t = \sum_{s=1}^{4} \delta_s D_{s,t} + u_t, \tag{12}$$

and it holds that $\mu = \sum_{s=1}^{4} \delta_s$, and that $\alpha_1 = \delta_4 - \delta_2$, $\beta_1 = \delta_1 - \delta_3$ and $\alpha_2 = \delta_4 - \delta_3 + \delta_2 - \delta_1$. There is no particular reason to favor one of the two models, except for the case where S is large, as I mentioned before. For example, when S is 52, a model like in (12) contains many parameters, of which many might turn out to be insignificant in practice. Additionally, the interpretation of these parameters is also not easy. In contrast, for the model in (10) one can choose to assume that some α and β parameters are equal to zero, simply as they are associated with deterministic cycles which are not of interest for the analysis at hand.

The constant seasonality model is applied widely in marketing and tourism. In finance, one might expect seasonality not to be too constant over time, basically as that would imply that traders could make use of it. Further, many macroeconomic data seem to display seasonality that changes over time, as is illustrated by for example Canova and Ghysels

(1994) and Canova and Hansen (1995). Seasonal patterns can change due to changing consumption patterns. For example, one nowadays needs to pay for next year's holiday well in advance. Also, one can eat ice in the winter, and nowadays have all kinds of vegetables in any season. It might also be that institutions change. The tax year may shift, the end-of-year bonus might be divided over three periods, and the timing of children's holidays can change. It may also be that behavior changes. For example, one can imagine different responses to exogenous shocks in different seasons. Also, it may be that certain shocks occur more often in some seasons. All these reasons suggest that seasonal patterns can change over time. In the rest of this section, I will discuss three basic models that can describe time series with changing seasonal patterns.

Seasonal random walk

A simple model that allows the seasonal pattern to change over time is the seasonal random walk, given by

$$y_t = y_{t-S} + \varepsilon_t. \tag{13}$$

It might not immediately be clear from this expression that seasonality changes, and therefore it is useful to consider the S annual time series $Y_{s,T}$. The seasonal random walk implies that for these annual series it holds that

$$Y_{s,T} = Y_{s,T-1} + \varepsilon_{s,T}. \tag{14}$$

Hence, each seasonal series follows a random walk, and due to the innovations, the annual series may switch position, such that "summer becomes winter".

From graphs it is not easy to discern whether a series is a seasonal random walk or not. The observable pattern depends on the starting values of the time series, relative to the variance of the error term, see the graphs in Figure 9. When the starting values are very close to each other, seasonal patterns seem to change quite rapidly (the series y) and when the starting values are far apart, the graph of the x series suggests that seasonality is close to constant, at least at first sight.

This demonstrates that simply looking at graphs might not be reliable. Here, a look at the autocorrelations of the series $(1 - L^S)y_t$ could be helpful. In the case of a seasonal random walk, the estimated autocorrelation function should look like a white noise series, while such a function for a

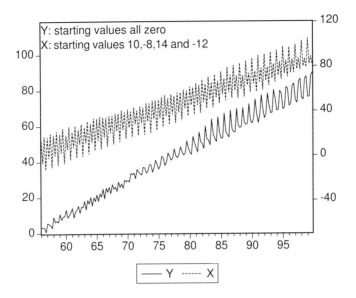

Figure 9: The two quarterly variables are seasonal random walks, with different starting values.

$(1 - L^S)$ transformed deterministic seasonality series, would result in an error process like $u_t - u_{t-4}$, with a theoretical fourth order autocorrelation of value -0.5, see Franses (1998).

Remarkably, even though the realizations of a seasonal random walk can show substantial within-sample variation, the out-of-sample forecasts are deterministic. Indeed, at time n, these forecasts are

$$\hat{y}_{n+1} = y_{n+1-S}$$
$$\hat{y}_{n+2} = y_{n+2-S}$$
$$\vdots$$
$$\hat{y}_{n+S} = y_n$$
$$\hat{y}_{n+S+1} = \hat{y}_{n+1}$$
$$\hat{y}_{n+S+2} = \hat{y}_{n+2}.$$

Another way of allowing for seasonal random walk type changing pattern, is to introduce changing parameters. For example, a subtle form of changing seasonality is described by a time-varying seasonal dummy

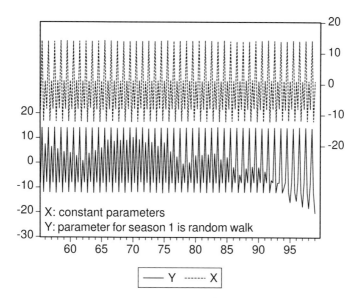

Figure 10: Time series with constant seasonality (x) and with one seasonal dummy parameter as a seasonal random walk (y)

parameter model. For example, for $S = 4$ this model could look like

$$y_t = \sum_{s=1}^{4} \delta_{s,t} D_{s,t} + u_t,\tag{15}$$

where

$$\delta_{s,t} = \delta_{s,t-S} + \varepsilon_{s,t}.\tag{16}$$

When the variance of $\varepsilon_{s,t} = 0$, the constant parameter model appears. The amount of variation depends on the variance of $\varepsilon_{s,t}$. A illustration is given in Figure 10. Such a model is used as a test vehicle in Canova and Hansen (1995) to diagnose if there is changing seasonality in time series.

Airline model

It can be felt that the seasonal random walk model allows for too much variation in the seasonal pattern. Indeed, allowing each season to be a random walk might introduce too much variation. One way to accommodate this is to introduce a correction, for example by having an error term at the lag that corresponds with the filter with a parameter that comes close to unity. An example is

$$y_t = y_{t-S} + \varepsilon_t + \theta_S \varepsilon_{t-S}, \tag{17}$$

where θ_S can approximate -1. Bell (1987) demonstrates that when $\theta_S = -1$, the model reduces to

$$y_t = \sum_{s=1}^{S} \delta_s D_{s,t} + \varepsilon_t. \tag{18}$$

Clearly, this also gives an opportunity to test if there is constant or changing seasonality.

An often applied model, popularized by Box and Jenkins (1970) and named after its application to monthly airline passenger data, is the airline model. It builds on the above model by considering

$$(1 - L)(1 - L^S)y_t = (1 + \theta_1 L)(1 + \theta_S L^S)\varepsilon_t, \tag{19}$$

where it should be noted that

$$(1 - L)(1 - L^S)y_t = y_t - y_{t-1} - y_{t-S} + y_{t-S-1}. \tag{20}$$

This model is assumed to effectively handle a trend in the data using the filter $(1 - L)$ and any changing seasonality using $(1 - L^S)$. Strictly speaking, the airline model assumes $S + 1$ unit roots. This is due to the fact that the characteristic equation of the AR part, which is,

$$(1 - z)(1 - z^S) = 0, \tag{21}$$

has $S + 1$ solutions on the unit circle. For example, if $S = 4$ the solutions are $(1, 1, -1, i, -i)$. This implies a substantial amount of random walk like behavior, even though it is corrected to some extent by the $(1 + \theta_1 L)(1 + \theta_S L^S)\varepsilon_t$ part of the model. In terms of forecasting, it assumes very wide confidence intervals around the point forecasts. On the other hand, the advantages of this model are that it contains only two parameters and that it can describe a wide range of variables, which can be observed from the Eviews output in Figures 11, 12 and 13. The estimated residuals of these models do not obviously indicate mis-specification. On the other hand, it is clear that the roots of the MA polynomial (indicated at the bottom panel of these graphs) are close to the unit circle.

Dependent Variable: LC-LC(-1)-LC(-4)+LC(-5)
Method: Least Squares
Date: 04/07/04   Time: 09:48
Sample(adjusted): 1981:2 2001:2
Included observations: 81 after adjusting endpoints
Convergence achieved after 10 iterations
Backcast: 1980:1 1981:1

Variable	Coefficient	Std. Error	t-Statistic	Prob.
C	-0.000329	0.000264	-1.246930	0.2162
MA(1)	-0.583998	0.088580	-6.592921	0.0000
SMA(4)	-0.591919	0.090172	-6.564320	0.0000

R-squared	0.444787	Mean dependent var	-5.01E-05
Adjusted R-squared	0.430550	S.D. dependent var	0.016590
S.E. of regression	0.012519	Akaike info criterion	-5.886745
Sum squared resid	0.012225	Schwarz criterion	-5.798061
Log likelihood	241.4132	F-statistic	31.24325
Durbin-Watson stat	2.073346	Prob(F-statistic)	0.000000

Inverted MA Roots	.88	.58	.00+.88i	-.00 -.88i
	-.88			

Figure 11: Airline model estimation results: Quarterly log(consumption) in Japan

Dependent Variable: LM-LM(-1)-LM(-4)+LM(-5)
Method: Least Squares
Date: 04/07/04   Time: 09:50
Sample(adjusted): 1976:3 2004:1
Included observations: 111 after adjusting endpoints
Convergence achieved after 16 iterations
Backcast: 1975:2 1976:2

Variable	Coefficient	Std. Error	t-Statistic	Prob.
C	-0.000192	0.000320	-0.599251	0.5503
MA(1)	0.353851	0.088144	4.014489	0.0001
SMA(4)	-0.951464	0.016463	-57.79489	0.0000

R-squared	0.647536	Mean dependent var	-3.88E-06
Adjusted R-squared	0.641009	S.D. dependent var	0.032112
S.E. of regression	0.019240	Akaike info criterion	-5.036961
Sum squared resid	0.039981	Schwarz criterion	-4.963730
Log likelihood	282.5513	F-statistic	99.20713
Durbin-Watson stat	2.121428	Prob(F-statistic)	0.000000

Inverted MA Roots	.99	.00+.99i	-.00 -.99i	-.35
	-.99			

Figure 12: Airline model estimation results: Quarterly log(M1) in Australia

```
Dependent Variable: LI-LI(-1)-LI(-12)+LI(-13)
Method: Least Squares
Date: 04/07/04   Time: 09:52
Sample(adjusted): 1920:02 2004:02
Included observations: 1009 after adjusting endpoints
Convergence achieved after 11 iterations
Backcast: 1919:01 1920:01
```

Variable	Coefficient	Std. Error	t-Statistic	Prob.
C	2.38E-05	0.000196	0.121473	0.9033
MA(1)	0.378388	0.029006	13.04509	0.0000
SMA(12)	-0.805799	0.016884	-47.72483	0.0000

R-squared	0.522387	Mean dependent var	-0.000108
Adjusted R-squared	0.521437	S.D. dependent var	0.031842
S.E. of regression	0.022028	Akaike info criterion	-4.790041
Sum squared resid	0.488142	Schwarz criterion	-4.775422
Log likelihood	2419.576	F-statistic	550.1535
Durbin-Watson stat	1.839223	Prob(F-statistic)	0.000000

Inverted MA Roots	.98	.85+.49i	.85 -.49i	.49+.85i
	.49 -.85i	.00 -.98i	-.00+.98i	-.38
	-.49 -.85i	-.49+.85i	-.85 -.49i	-.85+.49i
	-.98			

Figure 13: Airline model estimation results: Monthly log(industrial production) in the USA

Basic structural model

Finally, a model that takes a position in between seasonal adjustment and the airline model is the Structural Time Series Model, see Harvey (1989). The basic idea is that a time series can be decomposed in various components, which reflect seasonality, trend, cycles and so on. This representation facilitates the explicit consideration of a trend component or a seasonal component, which, if one intends to do so, can be subtracted from the data to get a trend-free or seasonality-free series. Often, a Structural Time Series Model can be written as a seasonal ARIMA type model, and hence, its descriptive quality is close to that of a seasonal ARIMA model.

To illustrate, an example of a structural time series model for a quarterly time series is

$$y_t = \mu_t + s_t + w_t, \quad w_t \sim N(0, \sigma_w^2) \tag{22}$$

$$(1 - L)^2 \mu_t = u_t, \quad u_t \sim N(0, \sigma_u^2) \tag{23}$$

$$(1 + L + L^2 + L^3)s_t = v_t, \quad v_t \sim N(0, \sigma_v^2) \tag{24}$$

where the error processes w_t, u_t and v_t are mutually independent, and where the errors are normally and independently distributed. This model contains three unknown parameters, that is, the variances, and of course, also the variables μ_t, s_t and the error term w_t are unobserved. The interest is in estimating the trend and the seasonal component, which are associated with these features due to the lag polynomials $(1 - L)^2$ and $(1 + L + L^2 + L^3)$, respectively. For parameter estimation one relies on Kalman filter techniques.

Combining the three equations gives that y_t can also be described by

$$(1 - L)(1 - L^4)y_t = \zeta_t \tag{25}$$

where ζ_t is a moving average process of order 5. Notice that this description comes close to that of the airline model above. This can be substantiated by deriving the autocovariances γ_k, $k = 0, 1, 2, \ldots$, of ζ_t, which are

$$\gamma_0 = 4\sigma_u^2 + 6\sigma_v^2 + 4\sigma_w^2 \tag{26}$$

$$\gamma_1 = 3\sigma_u^2 - 4\sigma_v^2 - 2\sigma_w^2 \tag{27}$$

$$\gamma_2 = 2\sigma_u^2 + \sigma_v^2 \tag{28}$$

$$\gamma_3 = \sigma_u^2 + \sigma_w^2 \tag{29}$$

$$\gamma_4 = -2\sigma_w^2 \tag{30}$$

$$\gamma_5 = \sigma_w^2 \tag{31}$$

$$\gamma_j = 0 \quad \text{for } j = 6, 7, \ldots. \tag{32}$$

The only formal differences between this model and the airline model is that the latter implies a zero-valued third order autocovariance, and that $\gamma_3 = \gamma_5$.

Conclusion

There are various ways to describe a time series (and use that description for forecasting) with constant or changing seasonal variation. In the next section, more models will be proposed for describing changing seasonality.

In practice, of course, one needs to make a choice. To make such a choice, one usually zooms in on the key differences between the various models, and these mainly concern the number of unit roots assumed in the autoregressive or moving average polynomials. When these roots are associated with seasonal fluctuations, like for example $(1 + L)$ and $(1 + L^2)$, these roots are called seasonal unit roots. The next section will say more about this selection of models.

To conclude, an important message of this section is that model choice can not just be guided by an informal look at graphs or at autocorrelation functions. Various models can generate data that look very similar, and hence more formal tests are needed.

4. Advanced Models

The previous section reviewed various basic models without checking whether these filters match with the properties of the data. These filters assume a certain amount of unit roots, and it seems sensible to test whether these roots are present or not. In this section I discuss models that allow for a more sophisticated description of seasonal patterns, while allowing for the possible presence of zero frequency trends. Next, I will discuss models that allow the trend and season variation to be intertwined.

Seasonal unit roots

A time series variable has a non-seasonal unit root if the autoregressive polynomial (of the model that best describes this variable), contains the component $1 - L$, and the moving-average part does not. For example, the model $y_t = y_{t-1} + \varepsilon_t$ has a first-order autoregressive polynomial $1 - L$, as it can be written as $(1 - L)y_t = \varepsilon_t$. Hence, data that can be described by the random walk model are said to have a unit root. The same holds of course for the model $y_t = \mu + y_{t-1} + \varepsilon_t$, which is a random walk with drift. Solving this last model to the first observation, that is,

$$y_t = y_0 + \mu t + \varepsilon_t + \varepsilon_{t-1} + \ldots + \varepsilon_1 \qquad (33)$$

shows that such data also have a deterministic trend. Due to the summation of the error terms, it is possible that data diverge from the overall trend μt for a long time, and hence one could conclude from a graph that there are all kinds of trends with directions that vary from time to time. Therefore, such data are sometimes said to have a stochastic trend.

The unit roots in seasonal data, which can be associated with changing seasonality, are seasonal unit roots, see Hylleberg et al. (1990) [HEGY]. For quarterly data, these roots are -1, i, and $-i$. For example, data generated from the model $y_t = -y_{t-1} + \varepsilon_t$ would display seasonality, but if one were to make graphs with the split seasonals, then one could observe that the quarterly data within a year shift places quite frequently. Similar observations hold for the model $y_t = -y_{t-2} + \varepsilon_t$, which can be written as $(1 + L^2)y_t = \varepsilon_t$, where the autoregressive polynomial $1 + L^2$ corresponds to the seasonal unit roots i and $-$i, as these two values solve the equation $1 + z^2 = 0$.

Testing for seasonal unit roots

In contrast to simply imposing (seasonal) unit roots, one can also test whether they are present or not. The most commonly used method for this purpose is the HEGY method. For quarterly data it amounts to a regression of $\Delta_4 y_t$ on deterministic terms like an intercept, seasonal dummies, a trend and seasonal trends and on $(1 + L + L^2 + L^3)y_{t-1}$, $(-1 + L - L^2 + L^3)y_{t-1}$, $-(1+L^2)y_{t-1}$, $-(1+L^2)y_{t-2}$, and on lags of $\Delta_4 y_t$. A t-test is used to examine the significance of the parameter for $(1+L+L^2+L^3)y_{t-1}$, and similarly, a t-test for $(-1 + L - L^2 + L^3)y_{t-1}$ and a joint F-test for $-(1 + L^2)y_{t-1}$ and $-(1 + L^2)y_{t-2}$. An insignificant test value indicates the presence of the associated root(s), which are 1, -1, and the pair i, $-$i, respectively. Asymptotic theory for the tests is developed in Hylleberg et al. (1990), and useful extensions are put forward in Smith and Taylor (1998).

When including deterministic terms, it is important to recall the discussion in Section 2, concerning the seasonal dummies. Indeed, when the seasonal dummies are included unrestrictedly, it is possible that the time series (under the null hypothesis of seasonal unit roots) can display seasonally varying deterministic trends. Hence, when checking for example whether the $(1 + L)$ filter can be imposed, one also needs to impose that the α_2 parameter for $\cos(\pi t)$ in (11) equals zero. The preferable way to include deterministics therefore is to include the alternating dummy variables $D_{1,t} - D_{2,t} + D_{3,t} - D_{4,t}$, $D_{1,t} - D_{3,t}$, and $D_{2,t} - D_{4,t}$. And, for example, under the null hypothesis that there is a unit root -1, the parameter for the first alternating dummy should also be zero. These joint tests extend the work of Dickey and Fuller (1981), and are discussed in Smith and Taylor (1999). When models are created for panels of time series or for multivariate series, as I will discuss below, these restrictions on the deterministics (based on the sine-cosine notation) are important too.

Kawasaki and Franses (2003) propose to detect seasonal unit roots within the context of a structural time series model. They rely on model selection criteria. Using Monte Carlo simulations, they show that the method works well. They illustrate their approach for several quarterly macroeconomic time series variables.

Seasonal cointegration

In case two or more seasonally observed time series have seasonal unit roots, one may be interested in testing for common seasonal unit roots, that is, in testing for seasonal cointegration. If these series have such roots in common, they will have common changing seasonal patterns.

Engle et al. (1993) [EGHL] propose a two-step method to see if there is seasonal cointegration. When two series $y_{1,t}$ and $y_{2,t}$ have a common non-seasonal unit root, then the series u_t defined by

$$u_t = (1 + L + L^2 + L^3)y_{1,t} - \alpha_1(1 + L + L^2 + L^3)y_{2,t} \qquad (34)$$

does not need the $(1-L)$ filter to become stationary. Seasonal cointegration at the annual frequency π, corresponding to unit root -1, implies that

$$v_t = (1 - L + L^2 - L^3)y_{1,t} - \alpha_2(1 - L + L^2 - L^3)y_{2,t} \qquad (35)$$

does not need the $(1 + L)$ differencing filter. And, seasonal cointegration at the annual frequency $\pi/2$, corresponding to the unit roots $\pm i$, means that

$$w_t = (1-L^2)y_{1,t} - \alpha_3(1-L^2)y_{2,t} - \alpha_4(1-L^2)y_{1,t-1} - \alpha_5(1-L^2)y_{2,t-1} \quad (36)$$

does not have the unit roots $\pm i$. In case all three u_t, v_t and w_t do not have the relevant unit roots, the first equation of a simple version of a seasonal cointegration model is

$$\Delta_4 y_{1,t} = \gamma_1 u_{t-1} + \gamma_2 v_{t-1} + \gamma_3 w_{t-2} + \gamma_4 w_{t-3} + \varepsilon_{1,t}, \qquad (37)$$

where γ_1 to γ_4 are error correction parameters. The test method proposed in EGHL is a two-step method, similar to the Engle-Granger (1987) approach to non-seasonal time series.

Seasonal cointegration in a multivariate time series Y_t can also be analyzed using an extension of the Johansen approach, see Johansen and Schaumburg (1999), Franses and Kunst (1999a). It amounts to testing the ranks of matrices that correspond to variables which are transformed using the filters to remove the roots 1, -1 or $\pm i$. More precise, consider the $(m \times 1)$ vector process Y_t, and assume that it can be described by the VAR(p) process

$$Y_t = \Theta D_t + \Phi_1 Y_{t-1} + \cdots + \Phi_p Y_{t-p} + e_t, \qquad (38)$$

where D_t is the (4×1) vector process $D_t = (D_{1,t}, D_{2,t}, D_{3,t}, D_{4,t})'$ containing the seasonal dummies, and where Θ is an $(m \times 4)$ parameter matrix. Similar to the Johansen (1995) approach and conditional on the assumption that $p > 4$, the model can be rewritten as

$$\Delta_4 Y_t = \Theta D_t + \Pi_1 Y_{1,t-1} \tag{39}$$

$$+ \Pi_2 Y_{2,t-1} + \Pi_3 Y_{3,t-2} + \Pi_4 Y_{3,t-1} \tag{40}$$

$$+ \Gamma_1 \Delta_4 Y_{t-1} + \cdots + \Gamma_{p-4} \Delta_4 Y_{t-(p-4)} + e_t,$$

where

$$Y_{1,t} = (1 + L + L^2 + L^3) Y_t$$
$$Y_{2,t} = (1 - L + L^2 - L^3) Y_t$$
$$Y_{3,t} = (1 - L^2) Y_t.$$

This is a multivariate extension of the univariate HEGY model. The ranks of the matrices Π_1, Π_2, Π_3 and Π_4 determine the number of cointegration relations at each of the frequencies. Again, it is important to properly account for the deterministics, in order not to have seasonally diverging trends, see Franses and Kunst (1999a) for a solution.

Periodic models

An alternative class of models is the periodic autoregression. Consider a univariate time series y_t, which is observed quarterly for N years. It is assumed that $n = 4N$. A periodic autoregressive model of order p [PAR(p)] can be written as

$$y_t = \mu_s + \phi_{1s} y_{t-1} + \cdots + \phi_{ps} y_{t-p} + \varepsilon_t, \tag{41}$$

or

$$\phi_{p,s}(L) y_t = \mu_s + \varepsilon_t, \tag{42}$$

with

$$\phi_{p,s}(L) = 1 - \phi_{1s} L - \cdots - \phi_{ps} L^p, \tag{43}$$

where μ_s is a seasonally-varying intercept term. The $\phi_{1s}, \ldots, \phi_{ps}$ are autoregressive parameters up to order p_s which may vary with the season s, where $s = 1, 2, 3, 4$. For ε_t it can be assumed it is a standard white noise process with constant variance σ^2, but that may be relaxed by allowing ε_t to have seasonal variance σ_s^2. As some ϕ_{is}, $i = 1, 2, \ldots, p$, can take zero values, the order p is the maximum of all p_s.

Multivariate representation

In general, the PAR(p) process can be rewritten as an AR(P) model for the (4×1) vector process $Y_T = (Y_{1,T}, Y_{2,T}, Y_{3,T}, Y_{4,T})'$, $T = 1, 2, \ldots, N$, where $Y_{s,T}$ is the observation of y_t in season s of year T. The model is then

$$\Phi_0 Y_T = \mu + \Phi_1 Y_{T-1} + \cdots + \Phi_P Y_{T-P} + \varepsilon_T, \tag{44}$$

or

$$\Phi(L) Y_T = \mu + \varepsilon_T, \tag{45}$$

with

$$\Phi(L) = \Phi_0 - \Phi_1 L - \cdots - \Phi_P L^P, \tag{46}$$

$\mu = (\mu_1, \mu_2, \mu_3, \mu_4)'$, $\varepsilon_T = (\varepsilon_{1,T}, \varepsilon_{2,T}, \varepsilon_{3,T}, \varepsilon_{4,T})'$, and $\varepsilon_{s,T}$ is the observation on the error process ε_t in season s of year T. The lag operator L applies to data at frequencies t and to T, that is, $L y_t = y_{t-1}$ and $L Y_T = Y_{T-1}$. The $\Phi_0, \Phi_1, \ldots, \Phi_P$ are 4×4 parameter matrices with elements

$$\Phi_0[i,j] = \begin{cases} 1 & i = j, \\ 0 & j > i, \\ -\phi_{i-j,i} & i < j, \end{cases} \tag{47}$$

$$\Phi_k[i,j] = \phi_{i+4k-j,i}, \tag{48}$$

for $i = 1, 2, 3, 4$, $j = 1, 2, 3, 4$, and $k = 1, 2, \ldots, P$. For P it holds that $P = 1 + [(p-1)/4]$, where $[\cdot]$ is the integer function. Hence, when p is less than or equal to 4, the value of P is 1.

As Φ_0 is a lower triangular matrix, model (44) is a recursive model. This means that $Y_{4,T}$ depends on $Y_{3,T}$, $Y_{2,T}$, and $Y_{1,T}$, and on all variables in earlier years. Similarly, $Y_{3,T}$ depends on $Y_{2,T}$ and $Y_{1,T}$, and $Y_{2,T}$ on $Y_{1,T}$ and on all observations in past years. As an example, consider the PAR(2) process

$$y_t = \phi_{1s} y_{t-1} + \phi_{2s} y_{t-2} + \varepsilon_t, \tag{49}$$

which can be written as

$$\Phi_0 Y_T = \Phi_1 Y_{T-1} + \varepsilon_T, \tag{50}$$

with

$$\Phi_0 = \begin{pmatrix} 1 & 0 & 0 & 0 \\ -\phi_{12} & 1 & 0 & 0 \\ -\phi_{23} & -\phi_{13} & 1 & 0 \\ 0 & -\phi_{24} & -\phi_{14} & 1 \end{pmatrix} \quad \text{and} \quad \Phi_1 = \begin{pmatrix} 0 & 0 & \phi_{21} & \phi_{11} \\ 0 & 0 & 0 & \phi_{22} \\ 0 & 0 & 0 & 0 \\ 0 & 0 & 0 & 0 \end{pmatrix}. \tag{51}$$

A useful representation is based on the possibility of decomposing a non-periodic $AR(p)$ polynomial as $(1 - \alpha_1 L)(1 - \alpha_2 L) \cdots (1 - \alpha_p L)$, see Boswijk, Franses and Haldrup (1997) where this representation is used to test for (seasonal) unit roots in periodic models. Note that this can only be done when the solutions to the characteristic equation for this $AR(p)$ polynomial are all real-valued. Similar results hold for the multivariate representation of a $PAR(p)$ process, and it can be useful to rewrite (44) as

$$\prod_{i=1}^{P} \Xi_i(L) Y_T = \mu + \varepsilon_T, \tag{52}$$

where the $\Xi_i(L)$ are 4×4 matrices with elements which are polynomials in L.

A simple example is the $PAR(2)$ process

$$\Xi_1(L)\Xi_2(L)Y_T = \varepsilon_T, \tag{53}$$

with

$$
\Xi_1(L) = \begin{pmatrix} 1 & 0 & 0 & -\beta_1 L \\ -\beta_2 & 1 & 0 & 0 \\ 0 & -\beta_3 & 1 & 0 \\ 0 & 0 & -\beta_4 & 1 \end{pmatrix},
$$

$$
\Xi_2(L) = \begin{pmatrix} 1 & 0 & 0 & -\alpha_1 L \\ -\alpha_2 & 1 & 0 & 0 \\ 0 & -\alpha_3 & 1 & 0 \\ 0 & 0 & -\alpha_4 & 1 \end{pmatrix}.
\tag{54}
$$

This $PAR(2)$ model can be written as

$$(1 - \beta_s L)(1 - \alpha_s L)y_t = \mu_s + \varepsilon_t, \tag{55}$$

or

$$y_t - \alpha_s y_{t-1} = \mu_s + \beta_s(y_{t-1} - \alpha_{s-1} y_{t-2}) + \varepsilon_t, \tag{56}$$

as, and this is quite important, the lag operator L also operates on α_s, that is, $L\alpha_s = \alpha_{s-1}$ for all $s = 1, 2, 3, 4$ and with $\alpha_0 = \alpha_4$. The characteristic equation is

$$|\Xi_1(z)\Xi_2(z)| = 0, \tag{57}$$

and this is equivalent to

$$(1 - \beta_1 \beta_2 \beta_3 \beta_4 z)(1 - \alpha_1 \alpha_2 \alpha_3 \alpha_4 z) = 0. \tag{58}$$

So, the PAR(2) model has one unit root when either $\beta_1\beta_2\beta_3\beta_4 = 1$ or $\alpha_1\alpha_2\alpha_3\alpha_4 = 1$, and has at most two unit roots when both products equal unity. The case where $\alpha_1\alpha_2\alpha_3\alpha_4 = 1$ while not all α_s are equal to 1 is called periodic integration, see Osborn (1988) and Franses (1996). Tests for periodic integration are developed in Boswijk and Franses (1996) for the case without allowing for seasonal unit roots, and in Boswijk, Franses and Haldrup (1997) for the case where seasonal unit roots can also occur. Obviously, the maximum number of unity solutions to the characteristic equation of a PAR(p) process is equal to p.

The analogy of a univariate PAR process with a multivariate time series process can be used to derive explicit formulae for one- and multi-step ahead forecasting, see Franses (1996). It should be noted that then the one-step ahead forecasts concern one-year ahead forecasts for all four $Y_{s,T}$ series. For example, for the model $Y_T = \Phi_0^{-1}\Phi_1 Y_{T-1} + \omega_T$, where $\omega_T = \Phi_0^{-1}\varepsilon_T$, the forecast for $N+1$ is $\hat{Y}_{N+1} = \Phi_0^{-1}\Phi_1 Y_N$.

Finally, one may wonder what the consequences are of fitting non-periodic models to periodic data. One consequence is that such a non-periodic model requires many lags, see Franses and Paap (2004) and Del Barrio Castro and Osborn (2004). For example, a PAR(1) model can be written as

$$y_t = \alpha_{s+3}\alpha_{s+2}\alpha_{s+1}\alpha_s y_{t-4} + \varepsilon_t + \alpha_{s+3}\varepsilon_{t-1}$$

$$+ \alpha_{s+3}\alpha_{s+2}\varepsilon_{t-2} + \alpha_{s+3}\alpha_{s+2}\alpha_{s+1}\varepsilon_{t-3}. \tag{59}$$

As $\alpha_{s+3}\alpha_{s+2}\alpha_{s+1}\alpha_s$ is equal for all seasons, the AR parameter at lag 4 in a non-periodic model is truly non-periodic, but of course, the MA part is not. The MA part of this model is of order 3. If one estimates a non-periodic MA model for these data, the MA parameter estimates will attain an average value of the α_{s+3}, $\alpha_{s+3}\alpha_{s+2}$, and $\alpha_{s+3}\alpha_{s+2}\alpha_{s+1}$ across the seasons. In other words, one might end up considering an ARMA(4,3) model for PAR(1) data. And, if one decides not to include an MA part in the model, one usually needs to increase the order of the autoregression to whiten the errors. This suggests that higher-order AR models might fit to low-order periodic data. When $\alpha_{s+3}\alpha_{s+2}\alpha_{s+1}\alpha_s = 1$, one has a high-order AR model for the Δ_4 transformed time series. In sum, there seems to be a trade-off between seasonality in parameters and short lags against no seasonality in parameters and longer lags.

Conclusion

There is a voluminous literature on formally testing for seasonal unit roots in non-periodic data and on testing for unit roots in periodic autoregressions. There are many simulation studies to see which method is best. Also, there are many studies which examine whether imposing seasonal unit roots or not, or assuming unit roots in periodic models or not, lead to better forecasts. This also extends to the case of multivariate series, where these models allow for seasonal cointegration or for periodic cointegration. An example of a periodic cointegration model is

$$\Delta_4 y_t = \gamma_s (y_{t-4} - \beta_s x_{t-4}) + \varepsilon_t, \tag{60}$$

where γ_s and β_s can take seasonally varying values, see Boswijk and Franses (1995).

For example, Löf and Franses (2001) analyze periodic and seasonal cointegration models for bivariate quarterly observed time series in an empirical forecasting study, as well as a VAR model in first differences, with and without cointegration restrictions, and a VAR model in annual differences. The VAR model in first differences without cointegration is best if one-step ahead forecasts are considered. For longer forecast horizons, the VAR model in annual differences is better. When comparing periodic versus seasonal cointegration models, the seasonal cointegration models tend to yield better forecasts. Finally, there is no clear indication that multiple equations methods improve on single equation methods.

To summarize, tests for periodic variation in the parameters and for unit roots allow one to make a choice between the various models for seasonality. There are many tests around, and they are all easy to use. Not unexpectedly, models and methods for data with frequencies higher than 12 can become difficult to use in practice, see Darne (2004) for a discussion of seasonal cointegration in monthly series. Hence, there is a need for more future research.

5. Recent Advances

This section deals with a few recent developments in the area of forecasting seasonal time series. These are (i) seasonality in panels of time series, (ii) periodic models for financial time series, and (iii) nonlinear models for seasonal time series.

Seasonality in panels of time series

The search for common seasonal patterns can lead to a dramatic reduction in the number of parameters, see Engle and Hylleberg (1996). One way to look for common patterns across the series $y_{i,t}$, where $i = 1, 2, ..., I$, and I can be large, is to see if the series have common dynamics or common trends. Alternatively, one can examine if series have common seasonal deterministics.

As can be understood from the discussion on seasonal unit roots, before one can say something about (common) deterministic seasonality, one first has to decide on the number of seasonal unit roots. The HEGY test regression for seasonal unit roots is

$$\Phi_{p_i}(L)\Delta_4 y_{i,t} = \mu_{i,t} + \rho_{i,1}S(L)y_{i,t-1} + \rho_{i,2}A(L)y_{i,t-1} \\ + \rho_{i,3}\Delta_2 y_{i,t-1} + \rho_{i,4}\Delta_2 y_{i,t-2} + \varepsilon_t, \tag{61}$$

and now it is convenient to take

$$\mu_{i,t} = \mu_i + \alpha_{1,i}\cos(\pi t) + \alpha_{2,i}\cos(\frac{\pi t}{2}) + \alpha_{3,i}\cos(\frac{\pi(t-1)}{2}) + \delta_i t, \tag{62}$$

and where Δ_k is the k-th order differencing filter, $S(L)y_{i,t} = (1 + L + L^2 + L^3)y_{i,t}$ and $A(L)y_{i,t} = -(1 - L + L^2 - L^3)y_{i,t}$. The model assumes that each series $y_{i,t}$ can be described by a $(p_i + 4)$-th order autoregression. Smith and Taylor (1999) and Franses and Kunst (1999a,b) argue that an appropriate test for a seasonal unit root at the bi-annual frequency is now given by a joint F-test for $\rho_{i,2}$ and $\alpha_{1,i}$. An appropriate test for the two seasonal unit roots at the annual frequency is then given by a joint F-test for $\rho_{3,i}$, $\rho_{4,i}$, $\alpha_{2,i}$ and $\alpha_{3,i}$. Franses and Kunst (1999b) consider these F-tests in a model where the autoregressive parameters are pooled over the equations, hence a panel HEGY test. The power of this panel test procedure is rather large. Additionally, once one has taken care of seasonal unit roots, these authors examine if two or more series have the same seasonal deterministic fluctuations. This can be done by testing for cross-equation restrictions.

Periodic GARCH

Periodic models might also be useful for financial time series. They can be used not only to describe the so-called day-of-the-week effects, but also to describe the apparent differences in volatility across the days of the week. Bollerslev and Ghysels (1996) propose a periodic generalized autoregressive conditional heteroskedasticity (PGARCH) model. Adding a periodic autoregression for the returns to it, one has a PAR(p)-PGARCH(1,1) model, which for a daily observed financial time series y_t, $t = 1, \ldots, n = 5N$, can be represented by

$$x_t = y_t - \sum_{s=1}^{5} \left(\mu_s + \sum_{i=1}^{p} \phi_{is} y_{t-i} \right) D_{s,t}$$

$$= \sqrt{h_t} \eta_t \qquad (63)$$

with $\eta_t \sim N(0,1)$ for example, and

$$h_t = \sum_{s=1}^{5} (\omega_s + \psi_s x_{t-1}^2) D_{s,t} + \gamma h_{t-1}, \qquad (64)$$

where the x_t denotes the residual of the PAR model for y_t, and where $D_{s,t}$ denotes a seasonal dummy for the day of the week, that is, $s = 1, 2, 3, 4, 5$.

In order to investigate the properties of the conditional variance model, it is useful to define $z_t = x_t^2 - h_t$, and to write it as

$$x_t^2 = \sum_{s=1}^{5} (\omega_s + (\psi_s + \gamma) x_{t-1}^2) D_{s,t} + z_t - \gamma z_{t-1}. \qquad (65)$$

This ARMA process for x_t^2 contains time-varying parameters $\psi_s + \gamma$ and hence strictly speaking, it is not a stationary process. To investigate the stationarity properties of x_t^2, (65) can be written in a time-invariant representation. Franses and Paap (2000) successfully fit such a model to the daily S&P 500 index, and even find that

$$\Pi_{s=1}^{5} (\psi_s + \gamma) = 1. \qquad (66)$$

In other words, they fit a periodically integrated GARCH model.

Models of seasonality and nonlinearity

It is well known that a change in the deterministic trend properties of a time series y_t is easily mistaken for the presence of a unit root. In a similar vein, if a change in the deterministic seasonal pattern is not detected, one might well end up imposing seasonal unit roots, see Ghysels (1994), Smith and Otero (1997), Franses, Hoek and Paap (1997) and Franses and Vogelsang (1998).

Changes in deterministic seasonal patterns usually are modelled by means of one-time abrupt and discrete changes. However, when seasonal patterns shift due to changes in technology, institutions and tastes, for example, these changes may materialize only gradually. This suggests that a plausible description of time-varying seasonal patterns is

$$\phi(L)\Delta_1 y_t = \sum_{s=1}^{4} \delta_{1,s} D_{s,t}(1 - G(t;\gamma,c)) + \sum_{s=1}^{4} \delta_{2,s} D_{s,t} G(t;\gamma,c) + \varepsilon_t, \quad (67)$$

where $G(t;\gamma,c)$ is the logistic function

$$G(s_t;\gamma,c) = \frac{1}{1 + \exp\{-\gamma(s_t - c)\}}, \qquad \gamma > 0. \tag{68}$$

As s_t increases, the logistic function changes monotonically from 0 to 1, with the change being symmetric around the location parameter c, as $G(c - z;\gamma,c) = 1 - G(c + z;\gamma,c)$ for all z. The slope parameter γ determines the smoothness of the change. As $\gamma \to \infty$, the logistic function $G(s_t;\gamma,c)$ approaches the indicator function $I[s_t > c]$, whereas if $\gamma \to 0$, $G(s_t;\gamma,c) \to 0.5$ for all values of s_t. Hence, by taking $s_t = t$, the model takes an "intermediate" position in between deterministic seasonality and stochastic trend seasonality.

Nonlinear models with smoothly changing deterministic seasonality are proposed in Franses and van Dijk (2004). These authors examine the forecasting performance of various models for seasonality and nonlinearity for quarterly industrial production series of 18 OECD countries. They find that the accuracy of point forecasts varies widely across series, across forecast horizons and across seasons. However, in general, linear models with fairly simple descriptions of seasonality outperform at short forecast horizons, whereas nonlinear models with more elaborate seasonal components dominate at longer horizons. Simpler models are also preferable for interval and density forecasts at short horizons. Finally, none of the models is found to be the best and hence, forecast combination is worthwhile.

To summarize, recent advances in modeling and forecasting seasonal time series focus at (i) models for panels of time series and at (ii) models which not only capture seasonality, but also conditional volatility and nonlinearity, for example. To fully capture all these features is not easy, also as various features may be related. More research is needed in this area too.

6. Conclusion

Forecasting studies show that model specification efforts pay off in terms of performance. Simple models for seasonally differenced data forecast well for one or a few steps ahead. For longer horizons, more involved models are much better. These involved models address seasonality in conjunction with trends, non-linearity and conditional volatility. Much more research is needed to see which models are to be preferred in which situations.

There are at least two well articulated further research issues. The first concerns methods to achieve parsimony. Indeed, seasonal time series models for monthly or weekly data contain a wealth of parameters, and this can reduce efficiency dramatically. The second concerns the analysis of unadjusted data for the situation where people would want to rely on adjusted data, that is, for decisions on turning points. How would one draw inference in case trends, cycles and seasonality are related? Finally, in case one persists in considering seasonally adjusted data, how can we design methods that allow for the best possible interpretation of these data, when the underlying process has all kinds of features?

References

Bell, W. R. and S. C. Hillmer (1984), Issues Involved with the Seasonal Adjustment of Economic Time Series (with discussion), *Journal of Business and Economic Statistics*, 2, 291–320.

Bell, W. R. (1987), A Note on Overdifferencing and the Equivalence of Seasonal Time Series Models With Monthly Means and Models With $(0, 1, 1)_{12}$ Seasonal Parts When $\theta = 1$, *Journal of Business & Economics Statistics*, 5, 383–387.

Bollerslev, T. and E. Ghysels (1996), Periodic Autoregressive Conditional Heteroscedasticity, *Journal of Business and Economic Statistics*, 14, 139–151.

Boswijk, H. P. and P. H. Franses (1995), Periodic Cointegration – Representation and Inference, *Review of Economics and Statistics*, 77, 436–454.

Boswijk, H. P. and P. H. Franses (1996), Unit Roots in Periodic Autoregressions, *Journal of Time Series Analysis*, 17, 221–245.

Boswijk, H. P., P. H. Franses and N. Haldrup (1997) Multiple Unit Roots in Periodic Autoregression, *Journal of Econometrics*, 80, 167–193.

Brendstrup, B., S. Hylleberg, M. O. Nielsen, L. L. Skippers, and L. Stentoft (2004), Seasonality in Economic Models, *Macroeconomic Dynamics*, 8, 362–394.

Canova, F. and E. Ghysels (1994), Changes in Seasonal Patterns: Are they Cyclical?, *Journal of Economic Dynamics and Control*, 18, 1143–1171.

Canova, F. and B. E. Hansen (1995), Are Seasonal Patterns Constant over Time?

A Test for Seasonal Stability, *Journal of Business and Economic Statistics*, 13, 237–252.

Darne, O. (2004), Seasonal Cointegration for Monthly Data, *Economics Letters*, 82, 349–356.

Del Barrio Castro, T. and D. R. Osborn (2004), The Consequences of Seasonal Adjustment for Periodic Autoregressive Processes, *Reconometrics Journals*, to appear.

Dickey, D. A. and W. A. Fuller (1981), Likelihood Ratio Statistics for Autoregressive Time Series with a Unit Root, *Econometrica*, 49, 1057–1072.

Engle, R. F. and C. W. J. Granger (1987), Cointegration and Error Correction: Representation, Estimation, and Testing, *Econometrica*, 55, 251–276.

Engle, R. F. and C. W. J. Granger (1991, eds.), *Long-Run Economic Relationships: Readings in Cointegration*, Oxford: Oxford University Press.

Engle, R. F., C. W. J. Granger, S. Hylleberg and H. S. Lee (1993), Seasonal Cointegration: The Japanese Consumption Function, *Journal of Econometrics*, 55, 275–298.

Engle, R. F. and S. Hylleberg (1996), Common Seasonal Features: Global Unemployment, *Oxford Bulletin of Economics and Statistics*, 58, 615–630.

Findley, D. F., B. C. Monsell, W. R. Bell, M. C. Otto, and B.-C. Chen (1998), New Capabilities and Methods of the X-12-ARIMA Seasonal-Adjustment Program (with Discussion), *Journal of Business and Economic Statistics* 16, 127–177.

Franses, P. H. (1991), A Multivariate Approach to Modeling Univariate Seasonal Time Series, Econometric Institute Report 9101, Erasmus University Rotterdam.

Franses, P. H. (1994), A Multivariate Approach to Modeling Univariate Seasonal Time Series, *Journal of Econometrics*, 63, 133–151.

Franses, P. H. (1996), *Periodicity and Stochastic Trends in Economic Time Series*, Oxford: Oxford University Press.

Franses, P. H. (1998), *Time Series Models for Business and Economic Forecasting*, Cambridge: Cambridge University Press.

Franses, P. H. (2001), Some Comments on Seasonal Adjustment, *Revista De Economia del Rosario (Bogota, Colombia)*, 4, 9–16.

Franses, P. H., H. Hoek and R. Paap (1997), Bayesian Analysis of Seasonal Unit Roots and Seasonal Mean Shifts, *Journal of Econometrics*, 78, 359–380.

Franses, P. H. and S. Hylleberg and H. S. Lee (1995), Spurious Deterministic Seasonality, *Economics Letters*, 48, 249–256.

Franses, P. H. and R. M. Kunst (1999a), On the Role of Seasonal Intercepts in Seasonal Cointegration, *Oxford Bulletin of Economics and Statistics*, 61, 409–433.

Franses, P. H. and R. M. Kunst (1999b), Testing Common Deterministic Seasonality, with an Application to Industrial Production, Econometric Institute Report 9905, Erasmus University Rotterdam.

Franses, P. H. and R. Paap (2000), Modelling Day-of-the-week Seasonality in the S&P 500 Index, *Applied Financial Economics*, 10, 483–488.

Franses P. H. and R. Paap (2004), *Periodic Time Series Models*, Oxford: Oxford University Press.

Franses, P. H. and D. J. C. van Dijk (2000), *Non-linear Time Series Models in Empirical Finance*, Cambridge: Cambridge University Press.

Franses, P. H. and D. J. C. van Dijk (2004), The Forecasting Performance of Various Models for Seasonality and Nonlinearity for Quarterly Industrial Production, *International Journal of Forecasting*, to appear.

Franses, P. H. and T. J. Vogelsang (1998), On Seasonal Cycles, Unit Roots and Mean Shifts, *Review of Economics and Statistics*, 80, 231–240.

Ghysels, E. (1994), On the Periodic Structure of the Business Cycle, *Journal of Business and Economic Statistics*, 12, 289–298.

Ghysels, E., C. W. J. Granger and P. L. Siklos (1996), Is Seasonal Adjustment a Linear or a Nnnlinear Data-Filtering Process? (with Discussion), *Journal of Business and Economic Statistics* 14, 374–397.

Ghysels, E. and D. R. Osborn (2001), *The Econometric Analysis of Seasonal Time Series*, Cambridge: Cambridge University Press.

Granger, C. W. J. and T. Terasvirta (1993), *Modelling Non-Linear Economic Relationships*, Oxford: Oxford University Press.

Harvey, A. C. (1989), *Forecasting, Structural Time Series Models and the Kalman Filter*, Cambridge: Cambridge University Press.

Haugen, R. A. and J. Lakonishok (1987), *The Incredible January Effect: The Stock Market's Unsolved Mystery*, New York: McGraw-Hill.

Hylleberg, S. (1986), *Seasonality in regression*, Orlando: Academic Press.

Hylleberg, S. (1992), *Modelling Seasonality*, Oxford: Oxford University Press.

Hylleberg, S., R. F. Engle, C. W. J. Granger, and B. S. Yoo (1990), Seasonal Integration and Cointegration, *Journal of Econometrics*, 44, 215–238.

Johansen, S. (1995), *Likelihood-Based Inference in Cointegrated Vector Autoregressive Models*, Oxford: Oxford University Press.

Johansen, S. and E. Shaumburg, (1999), Likelihood Analysis of Seasonal Cointegration, *Journal of Econometrics*, 88, 301–339.

Kawasaki, Y. and P. H. Franses (2003), Detecting Seasonal Unit Roots in a Structural Time Series Model, *Journal of Applied Statistics*, 30, 373–387.

Koopman, S. J. and P. H. Franses (2003), Constructing Seasonally Adjusted Data with Time-Varying Confidence Intervals, *Oxford Bulletin of Economics and Statistics*, 64, 509–526.

Löf, M. and P. H. Franses (2001), On Forecasting Cointegrated Seasonal Time Series, *International Journal of Forecasting*, 17, 607–621.

Maravall, A. (1995), Unobserved Components in Economic Time Series, in H. Pesaran, P. Schmidt and M. Wickens (eds.), *Handbook of Applied Econometrics* (Volume 1), Oxford: Basil Blackwell.

Ooms, M. and P. H. Franses (1997), On Periodic Correlations between Estimated Seasonal and Nonseasonal Components in German and US Unemployment, *Journal of Business and Economic Statistics* **15**, 470–481.

Osborn, D. R. (1988), Seasonality and Habit Persistence in a Life-Cycle Model of Consumption, *Journal of Applied Econometrics*, 3, 255–266.

Osborn, D. R. (1990), A Survey of Seasonality in UK Macroeconomic Variables, *International Journal of Forecasting*, 6, 327–336.

Osborn, D. R. (1991), The Implications of Periodically Varying Coefficients for Seasonal Time-Series Processes, *Journal of Econometrics*, 48, 373–384.

Osborn, D. R. and P. M. M. Rodrigues (2001), Asymptotic Distributions of Seasonal Unit Root Tests: A Unifying Approach, *Econometric Reviews*, 21, 221–241.

Shiskin, J. and H. Eisenpress (1957), Seasonal Adjustment by Electronic Computer Methods, *Journal of the American Statistical Association* 52, 415–449.

Smith, J. and J. Otero (1997), Structural Breaks and Seasonal Integration, *Economics Letters*, 56, 13–19.

Smith, R. J. and A. M. R. Taylor (1998), Additional Critical Values and Asymptotic Representations for Seasonal Unit Root Tests, *Journal of Econometrics*, 85, 269–288.

Smith, R. J. and A. M. R. Taylor (1999), Likelihood Ratio Tests for Seasonal Unit Roots, *Journal of Time Series Analysis*, 20, 453–476.

CAR AND AFFINE PROCESSES

Christian Gourieroux

CREST, Laboratoire de Finance-Assurance,
33, Bd. G. Peri, 92245 Malakoff, France
E-mail: gouriero@ensae.fr

CEPREMAP, Ecole Normale Supérieure (ENS),
48, Boulevard Jourdan, 75014 Paris, France
Department of Economics, University of Toronto,
150, St. George Street, Toronto, Ontanio M5S 3G7, Canada
E-mail: c.gourieroux@utoronto.ca

1. Introduction

Electronic trading systems on financial markets have been initially introduced to diminish the trading cost, to increase the traded volumes and to improve market transparency. They give also the opportunity to produce new data bases, in which every contract is registered, the so-called high frequency data, and to question standard econometric models used earlier for financial analysis. Contrary to earlier approaches, which focus on asset prices, the tick-by-tick data include a lot of other variables. More precisely, let us consider a given stock and a given trading day. The data are :

- the index n of the trading within the day;

- the trading time τ_n measured in seconds since the beginning of the day;

- the intertrade duration $d_n = \tau_n - \tau_{n-1}$, between consecutive trades numbered $n-1$ and n, respectively;

- the price of the stock p_n, or the intertrade price change $p_n - p_{n-1}$;

- the traded volume v_n in number of shares;

- the bid [resp. ask] curve, which provides the proposed sell price $b_n(v)$ [resp. buy price $a_n(v)$] posted in the order book corresponding to the given traded volume v;

- the sign of the trade : $+1$, if the trade is initiated by a buy order, -1, if the trade is initiated by a sell order.

The tick-by-tick data can be aggregated into new summary statistics to study the market at different calendar time frequencies, that is at 5 mn, 20 mn,... or daily. Associated daily data are :

- the index of the day t;

- the closing price p_t (resp. opening price $p_{t,0}$);

- the realized (historical) volatility at 5mn for day t, Σ_t;

- the number of trades N_t;

- the daily traded volume V_t.

The daily aggregated variables are generated from the tick-by-tick data as compound sums, that are sums over a stochastic number of terms . For instance the change of price during the day is :

$$p_t - p_{t,0} = \sum_{n=1}^{N_t} (p_{t,n} - p_{t,n-1}),$$

where $p_{t,n}$ denotes the stock price for trade n of day t; the daily traded volume is :

$$V_t = \sum_{n=1}^{N_t} v_{t,n};$$

the daily realized volatility-covolatility matrix at horizon one trade is :

$$\sum_t = \frac{1}{N_t} \sum_{n=1}^{N_t} (p_{t,n} - p_{t,n-1})(p_{t,n} - p_{t,n-1})',$$

(assuming that the intertrade price changes are zero-mean).

These data are generally domain restricted. For instance the time series of intertrade durations d_n correspond to positive variables, the sequence of signs of trades "buy-sell" to a series of dichotomous qualitative variables. The sequence of realized volatility matrices defines a time series of symmetric positive definite matrices, whereas the number of trades is an integer valued process.

The standard dynamic models considered in financial applications are not really appropriate to account for the nonlinear features of the data, especially for the domain restrictions discussed above. For instance the linear dynamic models, that are the autoregressive moving average processes, are closely related to Gaussian processes, and thus to variables which can admit any negative or positive real value, which can be predicted linearly without loss of information, or have a conditional distribution with thin tails and no skewness. Similarly the Autoregressive Conditionally Heteroscedastic (ARCH) type of models have been initially introduced for series of one-dimensional volatility, which explains the importance of the quadratic transformation in this specification, but seem less appropriate for more complicated domain restrictions such as the set of symmetric positive definite matrices encountered in volatility analysis in a multiasset framework. Even for one dimensional positive variables the quadratic transformation, which underlies the ARCH type model, does not necessarily correspond to the structural interpretation of the variable of interest. This is especially the case for the ACD-GARCH models introduced for intertrade duration variables.

The aim of the lecture is to describe and study an alternative class of dynamic models which :

i) takes care of the nonlinear domain restriction;

ii) provides simple (nonlinear) prediction formulas at any horizon;

iii) allows for large dimension, increased number of lags and mixing of different types of variables such as qualitative, integer valued and real variables;

iv) includes as special case Gaussian ARMA models and well-chosen (multivariate) stochastic volatility models;

v) admits continuous time counterparts.

Such dynamic models are the so-called Affine Processes initially considered by Duffie, Kan (1996), Duffie, Filipovic, Schachermayer (2003) for deriving affine term structure models (ATSM) in continuous time, and their discrete time analogues, called Compound Autoregressive (Car) models [see Darolles, Gourieroux, Jasiak (2006)]. Last, but not least, Car (or affine) dynamics are compatible with the recent literature on theoretical finance. Indeed they underly :

i) the affine and quadratic term structure models;

ii) the derivative pricing with stochastic volatility in a multiasset framework;

iii) the coherent specification of dynamics for stock prices, exchange rates, interest rates, corporate rates (including default risk);

iv) the analysis of the term structure of extreme risks.

The plan of the chapter is the following. In Section 2 we give a general presentation of Car (affine) processes. We especially describe the nonlinear prediction formulas and the interpretation of the processes in terms of compounding. In Section 3, we consider the autoregressive gamma (ARG) process, which is the time discretized Cox-Ingersoll-Ross (CIR) process. The ARG process is extended in Section 4 to a multidimensional framework. The Wishart Autoregressive (WAR) process is a natural dynamic specification for series of volatility-covolatility matrices and appears as a serious competitor to the various types of multivariate ARCH, or stochastic variance models. A WAR specification can typically be used to analyze the dynamics of daily realized volatility matrices. Section 5 discusses the importance of Car (affine) processes in financial theory. We first explain why Car processes are related with the so-called affine term structure models. Then we discuss how this approach can be used to analyze corporate risk and to get "quadratic" term structure models. Finally we show that WAR stochastic volatility models are appropriate to derive closed form derivative pricing formula in a multiasset framework. Section 6 concludes.

2. Compound Autoregressive Processes and Affine Processes

The compound autoregressive (Car) process shares the nice prediction properties of the Gaussian autoregressive process, but can feature nonlinear dynamics and apply to variates with restricted domain. In the first subsection we review the prediction properties of the Gaussian autoregressive process and highlight the importance of the conditional Laplace transform. The Car process is defined in subsection 2.2. Then we derive its marginal distribution (subsection 2.3) and its nonlinear prediction properties (subsection 2.4). The Car processes admits compounding interpretations which are useful for constructing flexible nonlinear dynamics (subsection 2.5).

2.1. The Gaussian Autoregressive Process

A one-dimensional Gaussian AR(1) model is defined by :

$$y_t = \rho y_{t-1} + \varepsilon_t, \tag{2.1}$$

where (ε_t) is a sequence of iid errors with Gaussian distribution $N(0, \sigma^2)$. The transition distribution of process y can be characterized in different ways :

  i) either by regression equation (2.1),

  ii) or by the conditional density function given by :

$$f(y_t | y_{t-1}) = \frac{1}{\sigma(2\pi)^{1/2}} \exp\left[-\frac{1}{2\sigma^2}(y_t - \rho y_{t-1})^2\right],$$

  iii) or by the conditional Laplace transform, which explains how to compute the short term predictions of exponential transformations of y_t possibly complex. The conditional Laplace transform (LT) is defined by :

$$\psi_t(z) = E[\exp(-zy_t)|y_{t-1}]$$

$$= \exp[-z\rho y_{t-1} + \frac{z^2 \sigma^2}{2}], z \in \mathbb{C}.$$

The transition above concerns short term horizon $h = 1$, but is easily extended to any horizon h. Let us first consider the regression interpretation. By recursive substitution we get :

$$y_{t+h} = \rho^h y_t + \varepsilon_{t+h} + \rho \varepsilon_{t+h-1} + \cdots + \rho^{h-1}\varepsilon_{t+1} \qquad (2.2)$$
$$= \rho^h y_t + \varepsilon_{t,h}, \text{say},$$

where : $V(\varepsilon_{t,h}) = \sigma^2(h) = \sigma^2 + \rho^2\sigma^2 + \cdots + \rho^{2(h-1)}\sigma^2 = \sigma^2(1-\rho^{2h})/(1-\rho^2)$.

This defines the regression equation at horizon h. Similarly the conditional pdf at horizon h is :

$$f_h(y_{t+h}|y_t) = \frac{1}{\sigma(h)(2\pi)^{1/2}} \exp\left[-\frac{1}{2\sigma^2(h)}(y_{t+h} - \rho^h y_t)^2\right],$$

whereas the conditional LT at horizon h becomes :

$$\psi_{t,h}(z) = E[\exp(-zy_{t+h})|y_t] = \exp[-z\rho^h y_t + \frac{z^2}{2}\sigma^2(h)].$$

Thus the predictive distributions at any horizon h are easily derived; they take the same Gaussian form with updated parameters : $\rho \to \rho^h, \sigma^2 \to \sigma^2(h)$. This nice property concerning the predictions is a consequence of a linear dynamic satisfied by the Gaussian autoregressive process. This linearity can be seen in two different ways.

i) First the regression function $E(y_t|y_{t-1})$ is a (linear) affine function of the lagged value y_{t-1}.

ii) Second the log-Laplace transform : $\log \psi_t(z) = -z\rho y_{t-1} + \dfrac{z^2}{2}\sigma^2$, is also a (linear) affine function of the lagged value y_{t-1}.

The standard time series literature extends either the first linearity property by considering processes satisfying $y_t = \alpha y_{t-1} + \beta + u_t$, where the sequence (u_t) corresponds to iid variables not necessarily Gaussian [see e.g. Grunwald et al. (2001) for the analysis of conditional linear AR(1) processes], or the pdf interpretation to include the generalized linear models and get the so-called GARMA processes [Benjamin et al. (2003)]. However these extensions do not allow to recover all nice nonlinear prediction properties of the Gaussian autoregressive process. We see in the next subsection that the linearity of the log-Laplace transform is the convenient tool to get the extension to nonlinear dynamic framework.

2.2. Definition of a Car Process

Let us consider a n-dimensional process $Y_t = (y_{1,t}, \ldots, y_{n,t})'$. The conditional Laplace transform defines the short term predictions of exponential linear combinations of the components. The function is given by :

$$\psi_t(z) = E[\exp(-z'Y_t)|\underline{Y_{t-1}}]$$

$$= E[\exp(-\sum_{i=1}^{n} z_i y_{i,t})|\underline{Y_{t-1}}], \qquad (2.3)$$

where $z = (z_1, \ldots, z_n)'$ belongs to $D \subset \mathbb{C}^n$ where D is the domain of existence of the LT, and $\underline{Y_{t-1}}$ denotes the information including all lagged values of the process, that are $Y_{t-1}, \ldots, Y_{t-p}, \ldots$.

Definition 1 : The n-dimensional process (Y_t) is a compound autoregressive process of order p, called Car(p), if and only if the conditional Laplace transform is :

$$\psi_t(z) = \exp[-a_1'(z)Y_{t-1} - \cdots - a_p'(z)Y_{t-p} + b(z)],$$

where $a_1, \ldots, a_p$ (resp. b) are n-dimensional (resp. one dimensional) functions of z.

Thus the conditional log-Laplace transform is an affine function of lagged values $Y_{t-1}, \ldots, Y_{t-p}$. In particular, since the conditional Laplace transform characterizes the transition pdf, the Car(p) process is a Markov process of order p.

The affine condition on the log-Laplace transform implies restrictions on appropriate conditional moments (when the moments exist). These conditions are derived by considering the series expansion of the log-Laplace transform in a neighbourhood of $z = 0$. For instance both conditional mean and conditional variance-covariance matrix of Y_t (when they exist) are affine functions[1] of the lagged values $Y_{t-1}, \ldots, Y_{t-p}$.

As, for Gaussian autoregressive processes, there is a trade-off between the autoregressive order and the dimension of the process. More precisely it is easily checked that if (Y_t) is a Car(p) process, the process $\tilde{Y}_t = (Y_t', Y_{t-1}', \ldots, Y_{t-p+1}')'$, obtained by stacking current and lagged values of the initial process, is a Car process of order 1. Therefore it is always possible to replace a Car(p) model by a Car(1) model after an appropriate increase of the process dimension. Without loss of generality we focus on Car(1) model in the rest of the chapter. Then the conditional LT reduces to :

$$\psi_t(z) = E[\exp(-z'Y_t)|Y_{t-1}] = \exp[-a(z)'Y_{t-1} + b(z)]. \qquad (2.4)$$

2.3. Marginal Distribution

If the process (Y_t) is stationary, its marginal distribution is easily related to its transition distribution. Let us denote by $E[\exp(-z'Y_t)] = \exp c(z)$, its marginal LT. By iterated expectation theorem, we get :

$$E[\exp(-z'Y_t)] = E[E(-z'Y_t)|Y_{t-1}],$$

or : $\quad \exp c(z) \qquad = E \exp[-a(z)'Y_{t-1} + b(z)] = \exp\{c[a(z)] + b(z)\}.$

By identifying both sides of the equality, we get the relationship :

$$c(z) = c[a(z)] + b(z). \qquad (2.5)$$

Thus the conditional LT can be equivalently parameterized by either functions a and b, or by functions a and c. We get :

---

[1] For a long time the affine condition on drift and volatility has been considered as the definition of affine processes in continuous time. Now it has been recognized that the condition has also to be written on cumulant conditional moments of higher order.

$$E[\exp(-z'Y_t)|Y_{t-1}]$$
$$= \exp[-a(z)'Y_{t-1} + b(z)]$$
$$= \exp(-a(z)'Y_{t-1} + c(z) - c[a(z)]). \qquad (2.6)$$

In the second representation the functional parameters have simple interpretations. Function c characterizes the marginal distribution whereas function a summarizes the whole nonlinear serial dependence.

2.4. Nonlinear Prediction Formulas

For a stationary process the marginal distribution considered in Section 2.3 coincides with the predictive distribution at very long horizon ($h = +\infty$). The iterated expectation theorem can also be applied recursively to derive the predictive distribution at any intermediate horizon h. More precisely we get the following property proved in Appendix 1.

Proposition 1 : The conditional Laplace transform at horizon h is given by :

$$\psi_{t,h}(z) = E[\exp(-z'Y_{t+h})|Y_t]$$

$$= \exp\{-a^{oh}(z)'Y_t + \sum_{k=0}^{h-1} b(a^{ok}(z))\}$$

$$= \exp\{-a^{oh}(z)'Y_t + c(z) - c[a^{oh}(z)]\},$$

where $a^{oh}(z)$ denotes function $a(z)$ compounded h times with itself and $c(z)$ is the same as in (2.5).

The result above is the direct generalization of the prediction formula for Gaussian VAR (1) process. Let us consider such a process defined by :

$$Y_t = MY_{t-1} + \varepsilon_t,$$

where ε_t is IIN $(0, \Sigma)$. Its conditional Laplace transform is :

$$\Psi_t(z) = \exp[-z'MY_{t-1} + \frac{1}{2}z'\Sigma z].$$

This is a Car(1) process with : $a(z) = Mz$ and $b(z) = \frac{1}{2}z'\Sigma z$. The a function is linear and we get $a^{oh}(z) = M^h z$. As expected for a Gaussian VAR process, the prediction at horizon h is performed by replacing the autoregressive matrix M by its power M^h (and keeping the same marginal Gaussian distribution).

The nonlinear prediction formula allows to derive a stationarity condition for the Car(1) process. Loosely speaking the process is stationary if the predictive distribution at long horizon ($h \to +\infty$) no longer depends on the initial condition. This implies :

$$\lim_{h \to \infty} a^{oh}(z) = 0, \forall z. \tag{2.7}$$

Moreover, when this condition is satisfied, we get :

$$\lim_{h \to \infty} \psi_{t,h}(z) = \exp c(z),$$

since the log-Laplace transform c is such that : $c(0) = \log E(\exp 0 | Y_t) = 0$. Thus at long horizon the predictive distribution is close to the marginal distribution and condition (2.7) appears as a necessary and sufficient condition for stationarity[2]. In the special case of Gaussian VAR model, the stationarity condition (2.7) reduces to $\lim_{h \to \infty} M^h = 0$. The condition is satisfied if the eigenvalues of autoregressive matrix M have modulus strictly smaller than one, which is the standard result.

Similarly it is possible to get a closed form expression of the LT of a future path [see Darolles, Gourieroux, Jasiak (2006)].

Proposition 2 : We get :

$$E\left[\exp(z'_{t+1} Y_{t+1} + \cdots + z'_{t+h} Y_{t+h}) | Y_t\right]$$
$$= \exp\left[A(t, t+h)' Y_t + B(t, t+h)\right],$$

where coefficients A and B satisfy the backward recursion :

$$A(t+j, t+h) = a[z_{t+j+1} + A(t+j+1, t+h)],$$
$$B(t+j, t+h) = b[z_{t+j+1} + A(t+j+1, t+h)] + B[t+j+1, t+h],$$

for $j < h$, with terminal conditions : $A(t+h, t+h) = 0, B(t+h, t+h) = 0$.

By considering $z_{t+1} = \cdots = z_{t+h} = z$, we get in particular the conditional LT of the integrated process $Y^*_{t,t+h} = \sum_{\tau=t+1}^{t+h} Y_\tau$.

---

[2] In fact this condition is necessary and sufficient for a weak definition of stationarity. A stronger condition is needed to get the convergence towards the stationary distribution at a geometric rate [see Darolles, Gourieroux, Jasiak (2006) for the discussion of geometric ergodicity of Car processes].

2.5. Compounding Interpretation

The Car processes admit an interpretation in terms of stochastic autoregression. This interpretation is useful to understand the properties of the
Car processes, simulate their trajectories, but also to construct various Car
dynamics.

2.5.1. Integer Autoregressive Process

It is easily seen why the standard linear autoregressive representation is not
appropriate for an integer valued process and how to modify the model to
be compatible with the integer state space. Let us consider a conditional
linear AR(1) model with iid errors :

$$y_t = \rho y_{t-1} + \varepsilon_t, \qquad (2.8)$$

say, where y_t can take values $0, 1, \ldots$ and $|\rho| < 1$. The right hand side takes
integer values only, for any integer y_{t-1}, if and only if the error also admits
integer values and ρ is integer. The latter condition with the stationarity
restriction $|\rho| < 1$ imply that $\rho = 0$. Therefore the single linear autoregres-
sive representation compatible with the integer state space corresponds to
a strong white noise.

   However integer values can be recovered by replacing the deterministic autoregression by a stochastic compound autoregression. More precisely let us consider a sequence of iid integer valued variables $X_{i,t}, i =
1, 2 \ldots, t = 1, 2, \ldots$, say, independent of the iid integer valued error terms
$\varepsilon_t, t = 1, \ldots, T$. Let us define :

$$y_t = \sum_{i=1}^{y_{t-1}} X_{i,t} + \varepsilon_t. \qquad (2.9)$$

By definition we get an integer value for the right hand side and any admissible drawing of $y_{t-1}, X_{i,t}, \varepsilon_t$. The deterministic autoregression has been
replaced by the stochastic (also called compound) sum : $\sum_{i=1}^{y_{t-1}} X_{i,t}$. The
conditional expectation of this term is : $E_{t-1} \left(\sum_{i=1}^{y_{t-1}} X_{i,t} \right) = y_{t-1} E(X_{i,t})$;
thus on average the linear autoregressive specification is recovered when-
ever $|\rho| = |E X_{i,t}| < 1$, but an additional randomness has been introduced
to satisfy the state space constraint.

It is easily checked that the process defined by (2.9) is a compound autoregressive process. Indeed let us represent the distributions of X and ε by their Laplace transforms :

$$E[\exp(-zX)] = \exp[-a(z)],\, E[\exp(-z\varepsilon)] = \exp b(z),\, \text{say.} \qquad (2.10)$$

We have :

$$E_{t-1}[\exp(-zy_t)]$$

$$= E[\exp(-z\sum_{i=1}^{y_{t-1}} X_{i,t} - z\varepsilon_t)|y_{t-1}]$$

$$= [E(\exp -zX_{it})]^{y_{t-1}} E[\exp(-z\varepsilon_t)]$$

$$= \exp[-a(z)y_{t-1} + b(z)].$$

This provides a new interpretation of the functional parameters. b characterizes the distribution of the error term ε, whereas a defines the law of the X variables involved in the stochastic autoregression.

Example : The Poisson INAR(1) process

When the error term follows a Poisson distribution $\mathcal{P}(\lambda)$, and the X variables are Bernoulli variables $B(1, \rho)$, the marginal distribution of the process is still a Poisson distribution with parameter $\lambda(1 - \rho)$. This Car process is the natural extension of the sequence of iid Poisson variables, and is used for marketing or insurance applications [see e.g. Brannas, Helstrom (2001), Gourieroux, Jasiak (2004)].

2.5.2. Nonnegative Continuous Variables

A similar approach can be followed to define Car processes for nonnegative one-dimensional processes. Loosely speaking the idea is to write a stochastic autoregression of the type :

$$y_t = \int_0^{y_{t-1}} X_{i,t} d(i) + \varepsilon_t,$$

where ε_t and $X_{i,t}$ are nonnegative continuous variables. More rigorously, we introduce two types of distribution.

i) The distribution of the error term admit the Laplace transform :

$$E[\exp(-z\varepsilon_t)] = \exp[b(z)].$$

ii) A second Laplace transform :

$$E[\exp(-zX)] = \exp[-a(z)],$$

is considered, such that the associated distribution is infinitely divisible. This means that for any nonnegative real value $\gamma : z \to \exp[-\gamma a(z)]$ is also a well-defined Laplace transform.
Then the function :

$$z \to \exp[-y_{t-1}a(z) + b(z)],$$

defines a conditional Laplace transform associated with a Car process. Loosely speaking a is the log-Laplace transform of the (stochastic) integral $\int_0^1 X_{i,t} d(i)$.

The discussion above shows that there exists a large class of Car processes with nonnegative values, since the distribution b and the infinitely divisible distribution a can be chosen arbitrarily.

2.6. Continuous Time Affine Processes

Since a large part of financial theory uses continuous time models, it is natural to consider what is the continuous time dynamics, which implies discrete time Car dynamics. We have already noted that the first and second order conditional moments of the Car process are affine functions of the conditioning value. Since diffusion models are characterized by their first and second order conditional infinitesimal moments, we get immediately the definitions below [Duffie, Filipovic, Schachermayer (2003)].

Definition 2 : i) An affine diffusion process is the solution of a stochastic differential system with affine drift and volatility :

$$dY_t = (\mu_0 + \mu_1 \; Y_t) \; dt + [\Sigma_0 + \sum_{j=1}^{n} y_{j,t} \; \Sigma_j]^{1/2} \; dW_t,$$

where (W_t) is a n-dimensional standard Brownian motion, μ_o a n-dimensional vector and $\mu_1, \Sigma_o, \Sigma_j$ are (n,n) matrices.

ii) A continuous time process is affine if and only if it admits an affine log-Laplace transform at any real horizon :

$$E_t[\exp(-z'y_{t+h})] = \exp[-a(z,h)y_t + b(z,h)], \forall h \in I\!R^+.$$

It is easily checked that any affine diffusion process satisfies the more general definition in terms of conditional Laplace transform. Moreover, the condition on the Laplace transform valid for any real h implies the same condition for integer h. Therefore a time discretized continuous time affine process is necessarily a Car process.

However the time coherency required at any small horizon for continuous time affine processes reduces considerably the set of affine processes. Let us for instance consider affine diffusion processes. The drift and volatility parameters have to satisfy some constraints. For instance the volatility parameters $\Sigma_0, \Sigma_1, \ldots, \Sigma_n$ have to be chosen to ensure a symmetric positive definite matrix $\Sigma_0 + \sum_{j=1}^{n} y_{j,t} \Sigma_j$ for any admissible values $y_{1,t}, \ldots, y_{n,t}$. Therefore the one-dimensional continuous time affine processes are essentially :

- The geometric Brownian motion :

$$dy_t = \mu_1 y_t dt + \sigma_1 y_t dW_t, \sigma_1 > 0;$$

- The Ornstein-Uhlenbeck process :

$$dy_t = (\mu_0 + \mu_1 y_t)dt + \sigma_0 dW_t, \sigma_1 > 0;$$

- The Cox-Ingersoll-Ross process :

$$dy_t = (\mu_0 + \mu_1 y_t)dt + \sigma_1 y_t^{1/2} dW_t, \sigma_1 > 0, \mu_1 < 0.$$

If the diffusion condition is not imposed, the one-dimensional continuous time processes includes also jump processes with bifurcations. Nevertheless the set of one dimensional continuous time affine processes is much smaller than the set of one-dimensional Car processes.

3. Autoregressive Gamma Process

The autoregressive gamma (ARG) process is a convenient dynamic specification for one-dimensional nonnegative time series. It can be used for the analysis of stochastic volatility [see Heston (1993), Ball, Roma (1994)], of inverse volatility [see Clark (1973)], of intertrade durations [see Gourieroux, Jasiak (2006)], of interest rates [see Cox, Ingersoll, Ross (1985)], or of time deformation [see Madan, Seneta (1990)]. In the first subsection some well-known results on gamma distributions are reviewed and we emphasize the compound interpretation of the noncentered gamma distribution. The ARG process is defined in subsection 3.2 and its prediction properties are described in subsection 3.3. Its relationship with the continuous time Cox, Ingersoll, Ross process is given in subsection 3.4. Finally we consider in subsection 3.5 the extension to any autoregressive order and the limiting unit root case.

3.1. Gamma Distribution

3.1.1. Centered Gamma Distribution

The gamma distribution with parameter ν is the continuous distribution on $(0, \infty)$ with pdf :

$$f(y) = \frac{1}{\Gamma(\nu)} \exp(-y) y^{\nu-1} \mathbf{1}_{y>0}, \tag{3.1}$$

where $\mathbf{1}_{y>0}$ denotes the indicator function of $(0, \infty)$, and $\Gamma(\nu) = \int_0^\infty \exp(-y) y^{\nu-1} dy$. This distribution is denoted $\gamma(\nu)$. Its Laplace transform is given by :

$$\psi(z) = E[\exp(-zy)] = \frac{1}{(1+z)^\nu}. \tag{3.2}$$

It is defined for $|z| < 1$.

3.1.2. Noncentered Gamma Distribution

The noncentered gamma distribution is a gamma distribution with a stochastic degree of freedom ν.

Definition 3 : The positive variable Y follows a gamma distribution with degree of freedom $\delta, \delta > 0$, and noncentrality parameter $\beta, \beta \geq 0$, denoted $\gamma(\delta, \beta)$, if and only if there exists a latent variable Z such that :

  i) X has a Poisson distribution $\mathcal{P}(\beta)$ with parameter β;
  ii) the conditional distribution of Y given X is the gamma distribution $\gamma(\delta + X)$.

  Since the family of gamma distributions is invariant by convolution, the noncentered gamma variable admits a compounding interpretation. More precisely we have :

$$Y = \sum_{i=1}^X W_i + \varepsilon, \tag{3.3}$$

where $\varepsilon, W_1, \ldots, W_n$ are mutually independent, with distributions $\gamma(\delta), \gamma(1), \ldots, \gamma(1)$, respectively, and are independent of X. The compounding interpretation explains the expression of the Laplace transform. We get :

$$\psi(z) = E[\exp(-zy)]$$
$$= E[\exp -z(\sum_{i=1}^{X} W_i + \varepsilon)]$$
$$= E\left[\frac{1}{(1+z)^{X+\delta}}\right]$$
$$= \sum_{x=0}^{\infty} \left(\frac{1}{(1+z)^{x+\delta}}\frac{\exp(-\beta)\beta^x}{x!}\right)$$
$$= \frac{1}{(1+z)^{\delta}}\exp\left(-\frac{\beta z}{1+z}\right), \tag{3.4}$$

that is :
$$\psi(z) = \exp\left[-\delta \log(1+z) - \beta\frac{z}{1+z}\right].$$

Thus the Laplace transform is exponential affine with respect to both parameters β and δ.

3.1.3. Change of scale

Finally a three parameter family is deduced from the gamma distribution by introducing a change of scale. We have :

$$Y \sim \tilde{\gamma}(\delta, \beta, c) \Longleftrightarrow Y/c \sim \gamma(\delta, \beta).$$

The associated Laplace transform is :

$$\psi(z) = E[\exp(-zy)] = \exp\left[-\delta \log(1+cz) - \beta\frac{cz}{1+cz}\right]. \tag{3.5}$$

3.2. The Autoregressive Gamma Process

The autoregressive gamma (ARG) process is the dynamic extension of a sequence of iid variables with noncentered gamma distribution.

Definition 4 : The process (y_t) is an autoregressive process of order 1, denoted ARG (1), if the conditional distribution of y_t given $\underline{y_{t-1}}$ is the generalized gamma distribution $\tilde{\gamma}(\delta, \beta y_{t-1}, c)$.

Thus the ARG(1) process admits the compound interpretation :

$$Y_t = \sum_{i=1}^{Z_t} W_{i,t} + \varepsilon_t,$$

where conditional on y_{t-1} :

$$i)\ \varepsilon_t \sim \tilde{\gamma}(\delta, 0, c),\ ii)\ Z_t \sim \mathcal{P}[\beta y_{t-1}],\ iii)\ W_{i,t} \sim \tilde{\gamma}(1, 0, c).$$

This is a special case of Car process with a conditional Laplace transform given by :

$$\psi_t(z) = E\left[\exp(-zy_t)|y_{t-1}\right] = \exp\left[-y_{t-1}\frac{\beta cz}{1+cz} - \delta\log(1+cz)\right]. \quad (3.6)$$

This conditional LT is :

$$\psi_t(z) = \exp[-a(z)y_{t-1} + b(z)],$$

$$(3.7)$$

where : $\qquad a(z) = \dfrac{\beta cz}{1+cz},\ b(z) = -\delta\log(1+cz).$

It is easily checked that the stationary distribution is such that :

$$\psi(z) = E[\exp(-zy_t)] = \exp c(z),$$

$$(3.8)$$

where : $\qquad c(z) = -\delta\log[1 + \dfrac{cz}{1-\beta c}].$

The stationary distribution is a centered gamma distribution up to a change of scale. Thus the ARG(1) process admits both marginal and conditional distributions in the generalized gamma family.

3.3. Nonlinear Prediction Formula

The nonlinear prediction formula is directly derived by considering function a compounded h times. We get :

$$a^{oh}(z) = \frac{\beta^h c^h z}{1 + c\dfrac{1-(\beta c)^h}{1-\beta c}z}.$$

This expression is similar to the expression of a, up to a change of parameters. We deduce the result below.

Proposition 3 : The conditional distribution of y_t given y_{t-h} is :

$$\tilde{\gamma}[\delta, \frac{\rho^h(1-\rho)}{c(1-\rho^h)}y_{t-h}, c\frac{1-\rho^h}{1-\rho}],$$

where $\rho = \beta c$.

Thus the change of parameters is :

$$1 \to h, \rho \to \rho^h, c \to c \frac{(1 - \rho^h)}{1 - \rho}.$$

We also note that the stationarity condition is : $|\rho| = |\beta c| < 1$. Under this condition the transition at horizon h tends to the stationarity distribution $\tilde{\gamma}(\delta, 0, \frac{c}{1 - \rho})$, when h tends to infinity.

In particular the conditional first and second order moments at any horizon h are immediately derived. We get :

$$E(y_{t+h}|y_t) = c \frac{1 - \rho^h}{1 - \rho} \delta + \rho^h y_t,$$

$$V(y_{t+h}|y_t) = c^2 \frac{(1 - \rho^h)^2}{(1 - \rho)^2} \delta + 2 \rho^h \frac{c(1 - \rho^h)}{1 - \rho} y_t.$$

The ARG(1) model is conditionally heteroscedastic with conditional first and second order moments, which are affine functions of the conditioning positive value y_t.

3.4. Link with the Cox, Ingersoll, Ross Process

In the subsection above, the (nonlinear) prediction formulas have been derived for any integer horizon h. Similar prediction formulas could be valid for fractional horizon $h = 1/2, 1/3, 1/4, \ldots$ This allows for the analysis of the process, when the observation frequency increases, that is when h tends to zero. It is expected that the ARG(1) process will tend to a continuous time diffusion process. The purpose of this subsection is to derive the form of the limiting diffusion process and the link between discrete and continuous time parameters.

Let us compute the infinitesimal drift and volatility per time unit, when $\rho > 0$. The infinitesimal drift is :

$$\lim_{h \to 0} \frac{1}{h} (E[y_{t+h}|y_t = y] - y)$$

$$= \lim_{h \to 0} \frac{1}{h} \left[c \left(\frac{1 - \rho^h}{1 - \rho} \right) \delta + (\rho^h - 1)y \right]$$

$$= \lim_{h \to 0} \frac{1 - \rho^h}{h} \left(\frac{c\delta}{1 - \rho} - y \right)$$

$$= -(\log \rho) \left(\frac{c\delta}{1 - \rho} - y \right).$$

The infinitesimal volatility is :

$$\lim_{h \to 0} \frac{1}{h} V(y_{t+h}|y_t = y) = -\frac{2c \log \rho}{1 - \rho} y.$$

More precisely we have the proposition below.

Proposition 4 : When $\rho > 0$, the stationary ARG(1) process is a time discretized Cox-Ingersoll-Ross process :

$$dy_t = a(b - y_t)dt + \sigma y_t^{1/2} dW_t,$$

where : $a = -\log \rho > 0, b = \dfrac{c\delta}{1 - \rho}, \sigma^2 = -\dfrac{2 \log \rho}{1 - \rho} c.$

3.5. Extensions

3.5.1. Autoregressive gamma process of order p

The ARG dynamics can be extended to any autoregressive order by introducing a stochastic degree of freedom function of several lagged values.

Definition 5 : The process (y_t) is an ARG(p) process, if the conditional distribution of y_t given $\underline{y_{t-1}}$ is the generalized gamma distribution $\tilde{\gamma}(\delta_1, \beta_1 y_{t-1} + \cdots + \beta_p y_{t-p}, c)$, where $\beta_1 \geq 0, \ldots, \beta_p \geq 0$.

The nonnegativity conditions on the sensitivity coefficients ensure a nonnegative parameter for the latent Poisson distribution. It can be shown that the process is stationary if and only if :

$$c(\beta_1 + \cdots + \beta_p) < 1.$$

It is interesting to note that the $ARG(p)$ model has no continuous time counterpart when $p \geq 2$.

4. Wishart Autoregressive Process

The Wishart Autoregressive (WAR) process is the extension of the Autoregressive Gamma (ARG) process introduced in Section 3 to the multidimensional framework. This extension is based on the following standard result concerning Gaussian variables : the square of any one-dimensional Gaussian variable follows a noncentral chi-square distribution, which is a special case of generalized gamma distribution. The Wishart process is defined in subsections 4.1 and 4.2 from outer products of vector autoregressive Gaussian processes.

4.1. The Outer Product of a Gaussian VAR(1) Process

Let us consider a (zero-mean) Gaussian VAR(1) process (x_t) of dimension n. This process satisfies :

$$x_{t+1} = Mx_t + \varepsilon_{t+1},$$

where (ε_t) is a sequence of iid random vectors with multivariate Gaussian distribution $N(0, \Sigma)$, where Σ is assumed positive definite. M is the (n, n) matrix of autoregressive coefficient. Thus the conditional distribution of x_t given x_{t-1} is Gaussian with conditional mean Mx_{t-1} and volatility matrix Σ.

Let us now consider the process defined by :

$$Y_t = x_t x_t'. \tag{4.1}$$

This process defines a time series of symmetric stochastic matrices, which are positive semidefinite with rank 1. They include squared component $x_{it}^2, i = 1, \ldots, n$ on the diagonal and cross products $x_{it}x_{jt}, i \neq j$, out of the diagonal. For instance for $n = 2$, we get :

$$Y_t = \begin{pmatrix} x_{1t}^2 & x_{1t}x_{2t} \\ x_{1t}x_{2t} & x_{2t}^2 \end{pmatrix}.$$

The main results of the literature [see Gourieroux, Jasiak, Sufana (2004)] are the following ones.

Proposition 5 : The conditional distribution of y_t given $x_{t-1}, x_{t-2}, \ldots$ depends on the past by means of the elements of y_{t-1} only, that is (Y_t) is a Markov process.

Moreover the transition of process (Y_t) is easily derived by means of its Laplace transform. At this stage it is important to define the LT in a way which is appropriate for matrix processes. Let us note that for two symmetric matrices Γ and Y of the same dimension, we have :

$$Tr(\Gamma Y) = \sum_{i=1}^{n} (\Gamma Y)_{ii} = \sum_{i=1}^{n} \sum_{l=1}^{n} \gamma_{il} Y_{li}$$

$$= \sum_{i=1}^{n} \gamma_{ii} Y_{ii} + 2 \sum_{i<j}^{n} \gamma_{ij} Y_{ij},$$

where Tr denotes the trace of a matrix, that is the sum of its diagonal elements. Thus any linear combination of the different elements of matrix Y can be written as $Tr(\Gamma Y)$. After a change of arguments $z_{ii} = -\gamma_{ii}, z_{ij} = -2\gamma_{ij}$, we can define the conditional Laplace transform as :

$$\psi_t(\Gamma) = E[\exp Tr(\Gamma Y_{t+1})|Y_t].$$

Proposition 6 : The conditional Laplace transform of process (Y_t) is :

$$\psi_t(\Gamma) = \frac{\exp Tr[M'\Gamma(Id - 2\Sigma\Gamma)^{-1}MY_t]}{[det(Id - 2\Sigma\Gamma)]^{1/2}},$$

where Id is the identity matrix, and is defined whenever $||2\Sigma\Gamma|| < 1$.

This log-Laplace transform is an affine function of the elements of Y_t, that is process (Y_t) is a Car process.

4.2. Extension to Stochastic Positive Definite Matrices

A drawback of the process introduced above is the rank restriction. Indeed we expect for applications to multivariate stochastic volatility matrices a process such that Y_t is of full rank almost surely.

A first idea to get such processes consist in summing a sufficient number of outer products of independent Gaussian VAR processes. More precisely let us consider the process defined by :

$$Y_t = \sum_{k=1}^{K} x_{kt}x'_{kt},$$

where the processes $x_{kt}, k = 1, \ldots, K$ are independent Gaussian VAR(1) processes with the same dimension n, autoregressive parameter M and innovation variance Σ :

$$x_{k,t} = Mx_{k,t-1} + \varepsilon_{k,t}, \varepsilon_{k,t} \sim N(0, \Sigma).$$

Analogues of Propositions 4.1, 4.2 can be derived. Process (Y_t) is a Markov process with conditional Laplace transform :

$$\psi_t(\Gamma) = \frac{\exp Tr[M'\Gamma(Id - 2\Sigma\Gamma)^{-1}MY_t]}{[det(Id - 2\Sigma\Gamma)]^{K/2}}. \tag{4.2}$$

The affine character of the log-Laplace transform is not lost, and its expression is just modified by a change of power in the denominator. The stochastic matrix Y_t has full rank almost surely whenever the number K of terms in the sum is larger than dimension n.

More generally the Laplace transform (4.2) can be extended to fractional degree of freedom, but the interpretation in terms of sum of outer products of Gaussian VAR is lost.

Definition 6 : A Wishart autoregressive process of order 1, denoted WAR (1), is a matrix Markov process with conditional Laplace transform :

$$\psi_t(\Gamma) = \frac{\exp Tr[M'\Gamma(Id - 2\Sigma\Gamma)^{-1}MY_t]}{[det(Id - 2\Sigma\Gamma)]^{K/2}}.$$

The conditional Laplace transform depends on parameters K, M, Σ. Parameter $K, K > 0$, is the degree of freedom, M the latent autoregressive coefficient, Σ the latent innovation variance. The stochastic matrix Y_t has full column rank whenever $K > n - 1$.

In the one-dimensional case $n = 1$, the Laplace transform becomes :

$$\psi_t(z) = \exp[-m^2 y_t \frac{z}{1 + \sigma^2 z} - \frac{K}{2}\log(1 + 2\sigma^2 z)],$$

with $z = -\gamma$. This is exactly the expression of the Laplace transform of an ARG(1) process with parameters : $c = 2\sigma^2, \beta = m^2/(2\sigma^2), \delta = K/2$.

4.3. Conditional Moments

The expressions of the first and second order conditional moments are directly deduced from the conditional Laplace transform. We get :

$$E_t(Y_{t+1}) = MY_t M' + K\Sigma,$$

$$Cov_t(\gamma'Y_{t+1}\alpha, \delta'Y_{t+1}\beta) = \gamma'MY_t M'\delta \; \alpha'\Sigma\beta + \gamma'MY_t M'\beta \; \alpha'\Sigma\delta$$
$$+ \; \alpha'MY_t M'\delta \; \gamma'\Sigma\beta + \alpha'MY_t M'\beta \; \gamma'\Sigma\delta$$
$$+ \; \gamma'\Sigma\beta \; \alpha'\Sigma\delta + \alpha'\Sigma\beta \; \gamma'\Sigma\delta;$$

for any n-dimensional vectors $\alpha, \gamma, \delta, \beta$. In particular the conditional moments above are affine functions of the lagged volatility matrix. For instance in the bidimensional framework, we get :

$$Y_t = \begin{pmatrix} Y_{1,1,t} & Y_{1,2,t} \\ Y_{1,2,t} & Y_{2,2,t} \end{pmatrix}.$$

The conditional means are :

$$E_t(Y_{1,1,t+1}) = (m_{1,1}, m_{1,2})Y_t \begin{pmatrix} m_{1,1} \\ m_{1,2} \end{pmatrix} + K\sigma_{1,1},$$

$$E_t(Y_{2,2,t+1}) = (m_{2,1}, m_{2,2})Y_t \begin{pmatrix} m_{2,1} \\ m_{2,2} \end{pmatrix} + K\sigma_{2,2},$$

$$E_t(Y_{1,2,t+1}) = (m_{1,1}, m_{1,2})Y_t \begin{pmatrix} m_{2,1} \\ m_{2,2} \end{pmatrix} + K\sigma_{1,2}.$$

There are 3 conditional variances and 3 conditional covariances :

$$V_t(Y_{1,1,t+1}) = 4\sigma_{1,1}(m_{1,1}, m_{1,2})Y_t \begin{pmatrix} m_{1,1} \\ m_{1,2} \end{pmatrix} + 2K\sigma_{1,1}^2,$$

$$V_t(Y_{2,2,t+1}) = 4\sigma_{2,2}(m_{2,1}, m_{2,2})Y_t \begin{pmatrix} m_{2,1} \\ m_{2,2} \end{pmatrix} + 2K\sigma_{2,2}^2,$$

$$Cov_t(Y_{1,1,t+1}, Y_{2,2,t+1}) = 4\sigma_{1,2}(m_{1,1}, m_{1,2})Y_t \begin{pmatrix} m_{2,1} \\ m_{2,2} \end{pmatrix} + 2K\sigma_{1,2}^2,$$

$$V_t(Y_{1,2,t+1}) = (m_{1,1}, m_{1,2})Y_t \begin{pmatrix} m_{1,1} \\ m_{1,2} \end{pmatrix} \sigma_{2,2}$$

$$+ (m_{2,1}, m_{2,2})Y_t \begin{pmatrix} m_{2,1} \\ m_{2,2} \end{pmatrix} \sigma_{1,1}$$

$$+ 2(m_{1,1}, m_{1,2})Y_t \begin{pmatrix} m_{2,1} \\ m_{2,2} \end{pmatrix} \sigma_{1,2}$$

$$+ K(\sigma_{1,2}^2 + \sigma_{1,1}\sigma_{2,2}), \dots$$

4.4. Continuous Time Analogue

Under restrictions on the dynamics parameters[3], a WAR(1) process is a time discretized continuous time affine process. The continuous time Wishart process satisfies a diffusion system :

$$dY_t = \left(KQQ' + \tilde{A}Y_t + Y_t\tilde{A}' \right) dt + Y_t^{1/2} d\tilde{W}_t Q + Q' d\tilde{W}_t' Y_t^{1/2},$$

where W_t is a (n, n) stochastic matrix, whose components are independent Brownian motions, and A, Q are (n, n) matrices. The state space of this

---

[3]The autoregressive matrix M has to be of an exponential form $M = \exp A$, where A is a (n, n) matrix. This excludes negative eigenvalues, recursive systems... often encountered in practice.

continuous time matrix process is the set of symmetric positive definite matrices. Indeed it is easily checked that $dY_t = dY'_t$, which explains the symmetry of the process. Moreover let us assume that, at time t, the matrix Y_t is positive semi-definite, such that $\beta'Y_t\beta = 0$. Thus we are on the boundary of the state space. In this situation the process becomes locally deterministic with a positive drift in the degeneracy direction, since :

$$\beta' dY_t \beta = \left(K\beta'QQ'\beta + \beta'\tilde{A}Y_t\beta + \beta'Y_t\tilde{A}'\beta \right) dt$$
$$+ \beta'Y_t^{1/2} d\tilde{W}_t Q\beta + \beta'Q' d\tilde{W}'_t Y_t^{1/2}\beta$$
$$= K\beta'QQ'\beta dt > 0.$$

5. Structural Applications

We have seen in the introduction that compound autoregressive models are naturally introduced in the analysis of high frequency data to account for the difference between calendar time and deformed time. They are also important in derivative pricing concerning either bonds, [Duffie, Kan (1996), Gourieroux, Sufana (2003), Gourieroux, Monfort, Polimenis (2006)], or stocks [Gourieroux, Sufana (2004)], to account for the evolution of latent risk. The aim of this Section is to show that these structural problems share a common structure, which involves the nonlinear prediction of the cumulated (or integrated) factor process : $Y^*_{t,t+h} = \sum_{\tau=t+1}^{t+h} Y_\tau$ at time t. Since the conditional Laplace transform of $Y^*_{t,t+h}$ is easily computed for any Car (affine) process, this family is the appropriate family to derive closed form solutions to all problems mentioned above.

5.1. Derivative Pricing

The analysis of derivative prices can be performed either with respect to the historical dynamics by introducing a stochastic discount factor, or with respect to the risk adjusted dynamics, called risk-neutral dynamics. The advantage of risk neutral dynamics is to facilitate the computations of derivative prices, but its main drawback is to correspond to a virtual world, which is not usual for econometricians [see e.g. the discussion in Dai, Singleton (2000)]. In the sequel we use the historical approach for analysing both term structures of interest rates and stock derivative pricing.

5.1.1. Affine Term Structures

In this section we are interested in bond pricing. The purpose is to find closed form formulas for the prices of zero-coupon bonds (and more generally bond derivatives), which are coherent with respect to both time and residual maturity. Let us denote by $B(t, t+h)$ the price at date t of a zero-coupon bond with residual maturity h. This is the price in \$ at date t of 1\$ paid with certainty at date $t+h$. This price summarizes both the discounting due to time and future uncertainty. It is known that, under the assumption of no arbitrage opportunity, the price of zero-coupon bond can be written as :

$$B(t, t+h) = E_t(M_{t,t+1} \ldots M_{t+h-1,t+h}), \qquad (5.1)$$

where E_t denotes the expectation conditional on the information available at time t and $M_{t,t+1}$ the stochastic discount factor (sdf) function of the information of date $t+1$. We assume that the information set includes the current and lagged values of some underlying factors Y_t, say, and that the sdf is an exponential affine function of the factor values at date $t+1$:

$$M_{t,t+1} = \exp[\alpha_0' Y_{t+1} + \alpha_1]. \qquad (5.2)$$

Then we get :

$$B(t, t+h) = E_t[\exp(\alpha_0' Y_{t+1} + \alpha_1) \ldots \exp(\alpha_0' Y_{t+h} + \alpha_1)]$$
$$= \exp(h\alpha_1) E_t \exp(\alpha_0' Y_{t,t+h}^*),$$

where : $Y_{t,t+h}^* = \displaystyle\sum_{\tau=t+1}^{t+h} Y_\tau$ is the integrated factor value.

Thus it is equivalent to looking for closed form expressions of the zero-coupon bonds, or for closed form expressions of the conditional Laplace transform of the integrated factor value (see Proposition 2).

5.1.2. Corporate Bonds

The approach above can be extended to the pricing of corporate bonds, which take account the possibility of default. If we assume a zero recovery rate when defaut occurs, the prices of corporate bonds can be written as :

$$B_c(t, t+h) = E_t[M_{t,t+1} \ldots M_{t+h-1,t+h} \Pi_{t,t+1} \ldots \Pi_{t+h-1,t+h}], \qquad (5.3)$$

where $M_{t,t+1}$ is the sdf and $\Pi_{t,t+1}$ the survivor intensity, which measures the probability of no default at date $t+1$, when the firm is still alive at date t. If we assume exponential affine functions of the factor for both $M_{t,t+1}$ and $\Pi_{t,t+1}$,

$$M_{t,t+1} = \exp[\alpha_0' Y_{t+1} + \alpha_1], \Pi_{t,t+1} = \exp(\beta_0' Y_{t+1} + \beta_1), \qquad (5.4)$$

we get :

$$B_c(t, t+h) = \exp[h(\alpha_1 + \beta_1)] E_t \exp[(\alpha_0 + \beta_0)' Y_{t,t+h}^*]. \qquad (5.5)$$

This is still a conditional Laplace transform of the integrated factor process.

Similarly the approach can be extended to include nonzero recovery rates (see Gourieroux, Monfort, Polimenis (2006)).

5.1.3. Stock Derivatives

The sdf based approach can also be used to price derivatives written on stocks. Let us for illustration consider a risky stock with price S_t and a riskfree asset with zero riskfree rate. Under the assumption of no arbitrage opportunity the price at t of a European call paying $g(S_{t+h})$ at date $t+h$ is :

$$C(g; t, t+h) = E_t[M_{t,t+1} \ldots M_{t+h-1,t+h} g(S_{t+h})]. \qquad (5.6)$$

It is known that all derivative prices can be easily computed if we know the prices of derivatives corresponding to exponential transform of the log-asset price :

$$g(S_{t+h}) = \exp(z \log S_{t+h}), \qquad (5.7)$$

where $z = z_0 i$ is a pure imaginary number.

For expository purpose let us now consider a one factor model. Let us assume that the sdf is an exponential affine function of this underlying risk factor :

$$M_{t,t+1} = \exp(\alpha_0 y_{t+1} + \alpha_1),$$

whereas the evolution of the stock price is given by :

$$\log S_{t+1} = \log S_t + \mu_0 y_{t+1} + \mu_1 + (\sigma_0^2 y_{t+1} + \sigma_1^2)^{1/2} \varepsilon_{t+1}, \qquad (5.8)$$

where (ε_t) is a sequence of iid standard normal variables. The price equation (5.9) corresponds to a standard Black-Scholes specification with a stochastic volatility and a risk premium [volatility-in-mean effect] introduced in the drift.

We deduce from equation (5.9) that :

$$\log S_{t+h} = \log S_t + \mu_0 y_{t,t+h}^* + \mu_1 h + (\sigma_0^2 y_{t,t+h}^* + h\sigma_1^2)^{1/2}\varepsilon, \qquad (5.9)$$

where ε is a standard Gaussian variable. Therefore the price of the derivative with payoff $g(S_{t+h}) = \exp(z \log S_{t+h})$ is :

$$C(z; t, t+h) = E_t\{\exp[\alpha_0 y_{t,t+h}^* + \alpha_1 h + z \log S_t + z\mu_0 y_{t,t+h}^* + z\mu_1 h$$
$$+ z(\sigma_0^2 y_{t,t+h}^* + h\sigma_1^2)^{1/2}\varepsilon\}$$

By integrating out the random term ε, we get :

$$C(z; t, t+h) = \exp[\alpha_1 h + z \log S_t + z(\mu_1 + \frac{1}{2}\sigma_1^2)h]$$

$$E_t \exp[(\alpha_0 + z\mu_0 + \frac{1}{2}z^2\frac{\sigma_0^2}{2})y_{t,t+h}^*].$$

These derivative prices have closed form expressions whenever the conditional Laplace transform of the integrated factor $y_{t,t+h}^*$ has a closed form expression.

6. Concluding Remarks

The compounding interpretations of daily data obtained by aggregating high frequency data and the role of the conditional Laplace transform in pricing derivatives on bonds and stocks explain the importance of Compound Autoregressive (Car) processes. The aim of this chapter was to define these processes, to describe their prediction properties and to highlight their use for derivative pricing. In practice the Car dynamics are often parameterized and the dynamic parameters have to be estimated from available data. The transition density of a Car process admits in general a rather complicated form. However the specification of the conditional Laplace transform :

$$E[\exp(-z'Y_t|\underline{Y_{t-1}}] = \exp[-a(z;\theta)'Y_{t-1} + b(z;\theta)], \forall z \in D,$$

can be rewritten as :

$$E\left\{[\exp(-z'Y_t) - \exp(-a(z;\theta)'Y_{t-1} + b(z;\theta))]|\underline{Y_{t-1}}\right\} = 0, \forall z \in D.$$

This specification provides an infinite set of conditional moment restrictions when z varies. This set can be used to derive asymptotically efficient estimators of parameter θ by applying GMM in an appropriate way.

References

Ball, C., and A., Roma (1994) : "Stochastic Volatility Option Pricing", Journal of Financial and Quantitative Analysis, 29, 589–607.

Benjamin, M., Rigby, R., and D., Stasinopoulos (2003) : "Generalized Autoregressive Moving Average Models", JASA, 98, 214–223.

Brannas, K., and J., Helstrom (2001) : "Generalizations to the Integer Valued AR(1) Model", Econometric Reviews, 20, 425–443.

Clark, P. (1973) : "A Subordinated Stochastic Process Model with Finite Variance for Speculative Prices", Econometrica, 41, 135–155.

Cox, J., Ingersoll, J., and S., Ross (1985) : "A Theory of the Term Structure of Interest Rates", Econometrica, 53, 385–408.

Dai, Q., and K., Singleton (2000) : "Specification Analysis of Affine Term Structure Models", Journal of Finance, 55, 1943–1978.

Darolles, S., Gourieroux, C., and J., Jasiak (2006) : "Structural Laplace Transform and Compound Autoregressive Models", Journal of Time Series Analysis, 27, 477–503.

Duffie, D., Filipovic, D., and W., Schachermayer (2003) : "Affine Processes and Application in Finance", Annals of Applied Probability, 13, 984–1053.

Duffie, D., and R., Kan (1996) : "A Yield Factor Model of Interest Rates", Mathematical Finance, 6, 379–406.

Gourieroux, C., and J., Jasiak (2004) : "Heterogenous INAR(1) Model with Application to Car Insurance", Insurance : Mathematics and Economics, 34, 177–189.

Gourieroux, C., and J., Jasiak (2006) : "Autoregressive Gamma Processes", Journal of Forecasting, 25, 129–152.

Gourieroux, C., Jasiak, J. and R., Sufana (2004) : "A Dynamic Model for Multivariate Stochastic Volatility : The Wishart Autoregressive Process", DP, HEC Montreal.

Gourieroux, C., Monfort, A., and V., Polimenis (2006) : "Affine Models for Credit Risk Analysis, Journal of Financial Econometrics, 4, 494–530.

Gourieroux, C., and R., Sufana (2003) : "Wishart Quadratic Term Structure Model", DP 0310, HEC Montreal.

Gourieroux, C., and R., Sufana (2004) : "Derivative Pricing with Multivariate Stochastic Volatility".

Grunwald, G., Hyndman, R., Tedesco, L., and R., Tweedie (2001) : "Non Gaussian Conditional Linear AR(1) Models", Australian and New Zealand Journal of Statistics, 42, 479–495.

Heston, S. (1993) : "A Closed Form Solution for Options with Stochastic Volatility with Applications to Bond and Currency Options", Review of Financial Studies, 6, 327–343.

Lando, D. (1998) : "On Cox Processes and Credit Risky Securities", Review of Derivative Research, 2, 99–120.

Madan, D., and E., Seneta (1990) : "The Variance-Gamma Model for Share Market Returns", Journal of Business, 63, 511–524.

Martellini, L., and P., Priaulet (2001) : "Fixed Income Securities", John Wiley and Sons.

Singleton, K (2001) : "Estimation of Affine Diffusion Models Based on the Empirical Characteristic Function", Journal of Econometrics, 102, 111–141.

Appendix 1

Prediction Formula

The prediction formula of Proposition 1 is derived by recursion.

i) First note that, for $h = 1$, we get :

$$\psi_{t,1}(z) = \exp[-a(z)'Y_t + b(z)],$$

which is the definition of the Car process.

ii) Moreover, if the prediction formula is valid for $h - 1$, we get :

$$\psi_{t,h}(z) = E\left[\exp(-z'Y_{t-h})|Y_t\right]$$

$$= \left\{E\left[\exp(-z'Y_{t-h})|Y_{t+1}\right]|Y_t\right\}$$

$$= E\left[\psi_{t+1,h-1}(z)|Y_t\right]$$

$$= E\left(\exp\left\{-a^{o(h-1)}(z)'Y_{t+1} + \sum_{k=0}^{h-2} b[a^{ok}(z)]\right\}|Y_t\right)$$

$$= \exp\left\{-a^{o(h)}(z)'Y_t + \sum_{k=0}^{h-1} b[a^{ok}(z)]\right\},$$

which is the expected formula.

MULTIVARIATE TIME SERIES ANALYSIS AND FORECASTING

Manfred Deistler

Department of Mathematical Methods in Economics, TU Wien
Argentinierstr. 8, A-1040 Wien, Austria
E-mail: Manfred.Deistler@tuwien.ac.at

A condensed presentation of linear multivariate time series models, their identification and their use for forecasting is given. General stationary processes, $ARMA$ and state space systems and linear dynamic factor models are described.

1. Introduction

In general terms, time series analysis is concerned with extraction of information from observations ordered in time. The ordering in time contains important information and the results obtained are, contrary to the classical case of i.i.d. observations, in general not invariant with respect to a permutation in the ordering of the observations. Here we only consider discrete-time, equally spaced data y_t, $t = 1, \ldots, T$; $y_t \in \mathbb{R}^n$.

The main aims in time series analysis are data driven modelling (also called system identification) on the one side and signal and feature extraction on the other side. In this contribution we mainly consider data driven modelling; the main issues here are:

- Model classes and structure theory
- Estimation of real-valued parameters
- Model selection

Here we only consider linear models in a stationary framework. When comparing with the univariate (i.e. $n = 1$) case, additional theoretical and practical problems arise in the multivariate ($n > 1$) case. In particular:

- certain theoretical features, such as the structure theory for linear systems are much more demanding
- typically, the dimension of parameter spaces increases at the rate n^2, whereas, clearly, the number of data points, for fixed sample size T, is linear in n

The contribution is organized as follows:

In section 2 we summarize main results from the theory of (wide sense) stationary processes. Such processes are the most important stochastic models for time series and the understanding of the structure of stationary processes is essential for a deeper understanding of time series analysis. In this section we are concerned with the structure of such processes, with forecasting and filtering and not with estimation.

In this contribution we do not discuss nonparametric estimation, such as smoothed periodogram estimators, also because this is not of primary interest in econometrics. In section 3 we consider identification for stationary processes with rational spectral densities, or, in other words for $ARMA$ or state space systems. The approach is semi nonparametric in the sense that model selection is performed in order to obtain finite dimensional parameter spaces after model selection.

For multivariate time series, the dimension of the parameter spaces for (unstructured) AR, $ARMA$ or state space systems may cause severe problems. In such cases cross-sectional dimension reduction by factor models may be very important. This is discussed in section 4. Clearly, linear models for nonstationary observations are very important in economic time series analysis. We do not deal with these models here, we only want to point out that cointegration models and factor models for panel data constitute important classes of factor models, not treated in section 4.

The contribution is intended to provide a condensed presentation, by describing main ideas and results and the basic structure of the problems. No proofs are given; for the sake of brevity in some cases compromises on the precision are made. In order to reduce the amount of referencing, the main references are given at the beginning of every section. In general, no original references are given.

2. Stationary Processes

Stationary processes are important models for time series. The central parts of the theory of wide-sense stationary processes, in particular spectral representation, Wold representation, spectral factorization, linear least squares forecasting, filtering and smoothing have been developed in the thirties and fourties of the last century by Khinchin, Kolmogorov, Wold, Wiener and others for the univariate case. In addition at the same time, the theory of strictly stationary processes and ergodic theory were studied. One of the first complete accounts on the multivariate theory was the book by Rozanov [20]. This book is the main reference for this section, see also Hannan [14] and Hannan and Deistler [15]. This theory is, in a certain sense, probability theory. Based on this theory the statistical analysis of stationary time series was developed, starting in the late fourties and early fifties of the last century with the work of Tukey and others.

Stationary processes with rational spectral densities correspond to finite dimensional linear systems (as treated in section 3) and are of particular practical importance for the statistical analysis. Also for important classes of nonstationary processes, such as for integrated processes, the theory of stationary processes in an important building stone. In this section we summarize important facts from the theory of wide sense stationary processes.

2.1. *Basic Definitions and Examples*

We commence with the following definition:

A stochastic process $(x_t | t \in \mathbb{Z})$, where $\mathbb{Z}$ are the integers and $x_t : \Omega \to \mathbb{R}^n$ are random variables, is called (*wide sense*) *stationary* if

- $Ex_t' x_t < \infty$ for all t
- $Ex_t = m$ (constant) for all t
- $\gamma(s) = \mathbb{E}(x_{t+s} - m)(x_t - m)'$ does not depend on t.

In other words, wide sense stationarity means existence and shift-invariance (in time) of first and second moments. Here a' denotes the transpose of a vector or a matrix a.

The covariance function $\gamma : \mathbb{Z} \to \mathbb{R}^{n \times n}$ is the "address book" of linear dependence relations between all pairs of (one-dimensional) process variables $x_{t+s}^{(i)}$ and $x_t^{(j)}$. A function $\gamma : \mathbb{Z} \to \mathbb{R}^{n \times n}$ is a covariance function if and only if it is a non-negative definite function, i.e. $\Gamma_T \geq 0$ holds for all T, where

$$\Gamma_T = \begin{bmatrix} \gamma(0) & \cdots & \gamma(-T+1) \\ \vdots & \ddots & \vdots \\ \gamma(T-1) & \cdots & \gamma(0) \end{bmatrix}$$

Examples for stationary processes are:

- *White noise*, defined by $E\epsilon_t = 0$, $E\epsilon_s \epsilon_t' = \delta_{st}\Sigma$, where δ_{st} is the Kronecker delta.
- *Moving average (MA) processes*, defined by

$$x_t = \sum_{j=0}^{q} b_j \epsilon_{t-j}, \qquad b_j \in \mathbb{R}^{n \times m}$$

  where ϵ_t is white noise
- *Infinite moving average processes*, which are of the form

$$x_t = \sum_{j=-\infty}^{\infty} b_j \epsilon_{t-j}, \quad \sum \|b_j\|^2 < \infty$$

  where here and throughout infinite sums are understood in the mean squares sense. Here $\| \ \|$ denotes a norm of a matrix. The class of infinite moving average processes is already a large class within the class of stationary processes.
- *(Stationary) Autoregressive (AR) processes* are the steady state solutions of stable vector difference equations (VDE's) of the form

$$a(z)y_t = \epsilon_t \qquad (1)$$

  where (ϵ_t) is white noise, z is the backward-shift operator (i.e $z((y_t|t\epsilon\mathbb{Z})) = (y_{t-1}|t\epsilon\mathbb{Z}))$ as well as a complex variable,

$$a(z) = \sum_{j=0}^{p} a_j z^j, \ a_j \in \mathbb{R}^{n \times n}$$

  and where the stability condition

$$\det a(z) \neq 0, \ |z| \leq 1 \qquad (2)$$

  holds. Here *det* denotes the determinant.

- *(Stationary) ARMA processes* are the steady state solutions of VDE's of the form

$$a(z)y_t = b(z)\epsilon_t$$

where

$$b(z) = \sum_{j=0}^{q} b_j z^j, \ b_j \in \mathbb{R}^{n \times n}$$

and the stability condition (2) holds. In most cases, in addition, the so called miniphase condition

$$\det b(z) \neq 0, \ |z| < 1 \tag{3}$$

is also imposed. This condition does not restrict the class of $ARMA$ processes.

- *Harmonic processes* are of the form

$$x_t = \sum_{j=1}^{h} e^{i\lambda_j t} z_j \tag{4}$$

where $\lambda_j \in (-\pi, \pi]$ are (angular) frequencies and $z_j : \Omega \to \mathbb{C}^n$ are complex valued random variables. W.l.o.g. we assume $\lambda_1 < \cdots < \lambda_h$; also the restriction of the angular frequencies to $(-\pi, \pi]$ does not restrict generality, since t varies over the integers. The highest observable frequency π is called the Nyquist frequency. By formula (4), (x_t) is a sum of harmonic oscillations with random amplitudes and phases. In general, (x_t) will not be stationary; in order to guarantee stationarity, we impose the following conditions:

$$Ez_j^* z_j < \infty$$

where $*$ denotes the conjugate-transpose

$$Ez_j = \begin{cases} 0 & \text{for all } j \text{ such that } \lambda_j \neq 0 \\ (Ex_t & \text{for } j \text{ with } \lambda_j = 0) \end{cases}$$

$$Ez_j z_l^* = 0 \text{ for all } j \neq l \tag{5}$$

Condition (5) means, that there is no linear dependence between the weights at different frequencies. In addition, since (x_t) is real-valued, we have: $\lambda_{1+i} = -\lambda_{h-i}$ and $z_{1+i} = \bar{z}_{h-i}, i = 0, \ldots, h-1$.

The *spectral distribution function* $F : [-\pi, \pi] \longrightarrow \mathbb{C}^{n \times n}$ of a harmonic process is defined by

$$F(\lambda) = \sum_{j:\lambda_j \leq \lambda} F_j,$$

$$F_j = \begin{cases} Ez_j z_j^* & \text{for all } j \text{ such that } \lambda_j \neq 0 \\ E(z_j - Ex_t)(z_j - Ex_t)^* & \text{for } j \text{ with } \lambda_j = 0 \end{cases} \quad (6)$$

The equation

$$\gamma(t) = \sum_{j=1}^{h} e^{i\lambda_j t} F_j \quad (7)$$

defines a one-to-one relation between covariance functions and spectral distribution functions, thus F contains the same information about the process as γ. For many applications however spectral distribution functions are preferred due to the way how this information is displayed: The diagonal elements $F_j^{(l,l)}$ of F_j are a measure of the expected amplitude at frequency λ_j in the l–th component of the process (x_t) and the off-diagonal elements $F_j^{(i,l)}$, $i \neq l$, which are complex in general, measure with their absolute values the strength of the linear relation between the i–th and the l–th component of (x_t) at frequency λ_j and the phase of $F_j^{(i,l)}$ is a measure of the expected phase shift between these components.

2.2. *The Spectral Representation of Stationary Processes*

The theorem below constitutes one of the central parts of the theory of stationary processes. It states that every stationary process can be obtained as the (pointwise in t) limit (in the mean squares sense) of a sequence of (stationary) harmonic processes. Let H_x denote the Hilbert space spanned by the one dimensional components $x_t^{(j)}$, $j = 1, \ldots, n$, $t \in \mathbb{Z}$ of (x_t) in the Hilbert space L_2 over the underlying probability space $(\Omega, \mathcal{A}, \mathcal{P})$.

Theorem 2.1: For every stationary process (x_t) there is a (in H_x unique) process $(z(\lambda)|\lambda \in [-\pi, \pi])$, $z(\lambda) : \Omega \to \mathbb{C}^n$ satisfying
$z(-\pi) = 0$, $z(\pi) = x_0$
$Ez^*(\lambda)z(\lambda) < \infty$
$\lim_{\epsilon \downarrow 0} z(\lambda + \epsilon) = z(\lambda)$

$E(z(\lambda_4) - z(\lambda_3))(z(\lambda_2) - z(\lambda_1))^* = 0$ for $\lambda_1 < \lambda_2 \leq \lambda_3 < \lambda_4$
such that

$$x_t = \int_{[-\pi,\pi]} e^{i\lambda t} dz(\lambda) \tag{8}$$

holds.

The process $(z(\lambda)|\lambda \in [-\pi, \pi])$ is called a process of orthogonal increments.

The importance of the spectral representation (8) is twofold. First it allows for an interpretation of a stationary process in terms of frequency components. Second, as will be seen in the next subsection, certain operations are easier to interprete and to perform in frequency domain.

For a general stationary process (x_t) its *spectral distribution function* $F : [-\pi, \pi] \to \mathbb{C}^{n \times n}$ is defined by $F(\lambda) = E\tilde{z}(\lambda)\tilde{z}^*(\lambda)$ where

$$\tilde{z}(\lambda) = \begin{cases} z(\lambda) & \text{for } \lambda < 0 \\ z(\lambda) - Ex_t & \text{for } \lambda \geq 0 \end{cases}$$

In this contribution from now on we will assume, that $Ex_t = 0$ holds.

If there exists a function $f : [-\pi, \pi] \to \mathbb{C}^{n \times n}$ such that

$$F(\omega) = \int_{-\pi}^{\omega} f(\lambda) d\lambda$$

where λ denotes the Lebesgue measure, then f is called the *spectral density*. If we assume $\Sigma ||\gamma(t)||^2 < \infty$ then the spectral density exists and there is a one-to-one relation between γ and f (or to be more precise the corresponding λ-a.e. equivalence class) given by

$$\gamma(t) = \int_{-\pi}^{\pi} e^{i\lambda t} f(\lambda) d\lambda \tag{9}$$

and

$$f(\lambda) = (2\pi)^{-1} \sum_{t=-\infty}^{\infty} \gamma(t) e^{-i\lambda t}$$

A function $f : [-\pi, \pi] \to \mathbb{C}^{n \times n}$ is a spectral density if and only if

$$f \geq 0, \ \lambda \ a.e.$$

$$|| \int f(\lambda) d\lambda || < \infty$$

and

$$f(\lambda) = f(-\lambda)'$$

hold. In particular we have

$$\gamma(0) = \int_{-\pi}^{\pi} f(\lambda)d\lambda$$

which may be interpreted as the decomposition of the variance-covariance matrix of x_t into the variance-covariance matrices $f(\lambda)d\lambda$ of the frequency components $e^{i\lambda t}dz(\lambda)$. The interpretation of F and f can be directly obtained from the interpretation of F in the harmonic case. In particular, the diagonal elements of f show the contributions of the frequency bands to the variance of the respective component process and the off-diagonal elements show the frequency band specific covariances and expected phase shifts between the component processes.

2.3. *Linear Transformations of Stationary Processes*

Linear transformations are the most important class of transformations of stationary processes. For (x_t) stationary let

$$y_t = \sum_{j=-\infty}^{\infty} a_j x_{t-j}; \ a_j \in \mathbb{R}^{n \times m} \tag{10}$$

hold. Then we say that (y_t) is obtained by a linear, time-invariant transformation from (x_t). If $\Sigma||a_j|| < \infty$ then the infinite sum in (10) exists for every stationary (x_t); if the condition $\Sigma||a_j||^2 < \infty$ holds, then this sum exists e.g. for white noise. The *weighting function* of the linear transformation is given as $(a_j|j \in \mathbb{Z})$. The transformation is called *causal* if $a_j = 0$, $j < 0$ and *static* if $a_j = 0$, $j \neq 0$ holds. As easily can be seen, $(x_t', y_t')'$ is stationary and, using an evident notation,

$$y_t = \int_{[-\pi,\pi]} e^{i\lambda t} dz_y(\lambda) = \int_{[-\pi,\pi]} e^{i\lambda t}(\sum_{j=-\infty}^{\infty} a_j e^{-i\lambda j})dz_x(\lambda) \tag{11}$$

holds for all $t \in \mathbb{Z}$. *The transfer-function*

$$k(z) = \sum_{j=-\infty}^{\infty} a_j z^j$$

is in one-to-one relation with the weighting function $(a_j | j \in \mathbb{Z})$.
From (11) we see that

$$dz_y(\lambda) = k(e^{-i\lambda})dz_x(\lambda)$$

and thus the discrete convolution (10) corresponds to multiplication by
$k(e^{-i\lambda})$ in frequency domain.

If a spectral density f_x for (x_t) exists, then the corresponding transformation of the second moments is given by

$$f_{yx}(\lambda) = k(e^{-i\lambda})f_x(\lambda) \tag{12}$$

$$f_y(\lambda) = k(e^{-i\lambda})f_x(\lambda)k^*(e^{-i\lambda}) \tag{13}$$

where f_y is the spectral density of (y_t) and f_{yx} is the cross-spectrum between (y_t) and (x_t).

2.4. *The Solution of Linear Vector Difference Equations*

Consider the VDE

$$a(z)y_t = b(z)x_t \tag{14}$$

where

$$a(z) = \sum_{j=0}^{p} a_j z^j, \ a_j \in \mathbb{R}^{n \times n}$$

$$b(z) = \sum_{j=0}^{q} b_j z^j, \ b_j \in \mathbb{R}^{n \times m}$$

The steady state solution is then obtained by inverting the matrix-polynomial $a(z)$ in the lag operator z. This is done by inverting the matrix-polynomial $a(z)$, $z \in \mathbb{C}$:

Theorem 2.2: Let the stability condition

$$\det a(z) \neq 0, \ |z| \leq 1$$

hold. Then there exists a causal and stable solution of (14) of the form

$$y_t = \sum_{j=0}^{\infty} k_j x_{t-j} = k(z)x_t \tag{15}$$

where

$$\sum_{j=0}^{\infty} k_j z^j = k(z) = a^{-1}(z)b(z) = (\det a(z))^{-1}\mathrm{adj}(a(z))b(z); \ |z| \le 1 \quad (16)$$

Here *adj* denotes the adjoint.

2.5. *Forecasting Stationary Processes*

The forecasting problem is to approximate a future value x_{t+h}, $h > 0$, from the past x_s, $s \le t$. More specifically, in linear least squares forecasting the problem is to minimize $E(x_{t+h} - \sum_{j\ge0} a_j x_{t-j})'(x_{t+h} - \sum_{j\ge0} a_j x_{t-h})$ over the $a_j \in \mathbb{R}^{n \times n}$, $j = 0, 1, 2, \ldots$ (This is a slight restriction of generality, because there are processes (x_t), where the predictor $\hat{x}_{t,h}$, i.e. the approximation, cannot be represented as an infinite sum $\Sigma_{j\ge0} a_j x_{t-j}$ but as a limit of such linear transformations).

As is well known this forecasting problem has an interpretation as projection. Let $H_x(t)$ denote the Hilbert space spanned by $\{x_s^{(j)}|s \le t, j = 1, \ldots, n\}$ in the Hilbert space L_2. Then the predictor $\hat{x}_{t,h}$ for x_{t+h} is obtained by projecting the $x_{t+h}^{(j)}$, $j = 1, \ldots, n$ onto $H_x(t)$.

A stationary process (x_t) is called (linearly) *singular* if $\hat{x}_{t,h} = x_{t+h}$ for some and hence for all $t, h > 0$ holds. (x_t) is called (linearly) *regular* if

$$l.i.m._{h\to\infty} \hat{x}_{t,h} = 0$$

for one and hence for all t holds. Here $l.i.m.$ denotes the limit in the mean squares sense.

The next theorem is of central importance:

Theorem 2.3: (Wold decomposition)

- Every stationary process (x_t) can be represented in a unique way as $x_t = y_t + z_t$, where (y_t) is regular, (z_t) is singular, $Ey_t z_s' = 0$ for all s, t and (y_t) and (z_t) are causal linear transformations of (x_t) (which may have a slightly more general form than (10) and can be expressed, as $y_t^{(j)}, z_t^{(j)} \in H_x(t), j = 1, \ldots, n$).
- Every regular process (y_t) can be represented as *(Wold representation)*

$$y_t = \sum_{j=0}^{\infty} k_j \epsilon_{t-j}, \quad \sum_{j=0}^{\infty} ||k_j||^2 < \infty \quad (17)$$

where (ϵ_t) is white noise and where (ϵ_t) is a causal linear transformation of (y_t) (which may have a slightly more general form than (10)).

The Wold decomposition provides a deep insight in the structure of stationary processes. Its consequences for forecasting are:

- (y_t) and (z_t) can be forecasted separately
- for the regular process (y_t) we have:

$$y_{t+h} = \sum_{j=0}^{\infty} k_j \epsilon_{t+h-j} = \sum_{j=h}^{\infty} k_j \epsilon_{t+h-j} + \sum_{j=0}^{h-1} k_j \epsilon_{t+h-j}$$

and thus, by the projection theorem, the best linear least squares predictor is given by

$$\hat{y}_{t,h} = \sum_{j=h}^{\infty} k_j \epsilon_{t+h-j} \tag{18}$$

and the forecast error by

$$\sum_{j=0}^{h-1} k_j \epsilon_{t+h-j}. \tag{19}$$

Substituting ϵ_t in (18) by the causal linear transformation of y_s, $s \leq t$ gives the forecast-formula, expressing $\hat{y}_{t,h}$ in terms of y_s, $s \leq t$.

From (17) we see that every regular process can be approximated with arbitrary accuracy by an $(AR)MA$ process. Long memory processes, where in (17)

$$\sum \| k_j \| = \infty$$

holds, are examples of regular processes which are not of $ARMA$ type.

By Theorem 2.3, every regular process can be considered as the output of a causal linear transformation (or in other words of a causal linear system) with white noise inputs. Thus, from (13) we see that the spectral density of (y_t) is given as:

$$f_y(\lambda) = (2\pi)^{-1} k(e^{-i\lambda}) \Sigma k^*(e^{-i\lambda}) \tag{20}$$

where

$$k(z) = \sum_{j=0}^{\infty} k_j z^j, \qquad \Sigma = E\epsilon_t \epsilon_t'$$

For actual forecasting, in general, the population second moments and thus the k_j will not be known and have to be estimated from the data, by estimating a forecasting model. Thus in addition to the "theoretical" forecast error (19), an estimation error occurs. Despite the fact, that for consistent estimators, the estimation error converges to zero and thus asymptotically only (19) remains, for actual sample sizes the estimation error, in a certain sense, depends on the dimension of the parameter space. Forecasting models with (relatively) low-dimensional parameter spaces are discussed in section 4.

2.6. *Filtering*

Another important approximation problem is the filtering problem. We commence from a, say, $m + n$ dimensional stationary process $(x_t', y_t')'$ and we are interested in the best linear least squares approximation of y_t by (x_t), i.e. in the projection of $y_t^{(j)}$, $j = 1, \ldots, n$ on the Hilbert space H_x, the space spanned by $x_t^{(j)}$; $t \in \mathbb{Z}$, $j = 1, \ldots, m$. Then, if $f_x(\lambda) > 0$ holds for all λ, the transferfunction of the best linear least squares filter

$$\hat{y}_t = \sum_{j=-\infty}^{\infty} a_j x_{t-j}$$

(this again may be too restrictive for certain processes (x_t)) is given by the Wiener-filter formula

$$k(e^{-i\lambda}) = f_{yx}(\lambda) f_x(\lambda)^{-1} \qquad (21)$$

This is easily seen from (12) and the fact that the cross-spectrum between $(\hat{y}_t)$ and (x_t) is equal to f_{yx}.

3. Identification of Linear Systems

System identification is concerned with finding a good model from noisy data, i.e. with data driven modelling. An identification procedure is a rule (in the automatic case a function) attaching to each data string y_t, $t = 1, \ldots, T$, a system from the so called model class, that is the class of all a-priori feasible candidate systems. We are interested in both, construction of such rules and in their evaluation. Here only linear systems are considered, the emphasis in this section is on ARMA and state space systems. It should be noted that identification of linear systems is a nonlinear problem, since the mapping attaching parameters to the (sample second moments of the) data is nonlinear in general.

The main references for this section are Hannan and Deistler [15], Reinsel [19], Deistler [5] and Deistler [6]. As has been stated before, every regular stationary process has a Wold representation and thus may be approximated with arbitrary accuracy by an $ARMA$ process. On the other hand, $ARMA$ systems are described by a finite number of parameters and are thus statistically convenient. To be more precise, in the semi nonparametric approach described here, every regular stationary process can be approximately modeled by an $ARMA$ system, obtained in a two step procedure, consisting of model selection and estimation of real-valued parameters, as described below. Analogously, every causal Wiener filter can be approximately described by an $ARMAX$ system.

3.1. *The Three Modules in System Identification*

From a theoretical point of view, (in the semi nonparametric approach), we may distiguish three modules in system identification. Although these modules are dovetailed with each other, the problems can be solved in every module separately. The modules are as follows:

- *Structure theory*: Here an idealized identification problem is treated: We commence from the stochastic process generating the data (or, in the ergodic case, from an infinite trajectory) or from its (in particular second) population moments, rather than from data. The problem is to obtain from this information the parameters of interest. In more general terms, structure theory is concerned with the relation between "external behavior" (as described e.g. by population moments of the observed processes) and "internal parameters" (describing system and noise properties). Despite this idealized setting, structure theory turns out to be important for actual identification. Perhaps the best known part of structure theory is the theory of identifiability.
- *Estimation of real-valued parameters*: Here we commence from data and we assume that a finite-dimensional parameter space is given; the idealizing assumption here is, that we have no model selection

problem. By real-valued parameters we mean parameters that may vary e.g. in an open subset of an Euclidean space. A typical estimation procedure in this context is maximum likelihood estimation.

- *Model selection*: This concerns in particular input selection and dynamic specification. Here typically integer-valued parameters, such as e.g. maximum lag lenghts in the ARMA case, are estimated from data using information criteria or are obtained from test sequences.

As has been said already, here we only consider linear systems. For simplicity of notation, we restrict ourselves to systems with unobserved white noise inputs only, i.e. to systems with no observed inputs. For the case where also observed inputs are present we refer to [15].

3.2. *ARMA Systems and Rational Spectral Densities*

Consider an $ARMA$ system

$$a(z)y_t = b(z)\epsilon_t \tag{22}$$

satisfying the stability assumption (2) and the miniphase assumption (3). Then the steady state solution is given by

$$y_t = \sum_{j=0}^{\infty} k_j \epsilon_{t-j}, \quad k(z) = \sum_{j=0}^{\infty} k_j z^j = a^{-1}(z)b(z) \tag{23}$$

Note that, due to (3), (23) is the Wold representation. From (20) then we have

$$f_y(\lambda) = (2\pi)^{-1} a^{-1}(e^{-i\lambda})b(e^{-i\lambda})\Sigma\, b(e^{-i\lambda})^* a^{-1}(e^{-i\lambda})^* \tag{24}$$

Note that for an $ARMA$ system k as well as f_y are rational matrices. We also have:

Theorem 3.1: Every rational and nonsingular spectral density matrix may be uniquely factorized as in (24), where $k(z)$ is rational, analytic within a circle containing the closed unit disk, $\det k(z) \neq 0$, $|z| < 1$ and $k(0) = I$ and where $\Sigma > 0$.

Thus, under the assumptions of the theorem above, k and Σ can be uniquely determined from given f_y and thus from the population second moments of the observations. This is the justification for describing the external behavior of an ARMA system by its transfer function. In addition, it can be shown that every rational transfer function k with the properties given in the theorem above can be written as $k = a^{-1}b$ where the polynomial matrices a and b satisfy (2), (3) and $a(0) = b(0)$, and thus correspond to a stable and miniphase $ARMA$ system.

In order to obtain finite dimensional parameter spaces, subclasses have to be considered. There are several ways to break the class of all $ARMA$ systems into such subclasses. One is to fix the maximum degrees p and q of $a(z)$ and $b(z)$ respectively; in addition, it is assumed that $a(0) = b(0) = I$ holds. Then $\tau = vec(a_1 \ldots a_p, b_1 \ldots b_q) \in \mathbb{R}^{n^2(p+q)}$, where vec denotes columnwise vectorization, is a parameter vector. In the scalar (i.e. $n = 1$) case, common factors have to be excluded in order to avoid "redundant" $ARMA$ representations. The generalization of this idea to the multivariable case is as follows: We assume that a and b are relatively left prime, meaning that every left (polynomial matrix-) common factor u must be unimodular, i.e. $\det u(z) = const \neq 0$. It can be shown that under this assumption two $ARMA$ systems $(\bar{a}, \bar{b})$ and (a, b) correspond to the same transfer-function (i.e. $\bar{a}^{-1}\bar{b} = a^{-1}b$) and thus are observationally equivalent if and only if there exists a unimodular matrix u such that

$$(\bar{a}, \bar{b}) = u(a, b)$$

holds. Using this result, it is easy to show that the parameter space

$$
\begin{aligned}
T_{p,q} = \{\ & vec(a_1 \ldots a_p, b_1 \ldots b_q) \in \mathbb{R}^{n^2(p+q)} | \\
& \det a(z) \neq 0, |z| \leq 1,\ \det b(z) \neq 0, |z| < 1; \\
& a, b \text{ are relatively left prime, } a(0) = b(0) = I, \\
& rk(a_p, b_q) = n\ \}
\end{aligned}
$$

is identifiable, i.e. does not contain two different observationally equivalent systems. Here we identify (a, b) with $vec(a_1 \ldots b_q)$ and rk denotes the rank of a matrix. If we define the mapping π by $\pi(a, b) = a^{-1}b$, then identifiability means that π restricted to $T_{p,q}$ is injective. In addition, it can be shown that $T_{p,q}$ contains a nontrivial open subset of $\mathbb{R}^{n^2(p+q)}$ and that the inverse of the restriction of π to $T_{p,q}$ is continuous, where we endow sets of transfer functions with the topology of pointwise convergence of its power series coefficients. $T_{p,q}$ and $T_{p,p}$ are frequently used as parameter spaces; however for $n > 1$ they have the disadvantage that not every rational transfer function (satisfying our assumptions) can be described in this way.

Clearly AR systems are special $ARMA$ systems with $b(0) = I$. As can

be seen immediately a and I are always relatively left prime and the rank
of (a_p, I) is always n. This shows that, after having imposed stability and
$a(0) = I$, we do not have to take out additional points in order to obtain
identifiability. As a consequence structure theory for AR systems is much
simpler compared to the general $ARMA$ case. This is one reason why AR
systems are often prefered in applications, despite the fact that they are less
flexible in the sense that more parameters may be needed to approximate
a rational transfer function.

3.3. *State Space Systems*

A linear state space system is of the form

$$x_{t+1} = Ax_t + B\epsilon_t \tag{25}$$

$$y_t = Cx_t + \epsilon_t \tag{26}$$

where y_t are the n-dimensional outputs, (ϵ_t) is n-dimensional white noise,
x_t is the, say, s-dimensional state, and $A \in \mathbb{R}^{s \times s}$, $B \in \mathbb{R}^{s \times n}$, $C \in R^{n \times s}$ are
parameter matrices. The state dimension s is an integer-valued parameter.
The stability assumption is of the form

$$|\lambda_{max}(A)| < 1 \tag{27}$$

where $\lambda_{max}(A)$ denotes an eigenvalue of A of maximal modulus. Then the
steady state solution is given by the transfer function

$$k(z) = C(z^{-1}I - A)^{-1}B + I = I + \sum_{j=1}^{\infty}(CA^{j-1}B)z^j \tag{28}$$

In addition the miniphase assumption

$$|\lambda_{max}(A - BC)| \leq 1 \tag{29}$$

will be imposed. Then $k(z)$ in (28) corresponds to Wold representation.
In many cases state space systems are written with different white noise
processes for (25) and for (26), respectively, however such systems can be
always transformed to the so called innovations representation given in (25),
(26).

As easily can be seen, every $ARMA$ system (22) can be transformed to
a state space system (25), (26) with the same transfer function by defining
the state x_t as the vector formed by $y_{t-1} \ldots y_{t-p}, \epsilon_{t-1} \ldots \epsilon_{t-q}$. Clearly the

transfer function in (28) is rational. Thus every rational transfer function $k(z)$ satisfying the assumptions of Theorem 3.1 can be realized by (i.e. corresponds to the steady state solution of) an $ARMA$ or by a state space system. In other words, every stationary process with a rational spectral density can be described either by an $ARMA$ or by a state space system and both model classes describe the same class of stationary processes (namely those with rational spectral densities). Thus, in this sense, $ARMA$ and state space systems are equivalent.

The state x_t is unobserved in general. A state space system (A, B, C) is called minimal, if there is no state space system with the same transfer-function and with smaller state dimension.

The state has the following interpretation: Remember that $H_y(t-1)$ denotes the Hilbert space spanned by $y_s^{(j)}$; $s < t, j = 1, \ldots, n$, and project the variables $y_r^{(j)}$, $r \geq t, j = 1, \ldots, n$, onto $H_y(t-1)$. Then the space spanned by these projections, the so called state space, is finite dimensional if and only if the spectral density of (y_t) is rational and its dimension is equal to the state dimension s of a minimal system. Then s is called the order of the system. Every basis for this space may serve as a minimal state x_t. In this sense, the state space is the interface between the future and the past of (y_t).

Two minimal state space systems (A, B, C) and $(\bar{A}, \bar{B}, \bar{C})$ are observationally equivalent if and only if there is a nonsingular matrix T such that

$$\bar{A} = TAT^{-1}$$
$$\bar{B} = TB \qquad\qquad (30)$$
$$\bar{C} = CT^{-1}$$

hold.

Now, for fixed n and s, we can embed (A, B, C) in $\mathbb{R}^{s^2+2sn}$; by $S(s)$ we denote the set of all such (A, B, C) satisfying (27) and (29). $S(s)$ is of dimension $s^2 + 2sn$ and the subset $S_m(s)$ of all minimal (A, B, C) is open and dense in $S(s)$. As can be seen from (30), the equivalence classes in $S_m(s)$ are s^2-dimensional manifolds. Thus, in a certain sense, the dimension of the parameter space can be reduced to $2sn$.

We use ρ to denote the mapping attaching the transfer functions $k(z)$ to

(A, B, C) as described by (28). By $M(s)$ we denote the set $\rho(S_m(s))$. For the scalar case $(n = 1)$, $M(s)$ is equal to $\pi(T_{s,s})$ and in general $\pi(T_{p,p})$ is open and dense in $M(np)$. $M(s)$ can be shown to be a manifold of dimension $2sn$; for the case $s > 1$, however, $M(s)$ cannot be described by one coordinate system. For the description of $M(s)$ we refer to [15].

Note that $T_{p,q}$ is not the only parameter space used for $ARMA$ systems. In particular $M(n)$ may also be described in terms of $ARMA$ coordinate systems, see again [15].

3.4. *Estimation for a Given Subclass*

Up to now, we have been concerned with structure theory for $ARMA$ and state space systems. Now estimation can be treated in a rather general way: Let $T_\alpha \subset \mathbb{R}^{d_\alpha}$ be a "suitable", in particular identifiable parameter space, such as $T_{p,q}$ for the $ARMA$ or a coordinate set for $M(n)$ in the state space case. Let U_α denote the corresponding set of transfer functions. By $\psi_\alpha : U_\alpha \to T_\alpha$ we denote the inverse of π or ρ, respectively, restricted to T_α. This mapping is called a parametrization of U_α. We in addition require that ψ_α is continuous. This is important for the "well-posedness" of the estimation problem, because then convergence of transfer functions implies convergence of parameters. By $\tau \in T_\alpha$ we denote the (free) parameters for the transfer function. In addition by $\sigma \in \underline{\Sigma} \subset \mathbb{R}^{\frac{s(s+1)}{2}}$ we denote the stacked vector of all on and above diagonal elements of the positive definite symmetric matrix Σ and $\underline{\Sigma}$ is the set of all such vectors corresponding to such matrices. The overall parameter space for $\theta = (\tau', \sigma')'$ then is assumed to be of the form

$$\Theta = T_\alpha \times \underline{\Sigma}$$

Thus, in particular, we assume that there are no cross-restrictions between system and noise parameters.

An important observation is that many identification procedures, at least asymptotically, depend on the data only via their sample second moments

$$\hat{\gamma}(s) = T^{-1} \sum_{t=1}^{T-s} y_{t+s} y_t', \ s \geq 0$$
$$\hat{\gamma}(s) = \hat{\gamma}'(-s), \qquad\qquad s < 0$$

Now $\hat{\gamma}$ can be directly realized as an MA system, where "typically" the maximum lag q is equal to $T - 1$ and then, in general, its transfer function,

$\hat{\hat{k}}_T$ say, will be not be contained in U_α. From this point of view, in our case, estimation may be considered as consisting of two steps, namely:

- a model reduction step, where e.g. $\hat{\hat{k}}_T$ is approximated by a transfer function $\hat{k}_T$ in U_α. This is an information concentration step and is important for the statistical properties of the estimators. Note that $\hat{k}_T$ is a coordinate free estimator, since it does depend on the particular parametrization of U_α.
- a realization step, where the system parameters are estimated by $\psi_\alpha(\hat{k}_T) = \hat{\tau}_T$

The classical estimation methods are based on ($-2T^{-1}$ times the ln of) the Gaussian likelihood which, up to a constant, is given by

$$\hat{L}_T(\theta) = T^{-1} \ln \det \Gamma_T(\theta) + T^{-1} y'(T) \Gamma_T(\theta)^{-1} y(T) \qquad (31)$$

where $y(T) = (y_1', \ldots, y_T')'$ and $\Gamma_T(\theta)$ is the variance covariance matrix of a vector $y(T, \theta)$ whose parameters are θ. The maximum likelihood estimator (MLE) $\hat{\theta}_T$ then is obtained by minimizing $\hat{L}_T(\theta)$ over Θ. As is seen from (31), $\hat{L}_T$ depends on τ only via k, thus we have a coordinate-free MLE $\hat{k}_T$ of k and an MLE $\hat{\Sigma}_T$ of Σ.

For consistency and asymptotic normality we refer to [15] or in a more general, even nonlinear setting to [18].

There is no explicit formula for the $MLE's$ $\hat{\tau}_T = \psi_\alpha(\hat{k}_T)$ and $\hat{\Sigma}_T$ in general; then the $MLE's$ are approximated by numerical optimization procedures of Gauß-Newton type, commencing from a suitable initial estimator see [15], chapter 6. One important exception are AR systems, where the $MLE's$ are of least squares type and thus can be calculated explicitly, are asymptotically efficient and numerically fast and reliable; this is a main advantage of AR compared to more general $ARMA$ or state space systems.

Recently powerful methods for state space system estimation, such as subspace procedures or data driven local coordinates have been developed, see e.g. [7], in order to avoid or mitagate numerical problems occurring in numerically optimizing the likelihood. A modern approach to state space system identification is to use MLE for driven local coordinates and to use subspace procedures for initial estimation. Of course, estimators for $ARMA$ systems may also be obtained by estimating a state space system first and then to transform it to an $ARMA$ system.

3.5. *Model Selection*

In many applications the original model class (which corresponds to the a-priori knowledge available) is not finite dimensional; here the case, where this model class is U_A, the set of all $n \times n$ rational transfer functions $k(z)$, satisfying the conditions listed in Theorem 3.1, is considered. The set U_A has to be broken into bits U_α in order to allow for a convenient parametrization, see subsection 3.4. The development and evaluation of data driven procedures for the selection of such bits is one of the most important contribution to the system identification during the last thirty years.

Here we restrict ourselves to a special, but important case, namely to the estimation of $M(s)$ or in other words the estimation of the order s. In many cases, the estimators are obtained by minimizing a so called information criterion of the form

$$A(s) = \ln \det \hat{\Sigma}_T(s) + 2ns \; c(T)T^{-1}; \; 0 \le s \le S \qquad (32)$$

where $\hat{\Sigma}_T(s)$ in the MLE of Σ obtained by minimizing the likelihood over $\Theta = M(s) \times \Sigma$, $c(T)$ is a prescribed positive function and S is an upper bound for the order. The first term on the r.h.s of (32) is a measure for the goodness of fit to the data achieved by the MLE over $M(s) \times \Sigma$. It can be shown, that $\bar{M}(s)$, the closure of $M(s)$ in U_A, is equal to $\cup_{i=1}^{s} M(i)$. Thus $\bar{M}(s_1) \subset \bar{M}(s_2)$ holds for $s_1 < s_2$ and, as is easily seen, $\ln \det \hat{\Sigma}_T(s)$ is (not strictly) decreasing with increasing s. The idea behind criteria of the form (32) is to avoid overfitting by counterbalancing the first term on the r.h.s, which is a measure of fit, by the second term, which contains the dimension $2sn$ of $M(s)$ as a measure of complexity. In other words, an "optimal" tradeoff between fit and complexity necessary in order to achieve this fit is intended by minimizing $A(s)$. Note that such a procedure may be interpreted as a sequence of likelihood ratio tests, where the significance levels are implicitly prescribed by (32).

Now, $c(T)$ determines the tradeoff between fit and complexity; by far the most common choices for $c(T)$ are $c(T) = 2$, which gives the so called AIC criterion and $c(T) = \ln(T)$ which gives the BIC criterion. These criteria are derived from different reasonings, such as entropy minimization, optimal coding or Bayesian considerations.

As can be shown, the estimators of s, $\hat{s}_T$ say, obtained by minimizing $A(s)$

are consistent (under suitable assumptions) if $c(T)$ satisfies

$$\lim_{T \to \infty} c(T) T^{-1} = 0$$

and

$$\lim_{T \to \infty} \inf c(T) (\ln \ln T)^{-1} > 0 \qquad (33)$$

Thus BIC gives consistent estimates; as can be shown AIC does not give consistent estimators. It should be kept in mind, that, in most cases, model selection is an intermediate goal, e.g. estimation of the order s is rarely a final aim, but it is rather used to estimate a system e.g. in order to obtain forecasts.

An important and partly still unsolved question concerns the additional uncertainty in estimation of real-valued parameters coming from model selection (see [17]).

Information criteria such as AIC or BIC are also used in case of other parametrizations. Also note that, as has been stated in subsection 3.3, in the multivariate case, when considering $M(s)$, additional integer-valued parameters have to be estimated in order to obtain an identifiable parameter space.

4. Linear Dynamic Factor Models

As has been said already, a major problem in modelling multivariate time series with "unstructured" AR, $ARMA$ or state space models is the "curse of dimensionality" i.e. that the dimension of the parameter space is proportional to the square of the cross-sectional dimension n of the multivariate time series. There are several approaches to overcome this difficulty, one example is traditional structural modeling, where overidentifying restrictions, coming from theoretical a priori knowledge, are used to reduce the dimension of the parameter space. Factor models provide an alternative, more data-driven approach. The basic idea is to achieve cross-sectional dimension reduction by explaining the comovements between the components of a multivariate time series by a relatively small number of factors. Among the many possible references, we refer to Brillinger [3], Forni et al. [10] and Stock and Watson [22], see also [4], [1], [21], [11] and [13].

4.1. *The Basic Setting*

There are different classes of factor models, they all have the equation

$$y_t = \Lambda(z)\xi_t + u_t \tag{34}$$

in common; here (y_t) is the n-dimensional stationary process of the observations, (ξ_t) is the $r < n$ dimensional stationary factor process and (u_t) is the stationary noise process. The transfer function $\Lambda(z) = \sum_{j=-\infty}^{\infty} \Lambda_j z^j$; $\Lambda_j \in \mathbb{R}^{n \times r}$ is called factor loading matrix. In addition we assume

$$E\xi_t = 0, \ Eu_t = 0$$

and, unless the contrary has been stated explicitly,

$$E\xi_t u_s' = 0 \quad \text{for all} \quad t, s \in \mathbb{Z} \tag{35}$$

A factor model (34) is called *static*, if $\Lambda(z)$ is constant and if (ξ_t) and (u_t) are white noise. Static models are the classical factor models, see e.g. [1]. A factor model is called *quasi static*, if Λ is constant but (ξ_t) and (u_t) are not necessarily white noise.

The so called latent variables are defined as $\hat{y}_t = \Lambda(z)\xi_t$. One possible interpretation of (34) is that $\hat{y}_t$ are the true unobserved variables corresponding to the measured variables y_t. We assume throughout that the respective spectral densities exist and that moreover the covariances satisfy suitable summability conditions. (see [3]). Then, using an obvious notation, we obtain from (34) and (35)

$$f_y(\lambda) = \Lambda(e^{-i\lambda})f_\xi(\lambda)\Lambda(e^{-i\lambda})^* + f_u(\lambda) \tag{36}$$

Clearly the spectral density $f_{\hat{y}}(\lambda) = \Lambda(e^{-i\lambda})f_\xi(\lambda)\Lambda(e^{-i\lambda})^*$ is singular. We assume throughout that $f_\xi(\lambda)$ has rank r for all λ and that the same holds for $\Lambda(e^{-i\lambda})$. Then $f_{\hat{y}}(\lambda)$ has rank r for all λ and every $(n-r) \times n$ transfer function $w(z)$ satisfying

$$w(e^{-i\lambda})f_{\hat{y}}(\lambda) = 0$$

describes an exact linear dynamic relation

$$w(z)\hat{y}_t = 0 \tag{37}$$

for the latent variables. Throughout we assume that $w(e^{-i\lambda})$ has rank $n-r$ for all λ. Note that the relation (37) is symmetric in the sense that we do not have to distinguish a priori between inputs and outputs in $(\hat{y}_t)$ and we do not even have to know the number of equations $n - r$ (i.e. the number of outputs) a priori. Analogously

$$y_t = \hat{y}_t + u_t \tag{38}$$

gives a symmetric error model, where noise is allowed for observed inputs and outputs. Equations (37) and (38) give a linear dynamic errors-in-variables model. As is directly seen, in the static case, where Λ and w are constant, the factor models and the errors-in-variables models are equivalent, since the linear restrictions on the image of $\hat{y}_t$ are described by the image of the matrix Λ in the first case and by the kernel of w in the second case. For the dynamic case, we refer to [16].

In identification of factor models, the primary interest may be in the factor loading matrix Λ, in f_ξ and f_u, or in the unobserved processes (ξ_t) and $(\hat{y}_t)$. In general, for given f_y, these quantities of interest are not unique and we thus have an identifiability problem. If f_y is non-singular for all λ, as we will assume throughout, then, without further assumptions, every factor loading matrix Λ is compatible with this given f_y, i.e. the knowledge of f_y implies no restriction for Λ. Therefore additional structure has to be imposed in order to make identification meaningful. Additional assumptions imposed lead to the model classes discussed below.

Quasi static factor models are used for forecasting, in particular for high dimensional time series. The most common setting is to fit $AR(X)$ models to the estimated factors (either multivariate or r univariate models) and to forecast the latent variables using the factor forecasts and an estimate of Λ. The forecasts for the observed variables then are obtained form the forecasts of the latent variables, possibly combined with the forecasts of the univariate noise components (see e.g. [8]). In this way forecasting models with lower dimensional parameter spaces are achieved.

4.2. *Dynamic Principal Component Analysis*

For dynamic principal component analysis (PCA) [3] we commence from the eigenvalue decomposition of the spectral density f_y, written as

$$f_y(\lambda) = O_1(e^{-i\lambda})\Omega_1(\lambda)O_1(e^{-i\lambda})^* + O_2(e^{-i\lambda})\Omega_2(\lambda)O_2(e^{-i\lambda})^* \tag{39}$$

where $\Omega_1(\lambda)$ is the $r \times r$ diagonal matrix having the r largest eigenvalues of $f_y(\lambda)$ on its diagonal, ordered according to decreasing size, O_1 is the $n \times r$ matrix whose columns are the corresponding eigenvectors and the second term on the r.h.s. of (39) is defined analogously, where $\Omega_2(\lambda)$ is the $(n - r) \times (n - r)$ diagonal matrix consisting of the $(n - r)$ smallest eigenvalues of $f_y(\lambda)$, again ordered according to decreasing size.

By defining

$$f_{\hat{y}}(\lambda) = O_1(e^{-i\lambda})\Omega_1(\lambda)O_1(e^{-i\lambda})^*$$

and

$$f_u(\lambda) = O_2(e^{-i\lambda})\Omega_2(\lambda)O_2(e^{-i\lambda})^*$$

we attribute the first part on the r.h.s. of (39) to the latent variables and the second part to the noise. This gives a model of the form

$$y_t = O_1(z)\xi_t + u_t \tag{40}$$

with

$$\xi_t = O_1^*(z)y_t$$

$$\hat{y}_t = O_1(z)O_1^*(z)y_t$$

and

$$u_t = (I - O_1(z)O_1(z)^*)y_t = O_2(z)O_2^*(z)y_t$$

Throughout we assume that all eigenvalues of f_y are distinct; then the decomposition on the r.h.s of (39) is unique. It can be shown, that, for fixed r, this decomposition gives the smallest noise, in the sense that $Eu_t'u_t$ is minimal among all decompositions (34) where the rank of $\Lambda(z)$ is equal to r, for all λ. As also can be shown, for rational f_y, the spectral densities $f_{\hat{y}}$ and f_u are not necessarely rational. For decompositions with smallest noise under additional rationality assumptions (with bounded complexity), see [16].

If we commence from the eigenvalue decomposition of $\Sigma_y = Ey_ty_t'$ rather than of f_y, written as

$$\Sigma_y = O_1\Omega_1O_1' + O_2\Omega_2O_2' \tag{41}$$

where the quantities on the r.h.s of (41) are defined analogously to those on the r.h.s. of (39), we obtain a quasi-static PCA given by the model

$$y_t = O_1 \xi_t + u_t \qquad (42)$$

with $\xi_t = O_1' y_t$, $u_t = O_2 O_2' y_t$. Of course, if the true model is not quasi static, then, in general, (ξ_t) and (u_t) in (40) and (42) respectively are different. They coincide in the static case, where $f_y = (2\pi)^{-1} \Sigma_y$ holds and in the quasi-static case, where the kernel of $f_{\hat{y}}(\lambda)$ does not depend on λ, since Λ is constant. Note that in the quasi static case $E\xi_t u_s' = 0$ holds, whereas (35) is not true in general for (42), if the true model is not quasi static.

If forecasting of (y_t) is based on forecasting of the latent variables $(\hat{y}_t)$, then a problem arises, since $O_1(z)O_1^*(z)$ is in general a non causal transfer function and thus the "present" latent variable $\hat{y}_t$ may also be influenced by "future" observations y_s, $s > t$. For this reason, for forecasting, the quasi-static model, together with an (e.g. $AR(X)$) forecasting model for the factor process (ξ_t) is frequently used.

In a certain sense, the dimension r of the factor process (ξ_t) is not an intrinsic parameter, since for every $0 < r < n$ the decompositions (39) and (41) respectively may be performed. Usually r is fixed by heuristic considerations, e.g. relating to the fit achieved with the first term on the r.h.s. of (39) to the number of factors which have to be used to obtain this fit.

Once r has been fixed, for estimaton, f_y in (39) is replaced by a suitable spectral estimate, or Σ_y in (41) is replaced by the sample variance covariance matrix

$$\hat{\Sigma}_y = T^{-1} \Sigma_{t=1}^{T} y_t y_t'$$

and then the eigenvalue decompositions (39) or (41) are performed for the sample rather than for the population second moments in order to obtain the estimates for the quantities of interest.

4.3. *The Dynamic Factor Model with Idiosyncratic Noise (Dynamic Frisch Model)*

Here the additional assumption

$$f_u \quad \text{is diagonal} \tag{43}$$

is imposed in (34). By this assumption, the noise u_t represents the individual influence on y_t and the factors represent the influences common to the components of (y_t). By (43), the component processes of (y_t) are conditionally uncorrelated for given $(\hat{y}_t)$.

The structure theory for this case is rather involved, see [21] and there still exist a number of unsolved problems.

The identifiabilty problem may be decomposed into two parts:

- In the first part the concern is the uniqueness, if we restrict ourselves to the minimal r as we do throughout, of the decomposition of

$$f_y = f_{\hat{y}} + f_u \tag{44}$$

into $f_{\hat{y}}$ and f_u, where $f_{\hat{y}}$ is singular and f_u is diagonal (and both are spectral densities)
- The second part is concerned with obtaining $\Lambda(z)$ and f_ξ from $f_{\hat{y}}$

The main complication is connected with the first part. In general the decomposition (44) is not unique and even the dimension of the factor space (i.e. the rank of $f_{\hat{y}}$) is not unique for given f_y. In many cases only decompositions corresponding to the minimum possible number of factors, r_M say, are considered. If $r_M \leq \sqrt{n}$ holds, then, at least generically, for r_M factors, the decomposition (44) is unique. A number of estimation procedures have been proposed for this case, however neither a complete theory nor general methods are available.

4.4. *The Quasi-Static Frisch Model*

A simpler model class are *quasi-static Frisch models* where Λ in (34) is constant. Then we commence from

$$\Sigma_y = \Lambda \Sigma_\xi \Lambda' + \Sigma_u \tag{45}$$

where Σ_u is diagonal and where an obvious notation has been used. Considering all decompositions on the r.h.s. of (45), where $\Lambda \Sigma_\xi \Lambda'$ is singular and Σ_u is diagonal, analogously as above, in general we have no uniqueness, however, if we restrict ourselves to the minimal r as we do throughout, for $((n-r)^2 - n - r) \geq 0$ uniqueness can be achieved generically.

Once $\Sigma_{\hat{y}}$ is unique, we may assume $\Sigma_\xi = I$ and then Λ is unique up to postmultiplication by $r \times r$ orthogonal matrices, corresponding to factor rotation. If no assumption on Σ_ξ is imposed, then Λ is unique up to post multiplication by nonsingular matrices.

Note that, contrary to the PCA case, (and as in the dynamic idiosyncratic case), the factors ξ_t, in general, cannot be obtained as a function Ly_t of the observations y_t. Thus in estimating the factors, they are approximated by a linear function of the observations. Two methods for doing so are used:

- *Thomson's method*: Here ξ_t is approximated by the linear function $\hat{\xi}_t = Ly_t$ which minimizes the variance covariance matrix of $\xi_t - \hat{\xi}_t$. This approximation is given by

$$\hat{\xi}_t^{TH} = \Lambda' \Sigma_y^{-1} y_t \tag{46}$$

- *Bartlett's method*: Here the expression

$$(y_t - \Lambda L y_t)' \Sigma_u^{-1} (y_t - \Lambda L y_t)$$

  is minimized, which gives

$$\hat{\xi}_t^B = (\Lambda' \Sigma_u^{-1})' \Lambda' \Sigma_u^{-1} y_t \tag{47}$$

In the case where (ξ_t) and (u_t) and thus (y_t) are white noise, the negative logarithm of the Gaussian likelihood, up to a constant, has the form

$$L_T(\Lambda, \Sigma_u) = \frac{1}{2}T \ln(\det(\Lambda\Lambda' + \Sigma_u)) + \frac{1}{2}T \mathrm{tr}(\Lambda\Lambda' + \Sigma_u)^{-1} \hat{\Sigma}_y \tag{48}$$

Here we assume $\Sigma_\xi = I$; in addition assumptions guaranteeing uniqueness of Λ for given $\Lambda\Lambda'$ are imposed. Even if (ξ_t) and (u_t) are not white, minimization of L_T gives consistent estimators of Λ and Σ_u as long as $\hat{\Sigma}_y$ is consistent for Σ_y. A likelihood ratio test for the number of the factors has been suggested in [2]. Estimates for the factors are obtained by inserting estimates for Λ, Σ_y and Σ_u in (46) and (47) respectively.

For forecasting, again the (estimated) factors may be forecasted by an AR or ARX model. In addition, also the individual $u_t^{(i)}$ may be forecasted by

AR or ARX models in order to obtain a combined forecast for the observations [8].

4.5. *The Generalized Linear Dynamic Factor Model*

Generalized linear factor models are an important generalization of the Frisch model; they have been introduced for the static case in [4]. The dynamic case is treated e.g. in [10] and [11].

Generalized factor models have been developed for the case of a large cross-sectional dimension n; this situation is quite common now, e.g. for financial time series or for macroeconomic time series, for instance, in cross country studies, see e.g. [22]. The cross sectional dimension n may be even larger than sample size T. One of the basic challenges therefore is to extract information from such high dimensional time series and in particular to gain additional information not only from adding observations in time but also from adding in the cross sectional dimension, i.e. from adding time series; thus the task is compression of information in the time and in the cross sectional dimension.

The second main issue is that the assumption of the Frisch model, that f_u is diagonal, turns out to be too restrictive for many applications; the idea here is to allow for "weak" dependence of the noise components.

For the analysis of the generalized linear factor model, the cross-sectional dimension is not kept fixed. We consider a double sequence $(y_t^{(i)}|i \in \mathbb{N}, t \in \mathbb{Z})$ of observations. Let $y_t^n = (y_t^{(i)})^{i=1\ldots n}$. We assume that the stochastic processes $(y_t^n|t \in \mathbb{Z})$ have mean zero, are regular and stationary and that their covariances satisfy suitable summability conditions for every $n \in \mathbb{N}$. We also assume that the factors ξ_t are independent of n and in particular that r is constant. Then, using an obvious notation, we can write (34) as

$$y_t^n = \Lambda^n(z)\xi_t + u_t^n, \quad n \in \mathbb{N} \tag{49}$$

Here Λ^n, y_t^n, u_t^n are assumed to be "nested" in the sense that e.g. $u_t^{n+1} = (u_t^{n\prime}, u_t^{(n+1)})^\prime$

The main assumptions for the model sequence (49) are:

- the spectral densities $f_{\hat{y}}^n$ of the latent variables $\hat{y}_t^n = \Lambda^n(z)\xi_t$ have rank r (for $n \geq r$) and the associated nonzero eigenvalues diverge for $n \to \infty$, for all λ.

- all eigenvalues for the spectral densities f_u^n of the noise remain bounded for all n and λ.

White the first assumption formalizes strong dependence between the latent variables, the second assumption formalizes the notion of weak dependence of the noise components.

Identifiability in the sense of separation of $f_{\hat{y}}^n$ and f_u^n from f_y^n is achieved only asymptotically i.e. for $n \to \infty$.

As can be shown PCA and generalized factor model are asymptotically, i.e. for $n \to \infty$, equivalent in the sense that e.g. the PCA latent variables converge to the corresponding variables of the generalized factor models, see [10]. Based on this, estimation of quasi static and dynamic, respectively, generalized factor models may be performed by quasi static or dynamic, respectively, PCA. For an asymptotic analysis, for $T \to \infty$, $n \to \infty$, we refer to [11]. However, PCA is not the only procedure used for estimation of generalized factor models, see e.g. [12].

Again, forecasting in the context of generalized factor models may be done by forecasting the factors e.g. by $AR(X)$ models and by eventually combining these forecasts with the univariate forecasts for the noise components. However, for forecasting, dynamic PCA in general is not directly applicable, since in general

$$\hat{y}_t = O_1(z)O_1(z)^* y_t$$

is a noncausal filtering operation and thus $\hat{y}_t$ may depend on y_s, $s > t$.

One way to overcome this difficulty is to assume a rational $f_{\hat{y}}$, by e.g. assuming [12] that $\Lambda^n(z)$ is polynomial of degree q to assume that the factors are AR processes of order smaller than or equal to $q + 1$ and to write (49) as a quasi static model

$$y_t^n = (\Lambda_0^s, \ldots, \Lambda_q^s)(\xi_t', \ldots, \xi_{t-q}')' + u_t^n$$

with a higher dimensional factor.

Clearly, also in the context of generalized factor models, besides estimation of real valued variables, a number of model specification issues arises; for instance the question of determining the number of ("static" or "dynamic") factors from data.

References

1. T. W. Anderson, Estimating Linear Statistical Relationship, *Annals of Statistics*, 12, 1-45, 1984.
2. T.W. Anderson and H. Rubin, Statistical Inference in Factor Analysis, *Proceedings of the Third Berkeley Symposium on Mathematical Statistics and Probability V*, 111-150, 1956.
3. D.R. Brillinger, *Time Series: Data Analysis and Theory*, Holt, Rinehart and Winston, New York, 1981.
4. G. Chamberlain and M. Rothschild, Arbitrage Factor Structure and Mean Variance Analysis on Large Asset Markets, *Econometrica*, 51, 1281-1304, 1983.
5. M. Deistler, *Linear Dynamic Multiinput/Multioutput Systems*, in: D. Pena, et al. eds.: *A Course in Time Series Analysis*, Wiley, New York, Chapter 16, 2001.
6. M. Deistler, System Identification - General Aspects and Structure, in: G. Goodwin, ed.: *System Identification and Adaptive Control (Festschrift for B.D.O. Anderson)*, Springer, London, 3-26, 2001.
7. M. Deistler, *Linear Models for Multivariate Time Series Analysis*,, in: "Handbook of Time Series Analysis", Matthias Wintherhalder, Bjoern Schelter, Jens Timmer, eds., Wiley-VCH, Berlin, 283 − 306, 2006.
8. M. Deistler and E. Hamann, Identification of Factor Models for Forecasting Returns, *Journal of Financial Econometrics*, 3, 256-281, 2005.
9. M. Forni and M. Lippi, The Generalized Factor Model: Representation Theory, *Econometric Theory*, 17, 1113-1141, 2001.
10. M. Forni, M. Hallin, M. Lippi and L. Reichlin, The Generalized Factor Model: Identification and Estimation, *The Review of Economics and Statistics*, 80, 540 − 554, 2000.
11. M. Forni, M. Hallin, M. Lippi and L. Reichlin, The Generalized Dynamic Factor Model, Consistency and Rates, *Journal of Econometrics* 119, 231-255, 2004.
12. M. Forni, M. Hallin, M. Lippi and L. Reichlin, The Generalized Dynamic Factor Model, One Sided Estimation and Forecasting, to appear in: *Journal of the American Statistical Association*, 2005.
13. E. Hamann, M. Deistler and W. Scherrer, Factor Models for Multivariate Time Series, in: A. Taudes ed., *Adaptive Information Systems and Modeling in Economics and Management Science*, Springer, Wien, 243-252, 2005.
14. E.J. Hannan, *Multiple Time Series*, Wiley, New York, 1970.
15. E.J. Hannan and M. Deistler, *The Statistical Theory of Linear Systems*, Wiley, New York, 1988.
16. C. Heij, W. Scherrer and M. Deistler, System Identification by Dynamic Factor Models, *SIAM Journal on Control and Optimization*, 35, 1924-1951, 1997.
17. H. Leeb and B. Poetscher, The Finite Sample Distribution of Past-Model-Selection Estimators and Uniform Versus Nonuniform Approximations Econometric Theory, *Econometric Theory*, 19, 100 − 142, 2003.

18. B. Poetscher and I. Prucha, *Dynamic Nonlinear Econometrics Models*, Springer, Berlin-Heidelberg, 1997.
19. G.C. Reinsel, *Elements of Multivariate Time Series Analysis*, Second Edition, Springer New York, 2003.
20. Y.A. Rozanov, *Stationary Random Processes*, Holden Day, San Francisco, 1967.
21. W. Scherrer and M. Deistler, A Structure Theory for Linear Dynamic Errors in Variables Models, *SIAM Journal on Control and Optimization*, 36, 2418-2175, 1998.
22. J.H. Stock and M.W. Watson, Macroeconomic Forecasting Using Diffusion Indices, *Journal of Business and Economic Statistics*, 20, 147-162, 2002.

DH

330 .
015
195
ECO